'A really helpful guide to success. I love the positive spirit of this book, about making great things happen – for customers, staff and shareholders – great purpose and great fun at the same time.'

Brent Hoberman, Co-founder and CEO of lastminute.com

'May I congratulate you on a perfect summary of all important factors that contribute to success in business and private life. What a potential for better results – and ultimately success!'

Robert Salzl, CEO Arabella Hotel Holding International GmbH and Co

'One of the most stimulating and challenging reads in this field for a very long time. Often I wondered how the ideas could be applied – only to find the answer on the next page. It is not that we should agree on every idea – but that we should improve what we do by facing the challenges presented.'

Sir Digby Jones, Chairman, Confederation of British Industry

'Excellent management books should spur you into action. This one does! A thoroughly enjoyable and refreshing read, containing clearly-distilled views which do provoke even the most experienced leader to think again.'

Lord Leitch, Chairman of the Employment Panel, formerly CEO of Zurich Financial Services in UK and Asia

'Building a better world is a message that every business leader needs to listen to and turn into action. Patrick Dixon correctly suggests that purpose is always three sided: the satisfaction of performance goals for the enterprise must be hitched to the personal goals of those who lead it and those who work in it, and all has to be accomplished with an eye to the broader good of society at large. This is a must-read for those who care about our common future'.

Professor Derek Abell, Dean, European School of Management and Technology, Berlin

'Patrick Dixon is first among equals in "how-to" business writings. This brilliant book reveals how passion for your customers and your mission is vital in developing strong brands. For anyone who cares about business success, Building a Better Business is a must read.'

Professor Liping Cai, Director Purdue Tourism & Hospitality Research Center, Purdue University, USA

'It can be a little bit scary when you read a book like *Building a Better Business*. So much of it resonates instantly with one's own personal and business circumstances and experience. It is also comforting to realize that none of us are alone in trying to build better businesses and more particularly, as Patrick Dixon says, a better world.'

Paul O'Toole, Chief Executive, Tourism Ireland

'This book is a cracking good read, full of practical insights that will change your business life and understanding fundamentally. There is so much in this book that makes a positive difference to the way I run my own business.'
Paul Williams, Founder and CEO, MLS Business Centres

'Patrick Dixon's message is powerful, practical and important for every business leader. One of the most striking things about the Young Presidents Organisation's 10,000 business owners, with combined turnover of several trillion dollars a year, is a common desire to make a difference, to use business success to make important things happen in our wider world – and that is what this book is all about. The good news is that when we are truly passionate about making a difference in people's lives, our customers are better cared for, staff feel more committed, the community benefits – and our business is also more likely to be profitable, as well as personally fulfilling.'
Alex Cappello, Chairman Young Presidents Organisation,
Chairman and CEO Cappello Group

'If you want to be a great leader, you need to read this book. A vital guide to management and business success, full of practical examples which provoke, inspire, encourage and challenge. Tackles many of the most important issues in business today.'
Professor Prabhu Guptara, Executive Director, Organisational Development,
Wolfsberg, subsidiary of UBS

'Compelling and irresistible insights which provide a "quantum leap" and significant breakthrough to the current thinking about business. Connecting our passions and work purposes is a potent cocktail which releases, unlocks and transforms talent at an individual and corporate level. Patrick has done it again: a simple and powerful vision with a framework for action.'
Stuart McGreevy, Chairman, Transformational Business Network
and former CEO of Inter-Alliance plc

'Essential truths which we will come to see as pivotal in our understanding of how successful organizations will be led. Patrick Dixon's own passion and purpose are self evident and everyone in a leadership role will be invigorated by reading of his desire to build better business – and a better world.'
David Smith, CEO, Global Future Forum

'*Building a Better Business* combines irrefutable moral arguments for corporate social responsibility with a perceptive analysis of the corporate benefits of channelling the power of people's passion'
Karan F. Bilimoria CBE DL, Founder and Chief Executive, Cobra Beer

Dr Patrick Dixon is often described as Europe's leading futurist and has been ranked as one of the world's 50 most influential business thinkers alive today.[1] He is Chairman of Global Change Ltd, a Fellow of the Centre for Management Development at London Business School, author of 12 books, including *Futurewise*, and is a Visiting Professor at the European School of Management and Technology. He advises many global companies on a wide range of future trends including the digital society, virtual corporations, financial services, biotechnology, lifestyle changes, consumer behaviour, marketing, motivation, leadership, public policy, corporate ethics, activist movements and government regulation. His clients have included Hewlett-Packard, Microsoft, UBS, RBS, Credit Suisse, PricewaterhouseCoopers, Ford, IBM, Roche, GSK, UNIDO, Allianz, HSBC and BT.

Patrick Dixon has given presentations in more than forty countries, as well as at the World Economic Forum in Davos, the WEF Southern African Summit and the International Emirates Forum. He is also a past member of the World Bank technical assistance team in China.

He has taken part in hundreds of TV and radio broadcasts on networks such as CNN, CNBC, ABC News, Sky News, BBC, ITV, Channel 4 and Channel 5. He has written for many publications including *Time* magazine. His web-TV site (globalchange.com) has been visited by more than 6 million different people with up to 50 million words downloaded a day.

He is also involved in humanitarian projects in the poorest nations, and is the founder of ACET International – a global network of community-based AIDS care and prevention programmes. Patrick Dixon trained in medicine at Kings College, Cambridge, and Charing Cross Hospital, London. In 1979 he began his own IT-startup in medical computing before going on to specialize in the care of those dying of cancer. Born in 1956, he lives in West London with his wife and their four children.

---

1 Bloomsbury Publishing/Suntop Media global executive survey 2003 – www.thinkers50.com.

PATRICK DIXON

BUILDING A
BETTER BUSINESS

The key to future marketing,
management and motivation

Dear Tuber,
with thanks and warm
appreciation for many
interesting and thought-
provoking conversations on
these and related issues -
and with thanks also for
all your encouragement.
Your Patrls D

P

PROFILE BOOKS

First published in Great Britain in 2005 by
Profile Books Ltd
58A Hatton Garden
London ECIN 8LX
www.profilebooks.com

10 9 8 7 6 5 4 3 2 1

Typeset in Minion by MacGuru Ltd
info@macguru.org.uk

Printed and bound in Great Britain by
Bookmarque Ltd, Croydon, Surrey

A CIP catalogue record for this book is available from the
British Library.

ISBN 1 86197 753 0

To Sheila, my best friend for more than thirty years
and source of endless encouragement

CONTENTS

PREFACE

I would like every chairman, CEO, manager, leader, coach, consultant, business student, investor, politician and teacher to read this book. I believe it could be the most important guide to marketing, management and motivation that you have ever read and that it will change how you think about yourself, your job, your family and your future. It tells you how to:

- add value to your brand
- sell more with less marketing budget
- increase customer loyalty
- generate more passion at work
- increase loyalty, productivity and quality
- reduce staff turnover
- save costs faster
- manage change more easily.

One four-word principle of life is the secret of all leadership, marketing, management and motivation. It's the key to making things happen, the basis of every healthy business, advertising slogan and mission statement, and will impact on every decision made.

ACKNOWLEDGEMENTS

I am indebted to a host of thinkers, leaders, debaters, speakers and writers whose work over the years has permeated my evolving view of the world – especially to those listed in the Bibliography, or who are quoted directly, but also to many others whose unconscious influence has been significant. I owe a huge amount to the thinking of people such as Charles Handy, Bill Pollard, Prabhu Guptara, Lynda Gratton, Jules Goddard, David Stanley, Ian McMonagle, Dominic Houlder, Bill Leigh and Wes Neff. Peter Cox was helpful when the ideas first began to form, and Stephen Brough of Profile Books has been a huge encouragement in bringing the project to completion, nobly assisted by Linda Cayford and Anne Dixon.

I am also indebted to the thousands of senior executives who helped shape this book by their participation in discussions about building a better world, at conferences, workshops, seminars as well as teaching sessions at London Business School. I am thankful to many unnamed individuals who afterwards have shared deeply personal stories about the pressures of business life, the impact on those they love, and their desire to find greater purpose and meaning in what they do.

I am deeply grateful to others who have had a profound and lasting influence on my life: Sheila, my wife, our children John, Caroline, Elizabeth and Paul, who are all seeking to build a better world in different ways, my parents and many close friends including Naz Pambakian, Steve Clifford, Phil Wall and Gerald Coates who have shared parts of the journey.

A key inspiration has been the unfailing dedication and passion of a generation of people who have devoted their lives to causes they believe in – whether caring for those with AIDS and saving lives in the poorest nations through the work of ACET, or helping the vulnerable and marginalized in parts of the UK, as expressions of practical compassion.

Patrick Dixon

February 2005

http://www.globalchange.com

Quotations

It is always hazardous to quote those who have a high profile in public life on values they say are important. Leaders come and go, reputations can change, but in their words we find values that will endure and on which future success will depend.

THE FUTURE FEELS DIFFERENT

'Nothing great in the world has ever been accomplished without passion.'

Georg W.F. Hegel, 1770–1831, Berlin Professor of Philosophy

'Man is only truly great when he acts from the passions.'

Benjamin Disraeli, 1804–1881, British Prime Minister

Connect with all the passions people have – for themselves, their families, their communities and wider world – and they'll follow you to the ends of the earth. They will spread goodwill about your business, work hard for you, and buy your products, services and stock with pride. You will attract the best people, form highly motivated teams, collect loyal customers, sell the strongest brands with the greatest purpose and highest values, promising a better future.

The secret lies in knowing how to do it, which means understanding:

- why we act as we do
- why we choose what we do
- why we work as we do
- why we live as we do.

This book sets out to do that and explains how to make things happen, how to motivate, how to sell and how to win in a future where everything is changing – *including the definition of winning.*

On one level, it is about:

- the fire in your heart
- the passion in your life
- what makes people achieve greatness.

More practically, it explains *why*:

- so many leaders can't motivate their teams
- change management is often frustrating
- old work incentives don't work any more
- people are leaving well-paid jobs
- everyone is talking about 'getting a life'
- old marketing slogans are looking so tired
- values are changing dramatically.

… and why so many people get much more fulfilment *working for nothing* than they do from their job. Understanding this is crucial when it comes to managing and motivating people, and also in marketing.

Recently, I was with a business leader who was upset at losing one of his best people. 'I don't understand,' he said. 'We've offered him a bonus of half a million dollars to stay.'

What he had not realized was that his colleague's passion for what he wanted to do instead was such that he didn't mind whether he was paid a single cent.

'Being in touch with fire and passion seems to be an essential need for the soul of a human being.'

David Whyte in *The Heart Aroused*

A revealing exercise

Get people to share stories about work they do for nothing, the causes and community groups they or their family are involved in, or used to be and would still support if they had time. Their accounts may surprise you, warming your heart, making you smile and even moving you to tears. You could learn more about your fellow workers in ten minutes than in the last ten years.

'The most lasting happiness comes from finding something you believe in and then putting your strength into service.'

Martin E.P. Seligman, Professor of Psychology, University of Pennsylvania and author of *Authentic Happiness*

Seven out of ten people in the UK gladly work for nothing – 45 per cent help organizations as volunteers, while the remainder help others who are not part of their families, on a one-to-one basis. Their efforts are worth £40 billion or 4 per cent of GDP if we value each hour at the average wage.[1] We see also high figures in many other parts of Europe,[2] while 56 per cent of adults in the United States volunteer a total of 20 billion hours per year,[3] 44 per cent if you include only those working with organizations.[4]

But these figures are averages: 63 per cent of those earning more than £25,000 per year in the UK give unpaid time to organizations, and 40–54 year olds are generally the most likely to volunteer.[5] The vast majority of senior managers in the UK give time, and we see a similar pattern in other nations.

And the trend is growing. Volunteering has risen significantly since the 1980s, and so has the number of hours given by each person.[6]

> 'Nothing great was ever achieved without enthusiasm.'
>
> Ralph Waldo Emerson, 1803–1882

Another revealing question

At most conferences I ask people to put their hand up if they have given time in the last couple of years for a cause they believe in, whether it's helping out in the local school, shaking a tin for the Red Cross or doing the shopping for an elderly neighbour.

The immediate forest of hands always brings a smile. And as conference participants look around at all those waving arms, you can feel their spirits soar as they share the sense that they all want to change the world for the better.

Most managers in every group I have encountered in over 40 nations give time to the community, or give money to *others* so that *they* can give that time.

And even more interesting than learning what these time-givers do is to ask 'Why'? You will hear deeply moving reasons: a family tragedy, a friendship with someone who inspires passion to make a difference, a chance meeting with someone who was in desperate trouble, wanting to support children at the local school and so on, while others volunteer out of a sense of duty.

'My satisfaction comes from a commitment to advancing a better world.'

Faye Wattleton, President, Centre for the Advancement of

Women

Volunteering is a universal feature of human society – independent of wealth, status, language or culture. Wherever you travel, whether to Manhattan, Moscow, Madras, Milan, Melbourne or Madrid, you will find (if you ask) huge numbers of people, who gladly give small or large parts of their lives away without any thought of reward, save the knowledge that have helped make the world a better place.

In many wealthier nations, volunteering is a rapidly growing lifestyle choice by men and women of every age and ethnic group, in every office, factory, call centre, retail outlet, village, town and city. It is part of the air we breathe, a common passion even among the busiest executives, and a powerful force that every corporation needs to understand.

'People give freely to others not only where there is no hope of return, but also when no one is watching to applaud or approve of their generosity… People's wallets are returned without a penny removed. Charities benefit from large anonymous donations. … It does suggest how important altruism is in business.'

Nigel Nicholson, Professor at London Business School,

author of *Managing the Human Animal*

Listen and learn

Conference participants light up as people relate their

stories: heart-filled accounts of time and energy poured into places and people that need their help. If only they could put this strength of conviction into marketing campaigns, business challenges, management successes, product innovation, financial objectives, leadership strategies, operational plans, quality control, budgets or strategic targets. In some organizations such as well-run not-for-profit groups, they do, but in larger corporations it is rare indeed.

> 'What really counts in our lives and in our communities are the enduring values of giving back and helping others.'
>
> Colin L. Powell[7]

Contrast all this passion and commitment with the difficulties many organizations encounter in motivating their staff. You can spend a fortune on adopting the latest management fads, and on special publications, videos, conferences and internal training programmes, and make little or no difference. You need, instead, to connect with this intense desire of people to give their all for *absolutely nothing*.

The hours, days, weeks or months given by volunteers are often not talked about, perhaps out of modesty or because the motivation comes from something that is personal. But lessons we can learn from not-for-profit activity should be on the agenda of every executive board and management team, not least because what directors and managers do unpaid usually means *far* more to them than the profit-focused businesses they are paid so much to run.

Think about it: ten senior business leaders are sitting in a conference room for a whole day, battling with one business challenge after another. The total cost of that meeting is huge in terms of salaries plus add-ons, as well as in time that could otherwise be spent actually running the business. Most of the passion gathered *inside* that room has little to do with what is being discussed, but is about life *outside*: family, community and beyond.

If these people could just connect their business with even 20 per cent of their common passions for life *outside* work, and achieve that same linkage for everyone else across the entire corporation, most of the challenges they had spent all day discussing would rapidly melt away, and they would be better placed to answer such questions as:

- How can we get better performance?
- How can we increase our profits and share price?
- How can we encourage more rapid change?
- How can we get people motivated to save money?
- How can we make sure our sales team are on target?
- How can we increase customer and staff loyalty?
- How can we maintain our margins?
- How can we accelerate innovation?
- How can we maintain our competitive advantage?
- How can we improve our return on equity?
- How can we keep our shareholders happy?

> 'To succeed you have to believe in something with such a passion that it becomes a reality.'
>
> Anita Roddick, founder of Body Shop

What profit motive?

I have rarely met a chairman or CEO of a publicly listed corporation who is truly as passionate about shareholder value, bottom-line profit or return on equity as they are about their children, leisure interests, community causes they are involved in, or whatever else they give energy to *outside* the business. After all, when the paid job ends, they walk away. You don't see many coming back with offers to help out in their own time.

It is strange, then, that board members of public corporations should be deluded into imagining that anyone *else* will be deeply inspired by a vision that is dominated by increasing bottom-line profits year on year. You can promise big rewards for reaching targets, but short-term targets may be met with no passion at all for the overall mission, merely a desire to earn fast and retire early.

'No one, apart from investment managers, goes to work early because he or she is eager to make shareholders wealthy.'

Michael Hammer, author of *Re-engineering the Corporation*

Of course, those with large ownership stakes in the firms they work for may have deeper emotional ties, and founder-owners may see their companies as being almost like children, but strong emotional connection remains unusual. In any case, you cannot expect a CEO to have true passion about the future of a shareholder-owned corporation, when the average length of service before being sacked or pushed out can be as short as three and a half years, depending on industry and country.

Looking for change

> 'The most exciting breakthrough of the 21st century will
> not occur because of technology but because of an expand-
> ing concept of what it means to be human.'
>
> John Naisbitt, author of *Megatrends 2000*

The desire to volunteer is part of the same radical shift that
has provoked new perspectives on work–life balance, corporate governance and social responsibility, and reflects
the revolutionary spirit that could drive every business into
future success.

> 'The purpose of life is a life of purpose.'
>
> Robert Byrne, author

Who still prefers to work for large corporations in any
case? Not many in the UK. Nine out of ten 35–45 year olds
want to leave conventional business jobs.[8] You can hardly
imagine a greater force for change at work.

They can be separated into groups such as:

- Cross-shifters. These comprise the largest group of
  those seeking change. They are successful people
  looking to branch out on their own and are still very
  ambitious about careers and their future, but they want
  life on their own terms, to work for themselves, to find
  their own way.
- New authentics. Of these, as many as seven out of
  ten would halve their salaries for 'a more meaningful
  life'. Many move to the country, or do voluntary
  work abroad, or retrain for jobs such as teaching or
  landscape gardening.[9]

Many successful cross-shifters later become 'older authentics', who look to put something back, for the greater good, after running their own business.

Job dissatisfaction is strongly linked to long hours, partly because it becomes so hard to pursue other interests. If purpose is found entirely outside work, that may be fine if working hours are limited. But the longer those hours become, the more likely it is that someone will begin to feel crushed, dissatisfied or even abused.[10]

In search of fulfilment

> 'People enter business as bright, well-educated, high-energy people, full of energy and desire to make a difference ... The potential of business to contribute towards dealing with a broad range of society's problems is enormous. We must learn how to harness the commitment of our people – then our commitment to building a better world will have some meaning.'
>
> Peter Senge in *The Fifth Discipline*, quoting Bill O'Brien, former President of Hanover Insurance[11]

Another UK survey shows that six out of ten 25–35 year olds feel unfulfilled in their careers.[12]

- 83 per cent believe they are suffering from a 'quarter-life crisis'.
- 90 per cent are looking for a higher purpose at work.
- 59 per cent say they haven't found a meaningful purpose in their work.
- 75 per cent say their bosses don't value the skills they

gain from volunteer roles in the community.
- 25 per cent are worried about the poor ethics of the company they work for.
- More than half are trying to leave their jobs.
- Almost all feel that older managers don't seem to understand.

Such responses are new, growing, becoming more heartfelt, and will, in some way, impact on every organization – from the smallest family business to the largest multinational, from hospitals to contractors, government to civil servants, every university and every business school, every charity and every family.

Young people are fed up with being told to put their heads down and work hard by an older generation whose hearts they feel beat to a different rhythm – if they beat at all.

Of those surveyed, 40 per cent of the men and 20 per cent of the women feel unfulfilled at work. The disparity may be partly because more women than men are working part-time and they are generally more balanced in terms of purpose in their lives.[13]

Remember that this is the generation of children who were brought up on 'worthy' TV or school campaigns, whose parents themselves have often given time or money to causes, who have been encouraged to help save the world by collecting drink cans to raise money for rainforests, or loose change to help blind children in Malawi. As adults, they now find themselves in organizations that fail to give them any satisfaction in terms of solving any of the world's problems or meeting anyone's real needs.

> 'The companies that flourish in this decade will do so
> because they are able to provide meaning and purpose,
> a context and a time-frame that encourages individual
> potential to flourish and grow.'
>
> Professor Lynda Gratton, London Business School,
> author of *Living Strategy*

Lack of passion at work is also common in the US. Less
than half of Americans say they are satisfied with their jobs
– the highest level of discontent since 1995. Decline in job
satisfaction is found among workers of all ages, across all
income brackets and regions.[14] Consider these statistics:

- 35 per cent of 'top performing' corporate employees are
  at high risk of leaving their jobs.
- 60 per cent feel pressure to work is too much.
- 83 per cent want more time with their families.
- 56 per cent are dissatisfied at work.[15]

One in five Americans has chosen to 'downsize' by cutting
their income and expenditure.[16]

Another survey found that less than half of all Americans were satisfied with their jobs. The decline was found
among workers of all ages, across all income brackets and
regions. Reasons included accelerating pace of change,
pressure to adapt, growing requirements to perform at ever-
higher levels and blurring of home/office time. Those aged
between 45 and 54 were most likely to be fed up – around
half of them.[17]

These tired and demoralized workers are restless,
feeling at times exploited and perhaps even embarrassed

or ashamed to work for corporations that attract negative media coverage.[18]

In Australia, 30 per cent of 30–59 year olds have chosen to downsize over the past ten years, if you include 7 per cent who have chosen to return to education or to start working for themselves. People downsize to spend more time with family, for a healthier balanced life, or to achieve greater personal fulfilment. Those on lower incomes are, if anything, slightly more likely to downsize than those earning more, and the vast majority achieve what they hope for.[19]

A random nationwide telephone survey of 1,002 adults, conducted in 2003 by Barna Research Group, concluded that good health, high integrity, a good marriage, good friends and a clear purpose for living were the top five goals among all respondents. Good health was named by nine out of ten adults as their highest goal, while four out of five respondents said they wanted to live with high integrity, and nearly the same number wanted to have one marriage partner for life.[20]

All this means that managers should be asking themselves huge questions. If we want passion at work, we need to ensure that work enhances health, long-term relationships, friendship and provides purpose for living.

In search of meaning

'Man's search for meaning is the primary motivation in his life.'

Viktor Frankl, author of *Man's Search for Meaning*

'… the sole purpose of human existence is to kindle a light in the darkness of mere being.'

Carl Jung, 1875–1961

Many business thinkers are now talking about the importance of engaging people's passion in their work. For myself, passion is everything. I would rather work with five people who really believe in what they are doing than 500 who just can't see the point.

Life's too short to waste time on projects that can't deliver, people who won't change and processes without purpose.

When you have been close to death, it makes you think about life. I started originally as a physician, caring for those dying of cancer: relieving pain, giving emotional support, helping them to live their last days with their families at home. Every day is a special day. You come to see things differently. Priorities change at such a time and you focus more on what is really important.

But now we are seeing the same thought processes in a younger generation of business managers, among students, and even in those leaving secondary education. They are asking profound questions about the purpose and direction of their lives.

'We give people their lives back by repairing and healing the human body. … We call it "a purpose beyond profit". Everyone who works for the company knows that's our goal.'

Sir Chris O'Donnell, CEO of Smith and Nephew[21]

Given the attitudes outlined above, it's not surprising that the following are the most common questions asked about work:

- What is my life for?
- Why am I doing this job and working for this company?
- Why am I putting up with this level of pressure?
- Do I really want to carry on like this?
- Why don't I do something that is important to me?
- How can I devote more time to family and others who matter to me?
- How much money do I really need to live a contented life?

Here is one of the greatest challenges to your business future. If you can show me what difference your management objective makes to other people's lives, you'll find it met faster than you could ever imagine, and better than you dared hope. If you can't, then forget it. The people who work with you will decide that there are other jobs to do, which are more worthwhile and fulfilling.

> 'Passion is the single most powerful competitive advantage an organization can claim in building its success.'
>
> Richard Chang, author of *The Passion Plan at Work*[22]

We are talking about a more far reaching issue than employee commitment. Similar issues are affecting consumer behaviour and investment. A poll of 25,000 individuals across 23 countries in six continents shows that people's image of companies is now shaped more by corporate citizenship (56 per cent) than the brand (40 per cent) or business fundamentals (34 per cent). For example, 77 per cent want their pension funds to adopt ethical investment policies so long as it does not mean lower growth. Two out of three people want companies to go beyond making profit, paying taxes, employing people and obeying laws; they want companies to contribute to broader social goals as well. What's more, one in five consumers has rewarded or punished companies in the past twelve months depending on whether they approve or disapprove of its ethics.[23]

So what does it all mean for leadership, marketing and management?

2

FOUR WORDS FOR EVERY BUSINESS

All this is the background to what has been a very signifi-cant personal discovery for me. Here is how it happened.

I remember the winter's day in February 2001. I was at a conference attended by hundreds of men and women who were all working for nothing, giving time to different causes they passionately believed in.

I had been thinking about the trends I have just outlined: restless managers, the desire for purpose, the way people are turned off by profit-making goals.

I was sitting in my room, catching up on e-mails, and at the same time trying to prepare a client lecture for the following week. But I was continually distracted by these people with their remarkable, raw energy for change. If only corporations could tap into just a fraction of that same work-for-nothing commitment …

Arthur Koestler once said that the more original a dis-covery, the more obvious it seems afterwards. Well, this may not be an original discovery as far as the rest of the world is concerned, more a stumbling upon a well-rounded principle of life and seeing a new application to business, selling, management, leadership and psychology. But it was a discovery for me, profound in consequence, and yet, with hindsight, simple and obvious.

A four-word phrase began to form and take root in my mind, until I was compelled to think about nothing else. With every hour that passed, that same familiar phrase from the past seemed to grow in power and significance. Here, perhaps, could be a missing factor, a key not only to the passion behind volunteerism, but also to business success and to making things happen.

What is more, this four-word phrase seemed to connect deeply with *all* the greatest passions people have – for themselves, those they care for, and far beyond ...

Just four words?

Surely, I thought, such a simplistic approach must be full of holes.

> 'All truths are easy to understand once they are discovered; the point is to discover them.'
>
> Galileo Galilei, 1564–1642

The $20,000 challenge

Not long after, I decided to issue a challenge to anyone who could prove that this universal principle of human life was flawed. Over the next few months I started with thousands of executives from all over the world – bankers, brokers, analysts, marketing directors, risk managers, board members, accountants, human resource managers, journalists, business thinkers and academics – who attended my seminars, workshops and business school classes. Surely, I thought, their combined decades of collective wisdom and experience were bound to expose every false premise in my principle in a very short time.

I began by offering anyone in my audience $100 if they could produce a single argument that would stand against this 'absurdly simple' idea.

But here is a very strange thing. There was no significant challenge of any kind, despite the fact that the idea at first seemed to them to be unsustainable, counter-intuitive, and not one they had considered before. Many tried, but quickly saw their proposed exceptions fall apart. And the more they considered the problem, the harder it seemed to become.

I raised the stakes to $1,000. Over more than two years, despite many informal discussions over coffee or dinner, or through e-mail correspondence, no one came up with any kind of sustainable flaw in the argument.

I would have been perfectly happy to find quite a number of minor exceptions which would have been helpful in understanding how to apply the general rule, or would have defined it more clearly, but I was shocked not to be presented with *any*. To be sure, I received many comments but, after some reflection, their supposed exceptions to the rule melted away into nothing.

In fact, the *opposite* happened: many senior business leaders have been similarly struck by their *own* moment of truth, a point of clarity about their *own* mission and purpose, by a fundamental fact about all human beings that they recognize almost immediately to be true and likely to dominate much of *their* future.

At one gathering I had several of America's leading

business publishers in the audience. A number immediately wanted to meet me. One declared: 'I've sat there for the last hour picking your theory to bits. I thought it was going to be easy but I have to say I'm defeated. Much to my surprise, I can't find anything against it.'

That's when I realized this book had to be written.

The $1,000 challenge goes something like this:

At the end of this presentation I'm going to reveal a single four-word phrase, which is the basis of every successful advertising slogan, every promotional campaign, every mission statement, every satisfied customer, every great product, every workplace and home-based motivation and all great leadership.

These *four words* explain every deliberate action we take, every human desire, all effective parenting, and are the foundation of every reasonable law or regulation. Every appeal to a jury hangs or falls upon this same principle, every organization exists because of it, and every government is elected in the hope of it.

They shed light on all past decisions in human history, make sense of our present and help predict our future.

As we will see, this principle is fundamentally different in character from most last-century (or more ancient) theories about behaviour or motivation. It will be a dominant factor driving every successful business in the next three decades.

And if anyone in the audience can find and e-mail me an exception to this four-word phrase, once revealed, I promise to give a reward to the first person who does so.

But, then, *you* already know the phrase. You have heard it many times before. But take great care: familiarity may lull you at first into a false sense of comfort, when the reality can be profoundly life-changing.

Here it is again, a well-recognized aim in life but applied in a new way, from a different perspective:

Building a better world

Just that ...

... in whatever way *you* choose.

'The supreme purpose of history is to build a better world.'

Herbert Hoover, US President 1929–1933

Each of us is unique, and *building a better world* also means different things at various stages of life, but it's essentially about a *better life* in some way for yourself, or perhaps for those you care for, for family and friends, or for the community you live in and beyond.

Everything you have ever done from the day you were born, from taking a sip of water to solving a problem or 'saving the world', is related to this universal human desire for a better life.

Improvement is the key – even if this is just your own feeling of satisfaction and fulfilment, or maybe personal comfort right now as you adjust your position slightly while reading this book.

This basic truth is expressed by business in hundreds of different ways and, as we will see, has been used or abused by leaders for good or bad reasons since time began.

The aim of every business is to make life better – and to be rewarded for doing so.

- All products are designed to be life-enhancing.
- All services are delivered to be life-enriching.

All business slogans are derived from this building a better world principle:

- 'Our aim is to improve people's lives.'
- 'Our purpose is your pleasure.'
- 'We aim to make dreams come true.'

The promise of every product is a better life, and profits are the reward for making it so. Every product is designed to please, to meet a need.

Core competence, competitive strategies, balanced scorecards and other similar business ideas all need to be connected with this same primary mission which is at the heart of every organization: a better future.

> 'In each case our goals for the project reflected our respective personalities and visions of a better world.'
>
> Jerry Kaplan, in his account of a Silicon Valley startup called
>
> Go Corporation[1]

'Building a better world' is, of course, a familiar phrase, in common use – you will find the exact wording on more than 37,000 web pages indexed by Google alone, and 'better world' alone as a phrase on over 650,000. 'Building a better world' is part of our heritage, part of our social 'DNA'. As I say, it explains the whole of human history, which is the cumulative result of the collective desires for a better future of every person who has ever lived.

> 'As we enter the twenty-first century, it is timely, perhaps even critical, that we recall what human beings have understood for a very long time, that working together can be a deep source of life meaning. Anything less is just a job.'
>
> Peter Senge, author of *The Fifth Discipline*[2]

Why not take the challenge yourself? With the publication of this book the value of the challenge has been raised to $20,000, for a chosen good cause. (See page 310.)

Recall a single deliberate action you have ever taken, or a decision by someone else, that was not driven by this same inescapable expression of human nature.

This universal principle of human action even applies to those who are emotionally unwell. However bizarre a consciously directed human behaviour may be, however apparently self-destructive or unproductive, you will find within it an inner prompt, based on a perception or belief that it will, in some way, improve something, relieve a symptom, feed an addiction or provide some other reward.

Sadly, as a physician, I have seen all kinds of people driven to self-harm, whether by cutting themselves, starving themselves or taking substances that they knew could kill them. And I have friends whose lives have at times been dominated by such things. But, in every case, you will find that the person feels some sense of relief, a lessening of psychological pressure, or some other kind of positive outcome for them or for others that makes their action feel worthwhile at the time.

Why we do what we do

Huge industries have grown up over the past two centuries in an attempt to make sense of why people do what they do. There are hundreds of schools of psychology, behaviour and psychometrics based on Freud, Jung, Adler, Maslow, Myers-Briggs and others. They still have huge followings despite the fact that many parts of their theories at first sight seem to be in outright conflict with each other. Yet all find a common home within this wide-ranging principle of human action.

We can debate about semantics – for example, the notion of 'building a better world' rather than 'experiencing' or 'existing within' or finding a 'state of being', resonates more in Western than Eastern culture – but the broad principle is the same: action leading to enhancement, enlightenment or improvement.

It's the same with spirituality: the sense of a 'better world', or existence, or place of being, is a universal, timeless and life-enhancing theme, running through the teachings of all the world religions, in different kinds of ways, and operating across all cultures. It is central to the teachings of Jesus, Mohammed, Buddha, Confucius, the Jewish and Hindu traditions and every other major religion.

Each religion interprets the universal principle in a different way but the foundations are similar. It may be a better experience of the world in this life, or the promise of the kingdom of God to come. It could be in the nature of spiritual experience, or a better world for one's neighbour, or for the whole of creation itself.

In every individual and in every generation there can

come an 'Aha' moment – a point of revelation. This is how it came for me, and also for many others who have since adopted this same universal guiding factor as a basis for future marketing, management, self-motivation, business strategies, parenting and other areas of life.

Too much obsession with self?

You may say: 'OK, so it may be true, but so *what*? Is it so very different from the way we all thought in the past about ourselves and life?'

The answer is that it is as different as optimism and pessimism: different world-views of the same reality, both of which contain truth and are vital to health and survival. For example, 'We can overcome' (optimist) versus 'We need to take care' (pessimist).

Just as we all need a certain optimism, balanced with sound judgement and caution, to succeed, so this building a better world principle takes us in many new positive directions when we think about marketing, management and motivation, compared to theories which have focused almost entirely on 'self' alone:

- self-actualization
- self-fulfilment
- self-development
- self-realization.

'The idea that human behaviour is governed entirely by self-interest and that altruistic ultimate motives don't exist has never been supported by either a coherent theory or a crisp and decisive set of observations ... Concern for others is one of the ultimate motives people sometimes have.'

Professor Elliott Sober, University of Wisconsin, and
Professor David Sloan Wilson, Binghampton University, in
Unto Others[3]

Despite billions of dollars spent on such self-books, self-courses, self-seminars and self-training programmes, the self-industry has not only promised everything and delivered almost nothing, but has also miserably failed to connect with passion – except, of course, the passion to learn even more about ourselves (but try to use *that* as a get-up-and-go strategy at work).

If self-theories actually work, why on earth are we still spending billions a year buying yet more self-help books, attending yet more self-courses, self-workshops and self-seminars on how to satisfy the 'real you', or on how to motivate the self inside those around you to try and make things happen? Self-books do have value in the right place, particularly to those who feel they have lost their way, have low self-esteem, who feel trapped by their own history, personality, expectations or current situation. But they don't solve the bigger challenge of purpose.

You can self-analyse for ever but self-understanding alone cannot itself lead to passion and motivation. On the contrary, too much self-introspection can *destroy* passion altogether just as it surely destroys relationships, as anyone who has ever tried to analyze love knows.

'Man's goodness is a flame that can be hidden but never extinguished.'

Nelson Mandela[4]

Self-oriented psychobabble has little or nothing to say to the majority of us who, as we know, want to make a difference to other people by acting in a relatively self-less way.

Ever thought about why we give money to a good cause? Why we help an old woman who falls on her face while crossing a busy road? Ever considered why people feed birds in winter, why we put rubbish in a bin? Or why a mother cares for her child? Or why we fall in love?

You can dig as deep as you like to find reasons for acts of spontaneous kindness (psychologists rarely agree), but it is, of course, as futile as trying to analyse how music connects to the human spirit.

Pick a symphony to bits note by note – you'll soon lose the emotional plot altogether.

Are people more or less motivated if you tell them the reason they care is because of a strong genetic impulse, primeval instinct, biological need or unconscious desire? Such pontification misses the point entirely, and can rob us all of joy and enthusiasm for living. What is more it fails to fit the reality of what we see and feel.

Common sense tells us that our lives have *always* been far broader and deeper than 'self' alone. Certainly, in a purist intellectual debate you could argue that people helping others are just satisfying a psychological self-need. But that's not how we sense we are, nor how we actually *live* and *work*.

'Most people have jobs that are too small for their spirit.'

Studs Terkel, author and broadcaster[5]

Ask yourself, or anyone you know, this one question: 'Are you mostly selfish or unselfish?'

Do you feel you are interested only in satisfying your own physical and emotional needs at the expense of those around you – or do you feel deep down that, on the whole, you are a person who also looks out for others?

And when you do something that others would say is unselfish, do you think they are right or do you think they are misled, and that you are just completely self-centred in every way?

In his book *Emotional Intelligence*, Daniel Goleman describes a couple who managed to save their drowning daughter, but in the attempt died themselves. In the terrible tsunami disaster of December 2004 such stories were multiplied many thousands of times over. Men, women, and children dying in the act of saving complete strangers.

> Seen from the perspective of evolutionary biologists, such parental self-sacrifice is in the service of 'reproductive success' in passing on one's genes to future generations. But from the perspective of a parent making a desperate decision in a moment of crisis, it is about nothing but love.[6]

Evolutionary biologists may also dismiss heroic acts by strangers as instinctive preservation of the species, but once again, such explanations can devalue the nature of the human spirit.

Most people think of themselves as warm-hearted free agents, not as self-obsessed or genetically controlled. As I say, it's all a question of perspective, just like the optimist and pessimist. But perspectives really do matter, as you will know if your entire team is dominated either by optimists or pessimists. Perspectives change how we see ourselves, alter our own decisions; they affect business, and influence people in the products they buy, the jobs they want to do and the lives they lead.

The narrow self-approach has made a rag-bag of self-experts a lot of money, but left millions of people as dissatisfied and unfulfilled in their personal lives as they were before; it has wrecked marriages and families, caused untold damage to people and profits, and a new generation is now demanding change.

That's part of the reason why so many are talking about time with those they love, work–life balance, corporate values, community action and a host of concerns for the wider world.

Don Burr, former founder and CEO of People Express, was asked by MBA students at Harvard why he started the airline. He said: 'MABW' – his own acronym for 'making a better world'. 'How can we grow an organization where our great-grandchildren might be proud to work?'[7]

These passions are hardly new; they are merely a redis-covery of ancient truths about human nature and society that were somehow lost in the materialistic orgy of the 1980s and the competitive pressures of the 1990s. But with the new millennium has come a reawakening.

Just look at the tens of thousands of single-issue and activist groups which have mushroomed on different con-tinents, as well as the rapid growth of spirituality, faith commitment, religious pressure groups and fundamentalist people-movements. Look at the sales of business titles on spirituality, business with soul and so on. These are evidence enough.

The changing meaning of 'success'

Despite all these warning signs, many corporations are still driving their strategies by profit considerations alone, with minor and often cosmetic concessions in the name of corporate governance and social responsibility. This narrow philosophy can be disastrous, as Nestlé found when it tried to recover a few million dollars of old debt from a nation of starving Ethiopians, or embarrassing and damaging, as the pharmaceutical industry discovered when forced by public outrage to permit 'illegal' manufacturing of low-cost life-saving generic drugs by the poorest nations.

So what does building a better world mean in your business, your personal life and beyond? How can we use the building a better world principle to add value to people's lives, make things happen, market more effectively, build customer loyalty, create more profitable business, gain shareholder approval, lead more powerfully, change organizations more rapidly and win the war for talent?

3

BETTER LEADERSHIP

'It is essential to have a value system that underpins every aspect of your life.'

Ken Costa, Chairman of Investment Banking for Europe,
Middle East and Africa, UBS[1]

Give people a convincing reason and they will lay down their very lives.

During the twentieth century, success meant making big profits for shareholders, with few questions asked, so long as it was broadly legal.

Real success in the future will be far more difficult to define. It will mean demonstrating how your corporation makes a real difference for everyone: for shareholders, of course, but also for customers, workers, the wider community and, in some small way, the whole of humanity – for example, by protecting the environment.

Global leadership requires a new set of competencies blended with a wholeness of emotional experiences. These include technological savvy, anticipating opportunity, personal mastery, constructive conflict, thinking globally, appreciating diversity, building partnerships, sharing

> leadership, creating a shared vision, demonstrating integ-
> rity, empowering people, leading change, developing
> people, ensuring customer satisfaction, and maintaining
> a competitive advantage.
>
> Warren Bennis in *Global Leadership*[2]

In some ways, leadership is the most important human
activity in the world, and the most important element
in any successful business. Leadership releases people
to be all they can be. It enables great projects to be
completed and goals achieved. It inspires, provokes, challenges, envisions, encourages. It is found everywhere, is
simple to do, hard to imitate, something that people
can fall into by accident and others struggle for years
to achieve.

Each person's leadership is unique – it is an expression of
their entire being, a fusion of all they are, all their interests
and passions in life, all their life experience, all their own
hopes and dreams, attitudes and convictions. Leadership
can be extrovert or introvert, noisy and exuberant or quiet
and restrained, self-confident to the point of arrogance, or
self-effacing with humility.

Leadership at best is a joyful, fun, exciting, life-enhancing
and exhilarating experience in which many people gladly
join forces in racing towards a common cause. At worst it
can be a frustrating, worrying, tedious and soul-destroying
process in which some are working against everything you
are trying to achieve.

It is hard to imagine a world without leadership: there
would be no organizations, no institutions, no significant

commercial life, no government, no law and order, no role models and no parenting.

Leadership is a profound mystery because, despite huge efforts to analyse its component parts, it cannot be turned on or off, cannot be packaged, nor placed in a neat box.

Great leadership – that is, leadership that persuades large numbers of people to follow – is timeless and goes far beyond culture or situation. Thus we see time-warp leadership in which a generation that lived hundreds or thousands of years ago reaches out to a future generation through the influence of oral traditions, writings, whether religious or secular, and more recently in sound and video recordings.

All great leaders make the same speech

Look at all the most powerful speeches that the greatest leaders in the world have ever made – they could have been written by the same speechwriter. They all point directly to a better future. Leaders of corporations today have a huge amount to learn from the emotional appeal of these giants of recent history, while also recognizing that running a business often requires a radically different style.

Here are the sorts of phrases that great leaders use:

That this nation, under God, shall have a new birth of freedom – and that *government of the people, by the people, for the people,* shall not perish from the earth.

Abraham Lincoln

And when that victory is gained you will find *you are in a better world: a world which can be made even more fair, more happy,* if only all the peoples will join together to do their part and if all classes of parties stand together to reap the fruits of victory as they are standing together to bear the terrors and menaces of war.

Winston Churchill

I would just like to remember some words of St Francis of Assisi which I think are really just particularly apt at the moment. 'Where there is discord, may we bring harmony. Where there is error, may we bring truth. Where there is doubt, may we bring faith. And where there is despair, may we bring hope' and to all the British people – howsoever they voted – may I say this. Now that the election is over, may we get together and strive to serve and strengthen the country of which we're so proud to be a part.

Margaret Thatcher

Changing Britain for better. For good. Not a society where all succeed equally – that is utopia; but an opportunity society where all have an equal chance to succeed; that could and should be 21st century Britain under a Labour Government. Where nothing in your background, whether you're black or white, a man or a woman, able-bodied or disabled, stands in the way of what your merit and hard work can achieve.

Tony Blair

For our country to succeed requires the combined efforts of all of us, in all walks of life. *Our achievements so far have shown what can be done when we set aside petty differences and together pursue the common good.*

Nelson Mandela

Together *let us work with other nations for peace and happiness* across our continent and our globe.

Nelson Mandela

By *working together we can build the country of our dreams.*

Nelson Mandela

America, the richest and most powerful nation in the world, *can well lead the way in this revolution of values.*

Martin Luther King

After America was attacked [September 11, 2001] it was as if our entire country looked into a mirror and saw our better selves. We were reminded that we are citizens, with obligations to each other, to our country, and to history. We began to think less of the goods we can accumulate and more of the good we can do ... *We want to be a nation that serves goals larger than itself.*

George W. Bush

Lift your eyes beyond the dangers of today, to the hopes of tomorrow, beyond the freedom merely of this city, or your country, to the advance of freedom everywhere, to the day of peace with justice, beyond yourselves and ourselves to all mankind.

John F. Kennedy

We are here today to raise the flag of victory over the capital of our greatest adversary.... We're raising it in the name of the people of the United States who are *looking forward to a better world,* a peaceful world, a word in which all the people will have an opportunity to enjoy the good things

in life and not just a few at the top. Let us not forget that
we *are fighting for peace and for the welfare of mankind.* We
want *peace and prosperity for the world as a whole.*

Harry Truman, in Berlin, 1945

I offer you peace. I offer you love. I offer you friendship.
I see your beauty. I hear your need. I feel your feelings.
My wisdom flows from the Highest Source. I salute that
Source in you. *Let us work together for unity and love.*

Mahatma Gandhi

If you want to bring the whole thrust of their leadership
into a couple of sentences it would be this:

*'Follow me. Together I believe that we can build a better
kind of world for you, for your family, for the people you care
about, for your community, your city, our great nation and
for the whole of humanity ...'*

And they (almost always) add for good measure:

'In God we trust.'

And (depending on the country) end with:

'God bless America or wherever.'

That's the speech. It's the simplest, greatest, noblest, purest,
most powerful speech a leader can ever make. It takes the
moral high ground yet is as self-satisfying as you can get,
which is why similar speeches have been used by the worst

tyrants in history to promote evil purposes as morally great.

Such an appeal works at every level. We are swept along by our own self-interest, and by our concern for loved ones, our loyalty to our neighbours and friends, our common heritage and common values, by a sense of higher purpose, a sense of community and national identity and, beyond it all, by a call to identify with the good of all, wherever they may be and whoever they are.

Confidence in politicians and national leaders has sunk low, and we may at times be cynical about real motives and integrity, but the language they use is similar, because history shows it is the most powerful appeal that can be made.

There are many theories and styles of leadership ranging from visionary, strategist, commander, storyteller, systems architect, change agent and servant. But whatever method or style you adopt, 'building a better world' will be central to success.

Just imagine a different kind of speech:

'Follow me and I will satisfy your every personal need, give you loads of money, social status, faster cars, impressive job titles and the opportunity to learn new skills in challenging jobs that could lead to greater things.'

It hardly grabs you by the throat. It's hardly a speech to engage the deeper passions of a thousand people, let alone a city or an entire nation.

Why not?

Because the most powerful speeches always appeal to *all* the passions of the *heart*: not just to self, but to family concerns, community spirit and concerns for the future of our wider world.

Powerful speeches always touch a higher moral principle such as justice, liberty, relief of suffering or freedom. Consider the examples below:

> Sustainability – creating a better world for the future through our actions and decisions today – is at the heart of what we do. We define it by the actions we take, the values we uphold and the goals we set.
>
> Peter R. Dolan, CEO of Bristol Myers-Squibb

> Creating socially responsible corporations that help to make a better world is the auto industry's most important job in the 21st century.
>
> William Clay Ford, Jr, Chairman, Ford[3]

Speeches that appeal to high moral instincts and noble principles have been used to unleash powerful forces for both good and evil. The worst dictators that have ever lived have always used the same speech, because it is the only one that works for them, too. But the promise is *always* of a better world in a broad sense – for you, your family, neighbours, villages, communities, cities, our entire nation and for the whole of humanity. The more evil the nature of the regime, the stronger the apparent call to higher values, and the more the speech appeals to a broad vision of the future, because no other call is so effective at moving the heart of a nation, or a tribe or a group of people.

Always? There are some rare exceptions: 'Follow me and together we will wipe out all the other people and grab everything for ourselves.' In other words, let's make a better world for us, our families and our own communities but to hell with the rest.

Such a speech does sometimes work – so long as you are only speaking to criminals, psychopaths or people who have become dehumanized as a result (usually) of a terrible history of violence, atrocities, oppression, fear and insecurity. It works during armed conflicts at a local level – killings tend eventually to brutalize those on both sides – but it never works for long when nation-building in times of peace.

Terrorist groups also use the same 'building a better world' message, for example, to encourage suicide bombers: appealing to the individual (spiritual reward and honour if killed), the family (honour and financial/community support), the community (protection of 'our' people and promotion of the cause) and wider humanity (help usher in a new world order). Defeating terrorists depends not only on improved security but also on understanding the power of this appeal, and developing a stronger 'better world' message to replace it in the minds of rising numbers of disaffected people.

Strange, then, having seen how many good and evil regimes have successfully launched off the back of the same speech, that so many corporate leaders spend so much time and energy banging on the drum of naked self-interest and personal advancement in order to generate the maximum commitment to the corporate cause. They may be good leaders, but they will never achieve greatness, nor the deeper respect of their workforce, their community, their country nor indeed of the wider world.

Good and great leaders

'Good leaders create an organization with a purpose that rises above the bottom line; great leaders go a step further, finding ways to leverage the passion of each employee in order to create incentives that transcend financial rewards. The greatest leaders rely on a simple, timeless idea in order to create passionate, purposeful workplaces.'

Joe Morrow and Vince Cavasin,
Morningstar Consulting Group

Quiet leaders can be very effective

It is important not to confuse loudness with power, nor mere charisma with true greatness. Harvard Business School Professor Joseph Badaracco has described research into leadership of corporations that shows how effective quiet leaders can be.[4]

We don't need another hero, he says. Modesty and restraint, thoughtfulness in approaching moral dilemmas, caution in turbulent times and ability to find a working compromise – these characteristics may appear to hold a leader back, 'but often turn out to be the quickest way to make the corporation – and the world – a better place'.[5]

Jim Collins's research into carefully matched large corporations (published in *Built to Last*) also shows clearly that a charismatic maverick may move mountains, but can be a hard act to follow, especially if such a leader hinders the development of potential successors.

Quiet or loud, charismatic or reflective, all leaders need to engage with people's own sense of purpose, to convince them it's worth the effort to get up and follow.

'The key to successful leadership today is influence, not authority.'

Ken Blanchard, co-author of The One-Minute Manager

Why people follow leaders

Deeply buried in the human psyche is a social instinct which encourages us to relate to others, live in communities and follow leaders – people we instinctively recognize as those who know where they are going and how we need to get there together.

Some charisma is vital to successful leadership, so that others follow without feeling 'bossed around'; they are led through influence rather than authority:

Leadership is the practice of helping people envision, and then participate in creating a better world than the world they came into. It means raising individuals, organizations and communities to higher levels of moral development.

Kevin Freiberg, author of Nuts!, Southwest Airlines' Crazy Recipe
for Business and Personal Success[7]

Being a strong leader

'A good leader can't get too far ahead of his followers.'

Franklin D. Roosevelt, US President 1933–1945

How do you know if you are a strong leader? Just look over your shoulder at the people who are following some of your ideas or values, goals or life-targets – not primarily because of some organizational role, or job title, but simply because of the nature of who you are, the values you have, the vision you hold, the friendships you form and what you mean to those people's lives.

Most leadership is by example, and the effect of example can be very enduring. Depending on your stage in life, your greatest leadership influence may now be through the lives of all those you influenced, mentored, encouraged and taught some years ago. That is why leadership influence can span several generations, commonly seen in families, but also in all long-term organizations.

> 'When I hear corporate leaders refer to values as "soft" issues, I wonder what they regard as "hard". In my experience, cultural beliefs are the heart and soul of all business matters. More than heroic working hours, more than pay incentives, certainly more than strategy alone, shared beliefs, values, can be the key to unleashing the talents of all the people in an organization.'
>
> Eli Lilly, former CEO of Randall Tobias

Ten steps to powerful leadership

Do you want to lead more powerfully?

1 Let your passion show.
2 Be the person you know you were made to be.
3 Have the courage of your convictions.
4 Focus on things that are important to you and others.
5 Decide to make a significant difference.
6 Dump trivial and unimportant things.
7 Go for it with all your heart and mind.
8 Live just as you want others to live.
9 Show people how you are going to build a better world,

FedEx – Passion to deliver more than a package

'When I started Federal Express back in 1973, we had a small group of employees, an even smaller fleet of aircraft, and an idea ... Twenty-seven years later this passion still burns strong. In fact it is the heart of the entire FedEx Corporation. As market conditions and strategies have changed – and as our business has grown – our passion has remained constant. A passion to deliver more than packages. It's a passion to deliver success for every customer...Passion can build better companies, create better products and services and improve the lives of all those it touches – customers, employees, partners and communities ...'

Fred Smith, CEO FedEx[8]

with or without their help, and get on with making it a reality.

10 Have fun!

Why should people follow you?

People will only follow you if they see you're ahead, are convinced you know the route, trust you and want to get there too. Leaders have to prove they are worth following, as Fred Smith did when he founded Federal Express.

There is a crisis of leadership today because many no longer trust those in authority – their integrity, vision and wisdom. That's why character is fundamental to all successful leadership. Consistency, honesty and a willingness to admit the truth, even when embarrassing or humiliating, are required. It is not enough to be liked, or attractive, or a powerful speaker who can touch mind and emotion. Leaders need to be more than that if they are to survive close scrutiny and criticism.

Within every strong leader there is an unshakeable inner conviction of the rightness of their cause, matched by bold commitment to the way ahead, tempered by sound judgement. Strong leadership defies those around to challenge the vision. Yet strong leadership is like a magnetic force, drawing people and resources into action. As Max Landsberg puts it:

> The leader is always more effective when he gets the relevant people to 'buy into' his proposals. The leader uses his interpersonal skills to excite his people, and helps them to see how they may themselves benefit from both the journey and the arrival. He helps them to see 'the word made flesh' … For a vision to guide a team or organization, it must be a compelling story – one that portrays real events: real people achieving a better tomorrow.[9]

Landsberg describes the essence of leadership as Vision × Inspiration × Momentum.

The characteristics of strong leaders

Strong leaders are always:

S *elf-aware*
T *arget-driven*
R *elationship-hungry*
O *rganization-influenced*
N *eighbourhood-linked*
G *lobally-concerned*

S *Self-aware*

All strong leaders know their own strengths and weaknesses. They know their limitations and what complementary skills they need in their teams to work most effectively. They are humble, teachable and quick to defer. What is more, they listen to the voice within, to their own thoughts and values about what really matters. They are sensitive to their own conscience as a higher principle and use it to assess every action they may be about to take, rather than simply rely on what is permissible in law and acceptable generally.[10]

T *Target-driven*

Strong leaders are driven by more than vague vision. They aim for clear targets – practical, achievable goals which inspire teams to great things. They are passionate about the higher purpose of all they do, and how each target fulfils their big mission.

In their book *The Balanced Scorecard*, Robert Kaplan and David Norton developed the idea of a plane cockpit, proposing new 'dials' and 'instruments' to provide ongoing feedback to business leaders about many different parts of their business. The scorecard has revolutionized target-setting in many corporations but, as the authors point out, the four parts of the scorecard (financial, customers, internal business processes and learning/growth) can be a straitjacket and may need rebalancing with softer variables such as employee satisfaction and community involvement.[11]

'If any one idea about leadership has inspired organizations for thousands of years, it's the capacity to hold a shared picture of the future we seek to create.'

Peter Senge, author of *The Fifth Discipline*

R *Relationship-hungry*

Strong leaders do it together. For them, relationships with men and women they can trust are of absolute importance. They spend time investing in key people, mentoring, coaching, encouraging, releasing and equipping – all things which help build morale.

'The best morale exists when you never hear the word mentioned. When you hear a lot about it, it's usually lousy.'

Dwight D. Eisenhower, US President 1953–61

O *Organization-influenced*

Strong leaders are always open and sensitive to those they are seeking to lead. They consult before they commit, listen before they leap, ask before they advance. They make themselves accountable to those they seek to serve in their leadership.

N *Neighbourhood-linked*

Strong leaders recognize that they are part of the wider local community and the company benefits from local talent, local resources and local trade. Strong leaders invest in neighbourhood schemes, and expect their corporations to benefit the area as a whole and, as a result, are seen as a community friend.

'You need to frame all your decisions in a wide view of your obligations to society and turn this into good business.'

Clive Mather, President and CEO of Shell Canada[12]

G *Globally concerned*

Strong leaders take the broad view, with a long-term perspective, committed to responsible planning rather than short-termism. They drive sustainable business practices and aim to leave the world in a better state than it would have been otherwise.

'Today, business leaders cannot begin to foster a climate of positive order if their sole concern is making a profit. They must also have a vision that gives life meaning, that offers people hope for their own future and those of their children.'

Mihaly Csikszentmihalyi, author of *Good Business*[13]

So we have seen what makes strong leaders but how do we improve the leadership we have? Can leadership be developed or is it a natural gift?

4

HOW TO DEVELOP BETTER LEADERS

'Leaders grow – they are not made.'

Peter F. Drucker[1]

Everyone is capable of leadership. We know this from child psychology. If you study families you will find that, almost without exception, an older child will naturally lead the younger, into safety or into danger, in play and in exploration – the natural 'pecking order'. If age and strength differentials are great enough, they usually override factors such as force of personality.

Anyone can provide leadership in crisis. Imagine a cinema attendant who discovers a fire, presses a fire alarm, runs into the auditorium to shout a warning and direct people to the exit. Inside that place may be some of the most powerful and influential leaders in the world, but they will follow her leadership.

Why? She has a clear vision of the future, which matters to everyone in the cinema, she communicates with passion and conviction, and has a clear and compelling strategy which inspires confidence, and her leadership fills a gap.

'I am a leader by default, only because nature does not allow a vacuum.'

Bishop Desmond Tutu

You could say that she is leading by proxy and her authority comes from her uniform or her role, but that is untrue. Any member of the public doing the same thing would also create leadership.

However, you can no more train an ordinary person to be a *great* leader than train someone to be a world-class musician. Both depend on a special quality, a presence, a charisma, a performance, an almost mystical ability to connect to large numbers of people.

Nevertheless, you can enhance someone's natural leadership. You can help them lead more effectively, but only by working with the spark of leadership that is already there. The one exception is, as I say, leadership by proxy. There are many examples in history and in business life where people have been able to lead in unexpected ways because they were in a subsidiary role to someone else who was providing strong, primary leadership.

In some institutions or situations the mantle of vested authority is so powerful that the person in post acquires huge authority and respect, able to command attention and make things happen.

You cannot train people to have a vision, nor train 'get up and go' into them. You can help them develop clear strategy and some aspects of communication. But you cannot train trust, nor humility, nor to be a worthy example. These are all things that come from within.

> **VICTOR leadership**
>
> **V** ision — great purpose and sense of mission
> **I** nitiative — get up and go
> **C** larity — practical strategy, route map
> **T** rust — truthful, reliable, upright, sincere, tough
> **O** penness — accountable, teachable, humble
> **R** ole-model — example worth following

Humility and willingness to serve are central. Other leadership styles based on aggressive domination and arrogance may succeed for a while, but such leadership tends to self-destruct for a very important and obvious reason. Leaders get the teams they deserve, and conceited bullies usually alienate other quality leaders, who tend to move away or refuse to work with the individual in the first place. As Jim Collins describes in his book *Built to Last*, such leadership may shine for a while, but succession is always a challenge since the talent base around the mega-star is usually so depleted.[2]

The second, and even more serious, risk in the shorter term is that the autocratic or bullying leader quickly becomes surrounded by those unwilling or unable to bring alternative points of view, so that leadership becomes blind to changes inside and outside the organization, with huge risks to the future of the organization.

Nelson Mandela has described in his own writings how a true leader is a shepherd, staying behind the flock and leading from behind. The most nimble sheep go on ahead and the others follow, not realizing that they are being directed from behind. In the New Testament, Jesus Christ called himself 'the good shepherd, who lays down his life for the sheep', and he also emphasizes in the words 'Whoever among you wishes to be great must become a servant' that to lead is to serve.

Trust, the T in VICTOR, is a make or break factor for all leaders, especially in our modern era of scandals and poor judgements. And trust is something that very often eludes aggressive and arrogant bullies. Their intense efforts to regain trust may simply raise more questions about their true character.

Such a person may be able to rebuild trust using a different approach, with openness, frankness, (probably) apology and careful listening, followed by genuine efforts to be more inclusive and respectful of others.

> 'Bad men live that they may eat and drink, whereas good men eat and drink that they may live.'
>
> Socrates, 469–399 BC

The 10-star double-trust rating: the *only* way to win trust

Corporations	Leaders
T ransparent	**T** ruthful
R esponsible	**R** eliable
U ncompromising	**U** pright
S uccessful	**S** incere
T emperate	**T** ough

Leaders who are trustworthy all demonstrate similar characteristics to varying degrees.

T *Transparent and Truthful*

First they are transparent: they don't have hidden agendas. What you see is what you get. They show integrity and refuse to get involved in underhand methods, deceptions and double-dealings. They delight in the truth. They like open discussions and are uneasy about secrecy. They are bad liars and, in their personal as well as corporate lives, demonstrate consistency with their stated values.

R *Responsible and Reliable*

They are responsible. They take upon themselves the obligations of leaders towards those who entrust authority to them, whether those who confer responsibility or those who choose to follow. Never reckless, always reliable, they are unafraid to take difficult decisions and necessary risks. They assume responsibility for actions by those who report to them, recognizing that accepting blame is different and implies dereliction of duty.

U *Uncompromising and Upright*

They are uncompromising. They are bound by unshakeable personal values and will not deviate to gain personal advantage or other benefit. They are guided by a strong sense of right and wrong, and have the courage to risk being criticized for it. They will not tolerate those who act in unethical ways.

'Real leadership is the way we do things: it's the values, but
then it's actually practising what you preach. It's saying to
the organization, "This is what I want us to do; what we
should do."'

John Steele, when Group Personnel Director, BT[3]

S *Successful and Sincere*

They are successful. They deliver consistently high performance. They are great at inspiring high levels of
achievement in others. They reach high targets, achieve
more than it would be reasonable to expect and delight
those who have the privilege to work with them. Their
track record gives them freedom to pursue the highest
ethical standards without concerns that, in doing so, they
may be sacrificing performance. They are sincere and
mean what they say.

T *Temperate and Tough*

They are temperate. They are balanced in public decisions
and private life. They do not attract sensation or scandal.
They have a clean track record. They are neither overcon-
fident and extravagant in good times, nor overhasty in
cutting when times are tough, able to use carefully stew-
arded reserves to maintain stability through business cycles.
Yet they are tough and unflinching when times call for
major action.

Transparent, truthful, responsible, reliable, uncompromising, upright, successful, sincere, temperate and tough
– these kinds of people are always trusted, unlike those who

are proven to be easy deceivers, irresponsible, willing to compromise and prone to excess.

'An effective corporate culture is increasingly a source of competitive advantage, which is why we pay such enormous attention to our corporate values, teamwork, respect, integrity and professionalism.'

Dolf van den Brink, former board member, ABN AMRO[4]

The nature of leadership

You can read hundreds of theories about leadership, but leading is something that *is*, rather than something to be dissected. After all, what is a leader without followers? In many ways, leadership is defined by the characteristics of followers, not by leaders themselves. Leadership is created by those who choose to follow, and can only be taken away by their own decisions.

True leadership is relational and not limited by structure: it derives from who the person is, rather than from the title or position they hold, which is why all powerful leaders exert profound influence not only on those who report to them, but also on their colleagues at many levels within the organization.

By the nature of who they are, true leaders have an irrepressible capacity to engage interest, provoke passion and win people over. They have a wide-ranging ability to change how people think, feel and behave, without them necessarily being aware that they have been affected in such a way, or ever having met the person. True leadership creates infectious agents of change, which are transmitted from one to another in attitudes, opinions, feelings and ideas which rapidly take root in each person's life.

Such leadership is usually largely unconscious, and the person who wields it is typically oblivious to many aspects of their extraordinary power. Strong leaders have so much 'unofficial' influence that they can inadvertently create paranoia further up and down the chain of command, especially if their opinions have greater impact than those who are supposed to be providing direction.

True leaders are extraordinarily powerful when placed in a situation where they are able to lead officially as well as informally, by right of their position as well as by reach of their general sphere of influence.

A leader is someone who others choose to follow

'It's your values that will mark you out as a leader.'
Paul Williams, CEO of MLS Business Centres[5]

The secret of building a large following is to capture hearts and minds by convincing people that, if they adopt your ideas, ways, attitudes, perspectives, vision, targets and goals, the result will be a better world than it would be if they try to follow someone else or follow no one at all.

'CEOs make the point over and over that the company must stand for something beyond mere profitability, although that is a precondition for success. Their companies must radiate these values over a long period of time, through swings in the business cycle and other business factors. They must communicate these values in a clear and understandable way to all their constituencies.'

Jeffrey Garten, author of *The Mind of the CEO*[6]

Can leadership be taught?

Most leadership strategies, courses and principles are a waste of time because they merely tinker around the edges.

Imagine that an executive has been overpromoted and is now alarmed to find himself leading a large business unit. Feeling out of his depth and vulnerable, he consults five leadership mentors, goes on ten leadership courses and reads fifty leadership books. Every night he rehearses his next steps along the leadership path to greatness and every day he is both amazed at how straightforward the methods are and disappointed at how little real impact they seem to have.

Yes, he knows how to run a meeting, set an agenda, keep to time, deal with deviants, drive discussion and delegate responsibility. He can set a decent target, measure performance and has sound reporting and appraisal systems. But lead? Ah, that is a very different thing. Manage, yes. Lead, maybe.

The trouble is that, however efficient he is as a manager, into that leadership vacuum will come all kinds of influences from above, below and from others on the same level, even within his own team. If he is not careful he may find himself feeling even more insecure, and he may deliberately not promote someone who is a natural leader into his team or may make it easier for a well-intentioned influential expert to move on.

'Imagine an expert, a well-intentioned expert. He wants to help all employees rise above their imperfections. He looks at all the fumbling inefficiency around him, and he knows, he just knows, that if only people would learn his simple steps, the world would be a better place. And everyone would thank him.'

Marcus Buckingham and Donald Clifton,
authors of *Now Discover Your Strengths*[7]

Dealing with strong unofficial leaders

Many managers think that a new promotion will automatically confer added authority. But true leadership comes from who you are, not from a new rank or title. We see this in 'unofficial leaders': workers who carry natural authority, which is not reflected in their official responsibilities. The scenario is common and the options for managers are few:

1 Bring them into the fold

Work with those who carry others with them, honour their contribution, be honest about your concerns, express your appreciation and draw them into the team. This can be the most successful leadership strategy of all, so long as you can convince the person that your own goals, objectives and strategy are going to create a better world than the alternatives. The risk is that the other person gains privileged access and a more powerful platform to promote a dissenting view. Bringing them into the fold is always the strongest option, assuming that the one 'in charge' has both the leadership capabilities to carry it out and the self-confidence to manage the extra electricity within the team.

2 Ignore and marginalize

Just hope the problem goes away. It may not. If the person is as gifted as you think he is, and as influential, it won't be long before he is talking informally to those you report to, who in turn may realize the importance of being close to what he is thinking – simply because of the far-reaching nature of his informal footprint. His insights into the organization as a whole may be invaluable. He is likely to be a great networker and could even network you out of a job.

3 Counsel him out

Talk with him and encourage him to spread his wings and apply for other internal posts where he can have room to flourish, open doors for him, invest in his success, and encourage him positively to change up a gear in thinking about other opportunities, perhaps elsewhere. This is a risky course that could also land you in legal trouble if he thinks he is being blocked for promotion in your own department for some reason or, even worse, is being victimized in terms of future employment.

Big organizations need big leadership

'Managers are people who do things right; leaders are people who do the right thing.'

Warren Bennis, author of *Leaders*

'The most powerful weapon on earth is the human soul on fire.'

Field Marshal Ferdinand Foch, 1851–1929

Passion releases energy. Passion drives us towards goals.

Passion wells up from the roots of our being. You cannot have strong leadership without passion. It is rare for followers to be more passionate and committed to a cause than the person they lead, and rare for a passionate leader to be thwarted by total lack of commitment from those who follow.

Few company leaders understand passion. For too long they have been forced to focus on short-sighted metrics, market price, fickle analyst perspectives and the harsh realities of an uncertain world.

Daniel Goleman[8] and others have influenced many with their promotion of emotional intelligence (EI), but this is about a far more fundamental transformation than EI. It is about vision:

> A vision builds passion, motivation, direction and purpose into our everyday lives. Without a compelling vision to pull our efforts together, a win becomes just a win, a deal becomes just a deal, and a sale becomes just a sale.
>
> Andy Stanley, author of *Visioneering*[9]

While at times a controversial figure, Bill Gates has a zeal about the future and a passionate belief in the positive contribution of Microsoft which is reflected in their corporate statements – and his own generous philanthropy.

One thing is certain: the smaller the organization, the smaller the vision needed to sustain motivation, and large organizations usually find it much harder to connect people with what the business is really all about.

Making a new sales assistant feel an essential part of the team is easy in a small family-owned corner store. But

> **Microsoft's vision, mission and values**
>
> **Vision**: 'We truly believe that our innovations have enabled people to accomplish great things.'
> **Mission**: 'To enable people and businesses throughout the world to realise their full potential.'
> **Values**: 'We are committed to the delivery of innovative, proven solutions that enable our customers to achieve their potential and do business in new and exciting ways.'

the same task can be almost impossibly difficult in a huge call centre belonging to a multinational, where a new team member is handling sales enquiries from perhaps another time zone and culture.

Not-for-profit organizations get round this problem by focusing on a mega-issue and are often able to attract good people at relatively low rates of pay, as well as generate huge amounts of passion, enthusiasm and personal commitment from large teams across many nations.

Both large and small businesses can learn a lot from not-for-profit organizations (see page 247).

All leaders are role-models

> 'Example is not the main thing in influencing others. It is the only thing.'
>
> Albert Schweitzer, 1875–1965

> 'A leader doesn't just get the message across. He is the message.'
>
> Warren Bennis

'Any closely held value, no matter how well concealed (even from yourself) inevitably prompts action that is consistent with it, because your people are boss-watchers, boss-students, boss-anthropologists of the first order.'

Tom Peters and Nancy Austin[10]

All leaders become role-models, whether they intend to or not. It is in human nature to follow an example, and this principle is fundamental to getting things done in the right way. A good or bad leader can change the atmosphere across a large organization quite rapidly, altering how people treat each other, the language they use, their work patterns and even the clothes they wear. Take care following a corporate scandal. You will often find the errors and attitudes of a few have infected the corporate culture far more widely than first appears – or have been shaped by it in the first place.

What you are can be multiplied a hundredfold in a short time: your own attitudes to clients, meetings, e-mail, time-keeping, taking holidays, claiming expenses, meeting dead-lines and so on.

A great leader can offset a hundred potentially demoti-vating factors in a job – but only if that leader has a compel-ling vision of a better future and values that fit with those of the organization:

To be effective in an organization, one's own values must be compatible with the organization's values. They do not need to be the same but they must be close enough to be able to co-exist. Otherwise they will be frustrated, but also the person will not be able to produce results.

Peter Drucker[11]

In summary, leadership is fundamental to motivation. Strong leaders are not only charismatic, dynamic, creative and visionary, but also encouraging: they energize, inspire and release others to do what they do best.

Strong leaders believe the best of those they invest in, look for opportunities to entrust them with responsibility, are open to criticism, honest about the pressures they face and are focused on the ultimate mission, while remaining sensitive to the price being paid by the team to achieve it.

CREATING BETTER TEAMS

'Most of what we call management consists of making it difficult to get their jobs done.'

Peter Drucker

'The difference between a boss and a leader; a boss says "go", a leader says "let's go".'

E. M. Kelly, author of *Growing Disciples*

All teams need targets, but most need better, more meaningful targets than they are traditionally given: ones that encourage action, innovation, creative dynamism and high efficiency.

Make sure that every target you agree conforms to these seven criteria:

- matters to you
- inspires others
- is clear
- is realistic
- is agreed
- is reviewed
- is rewarded.

Building loyalty

> 'People want to be caught doing things right and affirmed
> as a human being.'
>
> Ken Blanchard

Loyalty is a mission-critical issue in every sense. Frederich Reichheld's study of 150 years of business success in scores of corporations suggests that a 5 per cent increase in loyalty amongst employees, customers and investors can deliver 25–100 per cent increases in profitability depending on industry.[1] The best predictor of top-line growth is the answer to a single question: 'Would your staff or customers recommend your company to a friend?' And if your team is deeply loyal, those they look after – whether staff or customers – are more likely to be so too.

Your team will always be loyal so long as they are convinced that you are worth following, your heart is in the right place, your ideas are sound, your values are great, your friendship is important, the environment is fun, you listen well, treat people generously and fairly, with integrity and respect – and there is no other job they would rather do, or leader they would rather work for.

Democracy is a powerful principle in team-building, which can stretch across an entire organization, encouraging active participation by every member in discussions about direction, strategy and problem-solving. The result is greater agility, as well as stronger commitment.

> 'Each of us feels more engaged, more excited and more
> alive when we are in situations where we have freedom
> and a sense of shared purpose.'
>
> Lynda Gratton, author of *The Democratic Enterprise*[2]

How does your team score you?

1–5

1 Worth following ☐

2 Heart in the right place ☐

3 Knows what she's doing ☐

4 Values are great ☐

5 Her friendship is important ☐

6 Environment is fun ☐

7 Listens well ☐

8 Treats people generously, fairly, with integrity
and respect ☐

9 No other job I would rather do ☐

10 No other leader I would rather work for ☐

Total ☐

Scoring:

35 and above: Your leadership is likely to be strong, effective and enjoyable – for you and for others.

25 to 34: You need to look carefully at lower scoring areas and learn from other's whose leadership attracts you.

Less than 25: You will probably function far better as a supporter of other people's leadership, rather than trying to lead yourself.

How do you think you rate on a scale of one to five? How do your team members score *you*?

If there is a gap of ten points or more between your scoring of yourself and how others see you, then you need to listen more to your team, and get in touch with how they think and feel.

Sony's first mission statement:

'To establish a place of work where engineers can feel the joy of technological innovation, be aware of their mission to society, and work to their heart's content.'

Written by Masaru Ibuka, who started Sony in 1945[3]

Mission commitment

'The most distinguishing feature of winners is their intensity of purpose.'

Alymer Letterman

'You are only as strong as your purpose …'

Barry Munro

Mission is at the heart of what you do as a team. Goals are merely steps to its achievement. Mission has an eternal quality. Goals are time-bound: once achieved, they are replaced by others.

A true mission statement expresses an organization's reason for existence, and every team needs to know what part they play in the bigger picture. When your own team mission overlaps with the mission of many others, all kinds of things become possible.

And to arrive at a meaningful and effective overall mission statement, we have to understand what fires people up to achieve great things, the values people want their organization to share, how to run organizations, how to bring order out of chaos – and have a life at the same time.

> **Make your team GREAT**
>
> **G** ood
> **R** easons
> **E** nergise
> **A** ll
> **T** eams

Align behaviour with objectives

'I have absolutely no doubt that the senior team has to be
aligned to get maximum performance.'

Helen Alexander, CEO, The Economist Group[4]

Make sure that every strategy, decision, structure, layer of
management, control system, feedback mechanism and
performance indicator is directed towards only one goal:
doing a very important task even better.

Mission statements are a powerful way of developing
alignment; in fact, their main value can lie in the writing
of them. Every effective mission statement describes a
common aim: to build a better world – the only question is
for whom and in what way.

Create a powerful mission statement

'A business which makes nothing but money is a poor
business.'

Henry Ford, 1863–1947

All effective mission statements contain a compelling vision
expressed in a practical, down-to-earth, simple, direct and

inspiring way. People in a team may not be able to remember the exact wording of a corporate mission statement, but the core values and purpose should be part of the air they breathe.

Too many mission statements are full of bland, meaningless platitudes and business jargon, such as 'helping people achieve their potential' or 'providing customer satisfaction through quality support and services' or 'adding shareholder value by efficient service delivery'. These computer-speak phrases carry zero emotional energy and are not even worth the ink and paper used to reproduce them. Instantly forgettable, they add no value whatsoever to corporations looking to crystallize their purpose.

Mission statements can have the air of slogans. For example:

- 'For a great place to live and work that future generations will admire.'
- 'For peace and security.'
- 'Protecting your future wealth.'
- 'For safe, fast and reliable travel.'
- 'For attractive, comfortable clothing that you and your friends are proud to wear.'

Soul-friendliness
Teams with a strong sense of purpose can fire up the soul of an organization. In *The Spirited Business* Georgeanne Lamont describes how badly run companies can 'quietly take away your soul'.[5]

So what are the characteristics of soul-friendly companies and teams? Lamont suggests the following:[6]

- leadership that seeks to guide, help and support others, and gains pleasure when others succeed
- a culture that respects and values those at the bottom of the hierarchy – such as receptionists, factory operatives and cleaners who do many of the things that really matter
- a balance of personalities, genders, backgrounds, cultures and experience
- a belief in generosity, compassion, doing the right thing and caring about the wider community, working with decent people for something that is worthwhile
- valuing intangibles such as culture, a sense of belonging and team spirit, while also focusing on high performance and stretching financial targets
- standing up for what you know is right, taking risks for a greater future, encouraging creativity, believing in people
- Agape – a Greek word for love: unspoken but always there; love for what people are doing and affection for others; a deep concern for relationships.

Stirring the troops in crisis

'Singleness of purpose is one of the chief essentials for success in life …'

John D. Rockefeller, 1839–1977

A crisis provides an ideal opportunity to focus on what you and your team are doing and why it is so important. When one occurs:

1 **Tell them about it**. Take your time and tell the whole truth: what the crisis is, why it happened, why it really does matter, and what steps are already being taken to try to ensure that it doesn't happen again. If you want people to make a big effort, they need to know *all* the reasons for the crisis. If mistakes have been made, talk about them.

2 **Bring them into your confidence**. Let them see and feel for themselves what you are seeing and feeling. Share your perspective on the situation with them, and your hopes and your fears.

3 **Make yourself vulnerable**. Let them see how passionately you feel, how upset you will be if the crisis continues, and how determined you are to help. If few resources are available to throw at the problem, explain this and help people understand why.

4 **Make them feel important**. Honour them by affirming, praising and expressing your confidence in their abilities. Let them know (again) just how important they are to you and how you believe they could have a real impact.

5 **Ask them for ideas**. If you have done steps 1 to 4 correctly, you will be rewarded with a flood of new practical ideas (see Chapter 10 on innovation). Your team's greatest contribution may be insight rather than action. This stage is critical to encouraging ownership by the team as a whole.

6 **Give strong backing**. They need to know that they will have your full blessing and support for their best ideas and for team decisions taken once the flak starts flying around as it surely will when they get going.

7 **Lead by example**. Pull your weight in making all this happen. Model the kinds of behaviours you need from the team as a whole.

8 **Encourage each team member to mobilize as many others as possible**. Get them to use a similar approach and well-focused step-like objectives. Large tasks can be completed quickly when other teams come and help.

9 **Follow through**. Regular updates on the situation plus feedback sessions to monitor progress, review strategy and fine-tune decisions are vital in keeping teams focused on urgent tasks.

10 **Celebrate every achievement.** Most crises are solved in many small steps, in sequence or in parallel. Make sure that there are 'early wins', celebrate them, and honour those who had the idea and took initiative to make them happen.

Better ways to achieve cost control

The only reliable long-term way to control costs is to show people how much better things will be if they do so – better for them, better for others in the organization, better for clients or customers, better for shareholders, and better for the community as a whole.

People who are highly motivated to save money for a good cause usually succeed in doing so, and may also be far more successful than you dared to hope.

Too often the discipline of cost-cutting is seen as a negative, heartless, destructive activity driven more by greed than any sense of higher purpose. Jobs are culled, livelihoods destroyed, departments trashed and loyal workers dumped, apparently with no thought except that of making (more) money.

However, cost-cutting can be the most *caring* thing a person can do. The true nature of cost-cutting is prudency: it means making every hour and dollar count, spending time, energy and finance only on things that make a difference, give greatest value and are most worthwhile.

Jobs that are not central to fulfilling the mission may be lost, but if those people end up in other jobs in which they are able to make an important contribution, they will achieve a far more positive outcome than if they had continued in roles that make little difference to anyone.

Cost control is therefore a moral issue, since the opposite leads to reckless extravagance, wasted resources and irresponsible destruction of other people's wealth.

Outsourcing and offshoring

If you want to save money fast and take everyone with you, you have to convince those involved that the world will be a better place as a result. Take the high moral ground.

A good example of this has been tension over relocating call centres and software support from countries like the UK and the US to India and other Third World countries. Trade unions have protested that jobs are being destroyed in an immoral way. They argue that home communities are hit and that new jobs created in other countries pay very little and exploit the poor. They have often campaigned vigorously to block the process.

This has happened because many of the corporations concerned have failed to win the argument: that outsourcing will result in a better future in a broad sense, not just for shareholders; that it is, on balance, the only morally right thing to do.

First, you have to tell the bad news, and prepare the ground for how you are going to save the day. Whatever your business, outsourcing to a developing country should always be done in a way which complies with the building a better world principle.

The bad news

- We need to take urgent action to reduce costs.
- Customers will feel exploited by our high prices, and will go elsewhere.
- If we don't run our business efficiently, everyone could lose their jobs, and the business will close.
- People who have entrusted their savings and pensions provision to us will also lose their money.

The good news

- We can easily save costs, save the company, save most people's jobs, keep prices down and offer great service, by relocating some jobs to other, less expensive parts of the world.
- Highly skilled people are available in some of the poorest nations.
- Their daily costs of living are lower, and we can pay them less while still enabling them to enjoy a decent standard of living.
- People in these countries really do need our support and investment.

- Every job we create in these countries can create many others as new money flows into the national economy and is spent on local goods and services.
- By investing in these countries, we are also helping them develop into new markets for our own business, which is good for everyone.
- We are also doing our part to help tackle the greatest moral challenge of our time, which is the growing gap between richest and poorest nations, helping build international peace, prosperity and security for a better future.

In summary, if we continue as we are, the result will be disaster for everyone – customers, workers and the community. If we outsource, the future will be better for all, apart from a few, who we deeply regret will lose their jobs for the sake of those who remain. We are deeply indebted to them for the contribution they have made and are committed to their future. We will do all we can to help them find employment elsewhere.

Making a stronger case for high performance

Too many business leaders talk about high performance as a general aim without making a powerful enough case for it. They assume that everyone will automatically sign up to deliver high performance because by definition it is a *good thing*. But, in reality, demands for high(er) performance are often a *bad thing* for team members who suffer longer hours, and end up working even harder, chasing even more stressful targets. That's why we have to be convincing and passionate

Outsourcing pay tables – and buying power[7]

What about accusations of exploitation of low-wage workers in developing countries? While exploitation can be an important factor, the reality can be more complex. We need to compare not just salaries, but what those salary levels will actually buy in different places, in terms of things like the cost of housing, food, energy and so on. For example, an IT professional in India may be far better off in terms of lifestyle, even though paid only a quarter of the UK salary.

IT professional	Salary ($)	Purchasing power ($)
UK	96,000	93,120
India	26,000	159,380

about the reasons *why* high performance is so important.

Of course, for those who end up losing their jobs, the idea that they are sacrificing their own employment to save the rest of the company from extinction, even if this does give good employment to people in the Two-Thirds World, is not one that they may find easy to accept, especially if they feel the company is making good profits. You can't build a better world for every individual all the time. The building a better world principle applies to the overall situation: the best possible outcome for the greatest number, or some variation on this theme.

In many industries the answer to the performance question is obvious: safety. For example, air crews hardly need lecturing on the consequences of poor aircraft maintenance. But many other kinds of business struggle to make as convincing a case.

Consider the following typical examples:

- 'We want to reduce errors in the packages we send out because it is so annoying to be on the other end, and it takes us all ages to sort out.'
- 'When the software crashes, it's a complete waste of time and very frustrating.'

Sure, these things matter, but not as much as a plane crash; they are hardly matters of life and death, but the business activity *must* be a matter of life in some significant way if we are to engage passion.

Failing that, all we can resort to is a much more limited good news/bad news story, pointing out that, without higher performance, the entire corporation is at risk.

Better incentives linked to the right metrics

'Show me how a man is measured and I will tell you how he spends his time.'

Stuart Morris, Associate Partner,
Transformational Business Network

It is said that Albert Einstein kept a sign in his office which read: 'Not everything that can be counted should count, and not everything that counts should be counted.' Many organizations use financial incentives to encourage great performance. The trouble is that, all too often, the metrics used to measure that performance are too broad or just misleading. A common example is linking a bonus with group performance, to which the individual may have made very little (or even a negative) contribution. Another example is tying a bonus to sales figures rather than profits, encouraging aggressive pricing and unsustainable selling practices.

Performance-related pay can produce unexpected results. During the Battle of Britain, German fighter pilots were paid a bonus for every enemy Spitfire or Hurricane shot down. The result: the best shots became super-heroes, demoralizing the rest. They were also distracted from their job of protecting bombers and had a financial incentive to over-estimate their 'kills', which distorted the data received by German High Command.

In an article in the *Harvard Business Review*, Alfie Kohn has pointed out that management-by-reward, as part of a classic command and control structure, can be manipulative and controlling – and is simply a variation on 'Do this and you'll get a good kicking.' Management-by-reward produces movement rather than motivation, compliance rather than commitment. Rewards don't motivate people to do anything other than get rewards.[8]

Similarly, Frederick Herzberg has demonstrated that employee satisfaction and dissatisfaction are produced by very different factors. Bad pay may indeed create powerful disincentives, but generous terms do not necessarily build motivation.[9]

For a complex job, performance-related rewards give rise to a particular problem, in that performance measures may give a very simplistic view of what the job is actually about. Also, linking large rewards to individual targets can encourage cheating, creative data manipulation and other behaviour designed to please the boss rather than the customer.

It is safer to judge performance on a wider range of factors, including competitor comparisons, and to allow for special circumstances.

So, now that we have looked at the impact of building a better world on leadership and team-building, what about brands and marketing?

BUILDING BETTER BRANDS

'A brand for a company is like a reputation for a person. You earn reputation by trying to do hard things well.'

Jeff Bezos, founder and CEO of Amazon.com

'If people believe they share values with a company, they will stay loyal to a brand.'

Howard Schultz, CEO of Starbucks[1]

Every month we are exposed to $1 billion in advertising and 30,000 brand names clamour for our attention. The result is market fatigue, caused by overload. At the same time, many old brand-building techniques are dying. For example, it is now almost impossible to build high levels of national awareness through advertising on a limited number of peak-time TV shows, because of the huge increase in channels, online use, home cinema watching and so on.

A large corporation can easily spend more than half a billion dollars on a new branding exercise, coupled with new mission statement, corporate logos, identity, strap-lines and product relaunches.

What if we could add 10 per cent to the impact of every

global brand and 20 per cent to the power of every mission statement?

Too far fetched?

Let's pull back a little. Even if we only add 0.5 per cent to the impact of a marketing campaign, that may translate to a huge number of additional sales and a significant gain to the organization. But, in many cases, we may be able to do far better than that. And it's all about …

Warming up the brand

Branding is about how a product is perceived, rather than the nature of the product itself. So how do we adapt existing branding, logos, corporate image and advertising campaigns to the changing values of this new world?

The greatest and most valuable brands in the world are powerful symbols of our age – part of our history as well as our daily lives. Long-lasting brands are special: they gain the affection of more than one generation. Disney, Nike, Starbucks, Calvin Klein – these kind of brands connect with emotion, travel worldwide and transcend culture.

We see them in the food industry: think about a favourite food you enjoyed as a child and the chances are it's still sold in a similar way today.

But few brands last more than a couple of decades; most die even faster than the short-lived companies that invented them. Indeed, 60 per cent of new companies go out of business in under five years in the UK and US.[2] You never hear of them and you never miss them, or their logos, mission statements, brands and advertising campaigns.

Brands have to adapt or be left behind. You can focus all

The world's top ten brands in 2002[3]
Measured by $ billions value

1	Coca-Cola	69.6
2	Microsoft	64.1
3	IBM	51.2
4	GE	41.3
5	Intel	30.9
6	Nokia	30.0
7	Disney	29.3
8	McDonald's	26.4
9	Marlboro	24.2
10	Mercedes	21.0

you like on sales graphs and tables, brand mix, product lines and brand equity yet miss the most important fact of all: are your customers still as passionate about what you do?

People are changing in what they count as important, the brands they like and the advertising they approve of.

'Your premium brand had better be delivering something special, or it's not going to get the business.'

Warren Buffet

Future feeling

New emotion is replacing old thinking, so it is important to get a feel of the future. Old thinking is cerebral, whereas new thinking is visceral: from mind to heart, tangible to intangible.

One example of the new approach to life is the dramatic growth in alternative medicine, now used by 66 per cent of

Feel the future

Old thinking	*New feeling*
■ Science solves all	■ Science has limits
■ Facts	■ Feelings
■ Cool logic	■ Emotional intelligence
■ Objectivity	■ Empathy
■ Knowledge	■ Intuition
■ Detached	■ Involved
■ Processes	■ People
■ Structures	■ Purpose
■ Pragmatic	■ Spiritual
■ Conventional medicine	■ Alternative medicine
■ Left/right politics	■ Single-issue activism
■ What?	■ Why?

all 35–49 year olds, who are often reacting against rationalistic Western medicine and its formal research methods. The alternative medicine industry is worth around £1 billion per year in the UK, while in the US there are *well over half a billion consultations every year* with alternative therapy practitioners.[4]

Another example is the feminization of management, with a new emphasis on emotional intelligence, intuition, empathy, cooperation and relationships, and the rejection of a macho, aggressive, confrontational, task-oriented approach.

A third example is the boom in 'mind and spirit' book sales, offering a fusion between mental, emotional, mystical and spiritual worlds. Even brands are becoming like a religion.

Feeling → *faith* → *brand religion*

As we have seen, every marketing proposition is the promise of better things. Brand religion is all about the *belief* that a particular brand will indeed create a better world. It's usually linked to a similar *belief* in the values of the company.

> The time has passed when technical advantages alone can sell a product. It is the attributes to a brand and the emotional and non-material values associated with it, that create sales … Emotional values are replacing physical attributes as the fundamental market influence … Customers buy the company and everything it stands for.
>
> Jesper Kunde, author of *Corporate Religion*[5]

> I think that consumers are a pretty forceful pressure group on businesses and consumers are not as short-term as analysts and the media! … They are also asking – both when it comes to the brand and when it comes to company names – 'What long term intrinsic values do you carry and commit to?
>
> Antonia Axson Johnson, fourth-generation owner of
> Axel Johnson, Swedish food group[6]

Brands can create their own 'religions' or faith systems,[7] and we can actually watch this 'faith' process at work in people's minds. Nuclear magnetic resonance is used in medicine for high-resolution imaging of organs like liver and brain. Scientists can use it to 'watch' people think.

Different areas of our brains light up, linked to products we are using or consuming – or think we are. So people who *believe* they are drinking Coca-Cola rather than Pepsi reproduce their own classic 'Coca-Cola' brain activity patterns, even if the brand has been switched without their knowledge. It's all to do with brand image, suggestion, previous experience and emotion.

Emotional brands

Some brands are particularly linked to an emotional response – for example:

- Harley-Davidson
- Virgin
- Coca-Cola
- Nike
- Body Shop
- Disney
- Starbucks
- McDonald's
- Apple.

But what does it mean for a brand to be emotional? It means that we feel good when we use the brand or when other people associate us with it. Brand loyalty can run deep, even when we are disappointed in our recent experience. For example, people can lose a lot of money by investing in a corporation that has 'always done well in the past'. Marks and Spencer in the UK is just one example of a corporation that has generated passionate loyalty among a generation of older private investors who in many cases held shares longer than perhaps was wise.

Our own identity can be tied intimately to branding: the clothes we wear, the car we drive, the corporation we work for – all these things help shape our personal image. As Jonas

Ten steps to warming up a brand

Internal

- Write in two sentences why your product or service makes the world a better place.
- Explain clearly, in one sentence, why competing products and services are a poor substitute for your own presence in the market.
- In what way would the world be impoverished if your company did not exist?
- What makes your organization extra-special?
- Why would people choose to work for you rather than other similar organizations?

External

- Why are people passionate about your products or services?
- Why are they your unpaid unofficial sales team?
- If your customers had a dream, what would it be?
- How can you go beyond their reasonable expectations?
- What is the most powerful good-news story you can tell?

Ridderstrale and Kjell Nordstrom point out in their book *Karaoke Capitalism*, 'Harley-Davidson offers the ability for a 43-year-old accountant to dress in black leather, ride through small towns and have people be afraid of him'.[8]

So, then, the future of brands is all about emotion and beliefs, and both are changing. How we position our brands and our mission is vitally important.

It is one thing to have a brand, but it is another to market it. How can we improve our marketing practice?

7

BETTER MARKETING

'Marketing's work should not be so much about selling, but about creating products that don't need selling.'

Philip Kotler, Professor of International Marketing at Kellogg School of Management and author of *Ten Deadly Marketing Sins*

'Positioning is not what you do to the product. Positioning is what you do in the mind of the prospect.'

Al Ries, author of *Positioning: The Battle for the Mind*

'The key to success is to promise the consumer a benefit – like better flavour, better wash, more miles per gallon, a better complexion.'

David Ogilvy, author of *Confessions of an Advertising Man*

The promise of every product and every service is a better life. Profits are the prize for delivering on the promise.

In every marketing campaign we see the same core value – phrased in a thousand different ways. But will the promise be believed in a world where 65 per cent don't trust big companies any more, 56 per cent don't like global adverts simply because they are recognizably global and 69 per cent think big companies have no ethics?[1]

So much has been written about customer value proposition – what you are offering customers. It has become *the* mantra of marketing and product development. But the *only* customer value proposition that works is that these products provide a better life for you or for those you care about or improve things in some other way at a price you are prepared to pay.

All too often, the *real* value of the product is missed because business leaders drifted too far from the day-to-day concerns of ordinary people and lost trust along the way. Take car insurance, for example. You can sell on price and beat everyone else in the market – and forget entirely what insurance is for.

Of course, price is everything if insurance cover is just a nuisance that the law requires, but the *real* reason for insurance is to be there when there's trouble: when your car is stolen or damaged, you suffer a personal injury or worse. *Price* is about *value*, but *being there* is about *values*: price and values are two totally different things. Price is an absolute, hard item, instantly comparable in a savagely competitive marketplace. On the other hand, quality of care, trust, depth of support in a crisis, time-saving help are all far harder to measure and are therefore bought as a result of having faith in the organization.

In an online or telesales market where everyone is offering similar cover at almost identical prices, these 'soft' factors can make all the difference in differentiating one company from another.

Your marketing method is also important. Make sure that everything you do contributes to a better world. Consider, for example, the huge backlash against indiscriminate direct

---

'Only for you': better e-mail targeting

Skynet Belgacom signed up 500,000 people for special mailings based on their personal details and interests. Two out of three e-mail campaigns were entirely public service messages, while the remainder were commercials. The average mailing was to just 50,000 users, and response rates have been as high as 30–70 per cent.[2]

---

marketing. In June 2003 it became possible for people in the US to refuse direct mailings. In the first two hours of the scheme being launched, 250,000 opted out and 30 million had done so within six weeks. The rate of name removal is running at 600 per cent per year in some countries and 83 per cent of US citizens want a total ban on spam e-mail.[3] Marketing directors may be quite pleased with response rates of 2 per cent to a national mailing programme, but that means that 98 per cent failed to respond, of which the majority may have felt varying degrees of irritation or even outright hostility.

The answer is more accurate targetting. Opt-in programmes, where people actively participate in deciding on the kinds of marketing they will receive, are growing fast. By adopting this approach, corporations can achieve a 15 per cent reduction in marketing waste, a 12–19 per cent increase in response rates, a 100 per cent increase in sales leads and a 15 per cent increase in customer satisfaction.[4]

Direct mail continues to be very effective when targeted properly, and direct mail campaign spending has risen in many countries.

The IBM Focus 1:1 programme generated $594 million more revenue compared to a control group targeted with more conventional approaches, using consensual opt-in marketing, where department heads cooperated with IBM to make sure that the right e-mail addresses were in the IBM database with accurate information about responsibilities and buying power.[5] Another exponent of consensual marketing, Gary Dawson, in charge of marketing communications strategy at Hewlett Packard, says: 'HP has seen marketing waste cut by 50% or more. Moreover, program results have improved by 3 times or more. In very controlled programs response rates have been 30 per cent.'[6]

Believe in what you sell and others will too
Life's too short to sell things you don't believe in.

Working in advertising can be a tough assignment, selling your own ability to sell just about anything to anyone, regardless of how useful or useless the product is.

Slick campaigns attract attention and boost sales, but a career in advertising is hardly a mission in life unless you are convinced of the value of what you are promoting.

It makes a difference when those designing and running campaigns passionately believe in the product or service they are promoting. It affects the whole team, provides a higher sense of purpose and influences the quality of messages they develop.

The marketing message
All marketing messages are built around the same theme: making a better world. The primary appeal may of course be

to the world of the individual consumer, but is often wider than that. We will see in Chapter 9 on public relations what risks are taken by ignoring the wider principle.

Consider the examples below:

- Mary Kay: 'Enrich women's lives'.
- Ford: 'Striving to make the world a better place'.
- Merck: 'Business is preserving and improving human life'.
- American Red Cross: 'To Improve the Quality of Human Life'.
- Wal-Mart Stores: 'We exist to give ordinary folk the chance to buy the same things as rich people'.
- Walt Disney: 'We make people happy'.
- McDonald's: 'We offer the fast-food customer food prepared in the same high quality manner worldwide, tasty and reasonably priced, delivered in a consistent low-key décor and friendly atmosphere' – the corporation is now under pressure to make an alteration to 'healthy food'.
- BP's recent 'Beyond Petroleum', signals a leadership role in moving out of the fossil-fuel era.

Your marketing message must be connected to your sense of mission, and that raises another problem: most people in larger organizations are unable to explain, in simple, powerful terms, what their personal mission inside the corporation is all about, let alone explain how the organization makes the world a better place. It is not surprising, then, that we are seeing a crisis of motivation at work.

'Having written a 90 second pitch, the next step is to write
a 10 second one.'

Peter Knight, author of *The Highly Effective Marketing Plan*

Here is the 'Mission Test'

Can you explain to a ten-year-old child in two minutes why
what you do each day is so important? Try it. You'll know
if you've succeeded because the answer is usually the same:
'Cool! *I'd* like to do that when I grow up!'

You don't need many words if the mission is strong.
Here are some examples of the kinds of responses that any
employee should be able to generate spontaneously:

- GSK: 'We save lives and help cure disease'.
- BBC: 'We help inform the world'.
- Tesco: 'We provide low-cost, quality food'.
- Gillette: 'We provide a close, safe shave'.

Even advertising slogans do it

'You can do your homework (as an advertiser) from now
until doomsday, but you will never win fame and fortune
unless you invent big ideas. It takes a big idea to attract
the attention of customers and get them to buy your
product.'

David Ogilvy[7]

Just like mission statements, advertising slogans promise
better things, experience, life.

- 'Be all you can be' (US Army).
- 'All you have to do is drive one' (Suzuki).

- 'It keeps on going and going and going' (Energizer).
- 'Have a break' (KitKat).
- 'Better answers' (Compaq).
- 'Seeing beyond' (CIBC).
- 'Good to the last drop' (Maxwell House).
- 'Built tough' (Ford).
- 'Think different' (Apple Macintosh).
- 'For hair so healthy it shines' (Pantene).
- 'More power, more life' (Duracell).
- 'Drive safely' (Volvo).
- 'Coke is it' (Coca-Cola).

Since every successful marketing proposition is based on building a better world, every new campaign can be tested by asking the following questions:

- How powerful is the overall building a better world promise in the mind of the individual consumer?
- How many different promises are there?
- How important are they?

For example, a coffee company may make the following promises:

- We think it's the best-tasting coffee in the world.
- It's good value for your money.
- We also give coffee-growers a fair price.
- We help the poorest communities in the world.
- We take care of the environment.

Each of these promises may have varying significance for different consumers, with taste and value likely to be the

Waitrose anniversary advertising

In May 2004 UK grocery retailer Waitrose took out full-page adverts in the national press listing a hundred ways in which it improved people's lives and the wider world. These ranged from insisting on the highest standards of animal welfare, to a ban on genetically modified food (a sensitive issue for their upmarket client group) and so on.

most important. But they are all variations on the same theme.

People working for drink manufacturers, fashion, lifestyle and health companies tend to find it relatively easy to do the building a better world test. In contrast, those employed by banks, insurance companies, government departments, oil companies, airlines and component manufacturers often find it more difficult, by the nature of their work.

The strongest marketing campaigns are always based on simple messages that tell us something we didn't know before, which could make a significant difference to our lives.

When it comes to online shopping, the message is the same: keep it simple, fast and easy. For example, 98 per cent of online shoppers get frustrated and their main frustrations are as follows:[8]

- pop-up boxes while visiting/shopping (52 per cent)
- banner advertisements (50 per cent)
- congested web pages (35 per cent)
- slow load times (26 per cent)
- difficulty in finding a specific topic (20 per cent).

Brands are brittle and easily broken

'Billions of dollars have been wasted on marketing programs that couldn't possibly work, no matter how clever or brilliant. Or how big the budgets.'

Al Ries and Jack Trout, authors of
The 22 Immutable Laws of Marketing[9]

'People are not only turning advertising off, advertising itself is turning people off. Each year studies show that more and more people are taking less and less notice of ads than the previous year.'

Michael Newman, creative director, DNA[10]

You can have a world-class advertising campaign that successfully raises consumer awareness, only to find its entire value wiped out in a moment by a news story that suggests the corporation is in some way contributing to a worse kind of world (see Chapter 9 on public relations).

Consumers are becoming increasingly cynical and difficult to impress. Nowadays, they are sophisticated, fickle and wary as well as well-informed, with instant access to online informal reviews and comments about just about any product in the world.

Booking a holiday or a meal out? It is increasingly likely that within a few seconds of using a search engine you will find recent reviews online. What is more, the independent reviews may rank higher in the results than official websites or advertising.

Consumers are hypersensitive to exaggerated marketing claims, false promises and downright lies, and are now able to vent their fury or pleasure on public sites in very powerful ways. For a start, consumers are generally believed whereas advertising is not.

People have grown tired of hype and spin. That's why the future of marketing belongs to honest information, accurate data and clear claims based on truth.

There is often a beautiful jewel at the heart of an organization, but it may be almost entirely hidden beneath a stack of quite trivial and meaningless messages. Yet this hidden dimension may be exactly what is needed to help create high-impact campaigns with high memory retention and huge emotional appeal.

Marketing success is achieved by reminding people about, or revealing, the jewel in the form of a product or a service and telling them the facts about it, which will change how they think and feel, and their attitudes towards buying it.

> 'When you've got a good fact, get out of the way.'
>
> Dave Trott, creative director of Walsh, Trott, Chick and Smith

Conflicting messages don't help

Messages aimed at customers or shareholders are often in conflict, and this is becoming a major challenge for brand management, marketing and media relations. In the past, messages could be kept separate, but in a web-enabled world they collide in embarrassing and counterproductive ways.

Here are two diametrically opposed core messages:

- **Marketing:** 'We are here to serve you as a valued customer, making life better for you at a fair price. We believe in the value of what we do for you.'

- **Investor**: 'We are here to charge customers as much as we can get away with, creating as much wealth for shareholders as possible, without breaking the law.'

In a web-enabled world both messages are seen side-by-side by both groups, and the differences can be disturbing, as well as destructive.

Take an insurance company: try telling policy-holders that the company's only aim is to charge the largest amount possible (given competitive pressures), pay staff as little as possible, provide the absolute minimum to those whose relatives have died, look for every excuse not to pay theft or accident claims, and rip as much wealth out of the business as possible to give to shareholders. Sadly that is not so far from the public perception of the insurance industry in general, and is what you can expect if you follow the 'share-holder value' mantra to an ultimate extreme and are also overheard in public places, including the online world. The irony is that nothing could be further from the truth.

An insurance company exists for only one reason: to pay out in order to support those in the 'club' who have suffered a loss. Allied to that is a secondary purpose which is to enable members of the club to sleep at night, knowing that if disaster strikes, financial help will be available from pooled resources that the club has collected in the past. Insurance companies should never forget that their reason for existence is to allow people and organizations to share risk. But they often do forget.

Of course, their shareholders should be rewarded for their help, with dividends and the expectation of capital growth.

But you cannot drive a successful insurance company for long if you talk only about rewarding shareholders.

This is an issue of overwhelming importance. Insurance companies must remain connected with their primary mission of, in some way, creating a better future or they will lose customers and staff, both muddled by their mission and disturbed by their values.

But insurance companies are not an exception: all businesses exist to satisfy the requirements of their customers, in a mutually rewarding and profitable way. And every business sector is experiencing this same crisis of purpose to one degree or another – at least when it comes to the largest corporations.

Lessons from a small family-owned business

'The real purpose of business is to serve the needs of society like survival, safety, self-esteem, love and sense of higher purpose. When these are introduced, business does very well.'

Deepak Chopra, author of *Timeless Mind*

'The primary purpose of an organization is not to make a profit. It is to help human beings grow, express their creativity, contribute their life-source and make the world a better place.'

Lance Secretan, author of *The Reinvention of Work*

What about smaller companies? Imagine a restaurant where the mission statement on every menu says:

This restaurant exists to make a big fat profit out of feeding you. It also exists to make as much money every week for me, the owner, as I can possibly extract. We always use lower-cost ingredients where we suspect you can't taste the difference, pay our staff a pittance, spend the legal minimum on cleaning our kitchens, and charge you as much as we think we can get away with.

Such a restaurant would be out of business in a couple of months. Customers don't want to feel that the owner hates the restaurant and the people in it, would stop tomorrow if she could, and only does it for the money. They want a different kind of service. They want to feel that the whole focus of the restaurant is to give people a great eating experience in a wonderful environment. They want to feel that the owner really cares how the food is prepared, takes great personal pleasure and pride in every aspect of serving those who walk in through the door, is hospitable by nature and enjoys giving people a great time. And that is the image we need to market.

Of course, customers may be aware that it is partly a fantasy, but they want to feel it as a reality, as indeed it is in all long-term successful restaurants, except, of course, at fast-food outlets at the bottom end of the price range.

Develop the underlying message internally

The underlying marketing message is best defined by an organization's nature, mission and values. One of the biggest mistakes a company can make is to delegate to agencies or other outside organizations the job of defining its mission and values.

The message given out should be a revelation of what is there, not a synthetic creation to disguise what is not.

All too often, an agency is given only a partial brief and told to 'come up with something'. Account managers flounder about, learning what they can about the business, and try to develop attractive messages. In doing so, they may suggest to their client what the client's own core values are, in ways that are clearer and more vivid than the leadership have seen themselves.

But the underlying purpose of an organization is too important to be generated in a couple of afternoons by an external group. A campaign that is developed externally also risks overselling. Take, for example, a health insurance company which briefs an agency to come up with warm, friendly slogans. Let us suppose they come up with a general theme such as 'We care more about you'.

It sounds great, but such a slogan could expose the organization to raised expectations and invite public ridicule, as well as huge pressure from clients in future, unless it is true and based on reality – or at least based on a declared and well-understood aim of the organization as a whole.

What makes a great campaign?

You may think that the 'great news' advertising concept does not really apply in the same way to a mass-market commodity like Coca-Cola or Heineken beer. On the contrary, it does.

Take, for example, the crisis in Coca-Cola which erupted shortly after they launched a new product in the UK: pure bottled water branded as Dasani. The only trouble was that the water they were using was being taken straight from London's water supply, and then 'cleaned'. That might have been acceptable in the US, but not in Europe where people pay a premium for perfection and expect bottled water from a natural spring.

To make matters even worse, at the height of a series of media stories poking fun at Coca-Cola's new ways of selling tap water, disaster struck. Government tests revealed that the bottling plant had accidentally contaminated the 'specially purified' tap water with dangerous chemicals, introduced at the same time as other substances designed to make their bottled water taste better.

The damage to the brand was such that Coca-Cola not only recalled all 500,000 bottles, but cancelled the advertising campaign, closed the factory and ditched the entire project – not only in the UK but in other countries as well, except in the US where the brand and process had been well accepted since 1999.

So, what should Coca-Cola have done?

Coca-Cola's appeal and mission can be summarized as great drinks for all people everywhere. 'Great' means safe, enjoyable and, for anxious parents, healthy:

> Coca-Cola, the drinks people you can trust, working with you for a better, healthier future.

However, over time, Coca-Cola came under pressure over health: in particular, with regard to sugar content which contributes not only to obesity and diabetes but also to tooth decay.

So here was a great opportunity to gain moral ground with the healthiest drink known to human beings: pure water. No additives. No sugar. No preservatives. Just as nature intended. So launching a pure water product was, in itself, a great idea. We could express it like this:

> The purest water you can buy, from people you can trust, at a price you can afford.

> Healthy drinks for a better future.

Instead, it turned out to be more like this:

> Come to us for bottled tap water, purified by an industrial process, with added chemicals for better taste – made in a factory liable to accidents and dangerous contamination.

Coca-Cola lost face and a huge amount of money – and won't repeat the mistake in a hurry. Of course, it will take more than half a million bottles of recalled water to hit Coca-Cola significantly, but the impact would have been far greater for a smaller brand. Nevertheless, if Coca-Cola has the misfortune to be in the media a few more times with stories of contaminated drinks, it will be hit significantly.

Lesson: Even the strongest are vulnerable to blasts of bad publicity when they produce something that fails to contribute to a better world.

Who cares wins

What do Vodafone, Diageo, Avon, McDonald's, British Gas, Barclays, Cadbury, Trebor Bassett, Dollond & Aitchison,

> **Dollond & Aitchison opticians: World in Sight**
>
> Dollond & Aitchison have collected more than 750,000 pairs
> of discarded glasses and had them mended by prisoners and
> sent to developing countries.

Tesco, Fabergé, Walkers and News International all have in common?

They have all experienced the benefits of so-called cause-related marketing, or selling products and services linked to a 'good cause'. Partners have been as varied as The Alzheimers Society, Comic Relief, Help the Aged, Make A Wish Foundation, Mencap, Save the Children, as well as literacy and IT projects in schools.

Cause-related marketing

Cause-related marketing means:

- selling to people who believe in the cause more than differences between products
- partnership between business and charity to market products or services for mutual benefit.

> **J&B Rare Whisky: Care for the Rare programme**
>
> Diageo contributes to seven conservation projects and
> features the endangered species on local labels. Twenty-
> two projects have helped raise US$600,000, enhanced by
> a range of local activities for local markets. Tracked brand
> sales have increased by 37 per cent.[11]

These marketing tie-ins can be far more potent than traditional partnerships such as sports sponsorship, which may appeal to a narrower audience and be associated in people's minds with high-level advertising, and a more strictly commercial interest.

A major problem for most corporations is convergence in the marketplace – on price and specification as well as everything else. Product differentiation is a major challenge, and this is why value differentiation is becoming so important. Cause-related marketing makes that differentiation.

US spending on cause-related marketing jumped from $125 million in 1990 to $828 million in 2002.[12] In the same year £50.4 million was raised in the UK by 66 businesses benefiting 50 charities and good causes through 81 linked programmes. Over £17 million worth of gifts in kind were given as part of 23 community initiatives, and 27 corporations committed £13 million worth and 65,000 hours of staff time.

In the UK, 89 per cent of consumers have bought a product associated with a cause in which they believe and which influenced their decision to do so.[13] Research shows that 44 per cent of European consumers are willing to pay more for environmentally and socially responsible products.[14] In the UK and the US 98 per cent of consumers are now aware of at least one cause-related marketing programme, as compared with 88 per cent in 2000.[15]

- Seven out of ten consumers who participate in a cause-related marketing programme report a positive impact on their behaviour or perceptions.[16]

- 48 per cent of consumers show an actual change in behaviour, saying that they switch brands, increase usage or try or enquire about new products.[17]
- 46 per cent of consumers say that it makes them feel better about using the product, company or service.[18]
- 86 per cent of consumers have a more positive image of a company that is seen to be doing something to make the world a better place.[19]

When people share your values, they tend to be loyal.

Growing the bottom line by caring

What better way is there of making the most of the values you share than by giving money to an organization that your consumers, staff and shareholders also support or strongly approve of? Consider the evidence:

- 84 per cent of Americans say that, when price and quality are equal, they would switch brands or stores to those linked to a good cause.
- More than seven out of ten Americans tell friends about companies they think are responsible, and four out of ten do so frequently.
- Almost eight out of ten Americans have tried a new product because they've heard good things about the company.
- Six out of ten Americans have refused to buy 'quality' products because they don't like how the company operates.[21]
- Over 70 per cent of chief executives, marketing directors and community affairs directors believe that

Boys and Girls Club Movement (US)

Cause-related marketing is good news for not-for-profit organizations. The Boys and Girls Club Movement in America has benefited from alliances with Coca-Cola ($60 million), J.C. Penney ($7 million), Circuit City ($3 million), Crest/P&G ($3.3 million), Major League Baseball (official charity status – $1.5 million, annual ad campaign), Compaq ($7.5 million), Microsoft ($100 million), the Sports Authority ($3.3 million), and many others. The result has been not only hundreds of millions of dollars raised for the organization but also an unprecedented public profile.[20]

cause-related marketing will increase in importance over the next two to three years, with 75 per cent of them feeling that cause-related marketing can enhance corporate or brand reputation.[23]

We see similar results in the UK:[24]

- 81 per cent of consumers agree that, when price and

Tesco: Computers for Schools

Tesco customers collect one 'Computers for Schools' voucher for every £10 spent instore or on petrol. Schools collect tokens for computers and other items, which can be redeemed via a catalogue. Since 1992 Tesco has donated over £62.5 million worth of computers and related equipment to schools. This includes over 42,200 computers – more than one for every school in the UK.[22]

> **Walkers Snack Foods and News International: Free Books for Schools**
>
> In 1999 'Free Books for Schools' tokens were distributed in Walkers crisps packets and in various newspapers. Schools redeemed tokens for books, from a catalogue supplied by Walkers and News International, compiled with government advice. Walkers' market share of snacks grew over the period, and the *Sun* saw an increase in sales in a declining market. In 1999 over 2.3 million books, worth £12 million, were distributed to schools with over 98 per cent taking part, each receiving an average of 70 free books.

quality are equal, they are more likely to buy products linked to 'causes' they care about.

- 66 per cent say they would switch brands if price and quality are equal.
- 57 per cent say they would change their favourite retail outlet.
- 86 per cent say they think more of companies that are trying to make the world a better place.
- 67 per cent of consumers say that cause-related marketing should be part of every company's activities.

Senior executives are recognizing that this trend is totally compatible with protecting shareholder value, since it improves brand image and, hopefully, sales:

- 96 per cent of marketing and community affairs directors recognize the benefit of cause-related marketing to both business and the community.

> **Avon Cosmetics: the campaign against breast cancer**
>
> In the US, 400,000 independent sales reps raised more than $34 million in a high profile door-to-door campaign to raise money for breast cancer research, which generated goodwill about Avon cosmetics brands and improved rep morale. In the UK, Avon partnered with Breakthrough Breast Cancer and Macmillan Cancer Relief, donating a proportion of all sales. Avon also promoted sales of charity fundraising products, sponsored Fashion Targets Breast Cancer and also encouraged government action with consumer petitions. The campaign won Avon significant positive media coverage while also raising awareness of the issue and over £6.5 million for the cause.

- 77 per cent of chief executives, marketing directors and community affairs directors say that cause-related marketing can enhance corporate or brand reputation, and 69 per cent believe that cause-related marketing will grow in importance.

American surveys show that these links to great causes are very important to workplace motivation. One such survey[25] found that:

- 90 per cent of workers feel proud of their companies' values when they support a good cause.
- 87 per cent of workers feel a stronger sense of loyalty.
- 83 per cent of adults have a more positive image of companies who support a cause they care about.

- 65 per cent would be likely to switch brands or retailers to one associated with a good cause.
- 61 per cent agree that cause-related marketing should be a standard business practice.

However, all forms of sponsorship can promote cynicism and should be undertaken with care. Philip Morris spent $75 million on charitable donations in 1999 and $120 million on advertising that they had done so.

Moreover, sometimes cause-related promotions can go wrong. Cadbury's in the UK launched a new sports initiative for schools. The idea was to save chocolate wrappers, and eventually the school could send off for a free basketball. The Food Commission calculated how many calories a child would have to consume to get a free ball and found that a child would have to play basketball for 90 hours to work it all off. Eating all the promotional chocolate bars would have meant consuming 36 billion calories and 2 million kilograms of fat.[26]

The campaign was cancelled amidst much embarrassment. An idea aiming to create a better world (fitter, healthier children) was exposed as likely to create a worse world (fatter, less healthy children).

Coffee – telling a better story
Coffee is a big industry – it is the second most widely traded commodity in the world after crude oil. Many different global organizations sell different coffee brands.

Like the oil industry, the coffee industry has serious image problems – because of accusations that coffee farmers in poor nations are being exploited. A tiny and shrinking percentage of the revenue from supermarket coffee goes to the farmer. Many commodity prices fell over a number of years but coffee more than most, halving in a decade.

It ought to be a good-news story: a natural drink, benefiting both wealthy and poor.

A rural farmer plants coffee beans and cultivates bushes. After the third year he picks green beans, which are bagged, weighed and carried to market. These bean sacks are shipped to America and Europe, where they are roasted, ground, soaked in hot water and the pure extract is drunk. It should be a simple, sustainable, and elegant process. The impoverished father and mother have money to feed, clothe and educate their children, and for medicines when they are sick. The more affluent drinker enjoys a social activity – a conclusion to a great meal or a break at work.

However the image recently has been rather different – namely, 'Drink coffee, exploit the poor'. This has led to a campaign for 'ethical' coffee, alleging that the coffee industry is responsible for massive social injustice, falling prices for raw coffee beans, destitute farmers, rising retail prices and huge corporate profits.

The popularity of coffee drinking is flat or falling in much of the West. Coffee is not the cool drink it used to be, despite all the growth of niche market coffee houses and specialist coffee brands. That's why Starbucks and other coffee house chains have added fair-trade coffee to their brand mix. Farmers growing and selling coffee under this scheme get a better price for their product and hard work.

For the consumer the ethics of growing, selling and drinking coffee have become a big issue.

Ten steps to a better marketing plan

For many marketing executives, each year means yet another marketing plan. Here are ten steps to a better plan – dimensions you can add to your normal structure:

1 *Simplify your message*

Make sure that even a child can quickly understand what you are offering. A surprising number of advertising campaigns are confusing.

2 *Make a more powerful promise*

Meet a need and make sure you do it better than anyone else. Low price alone cannot build a brand. You need to interest people in buying it.

3 *Provide stronger facts*

The days of hype are over. In a web-enabled world you cannot provide too much supporting information. Let the facts speak for themselves.

4 *Make it more personal*

Make sure your best customers really know they matter. Keep close to your customers.

5 *Improve your targeting*

Targets are individual people. List all your target groups and plan for them. What do they like and dislike? What do they think about? Make sure you don't alienate people through general advertising or mailshots that have minority appeal.

6 *Respond more rapidly*

Make sure that calls are answered promptly and by people who know the business. Offer one-click telephone callback on websites. Answer all e-mail queries in 24–48 hours.

7 *Make your website more useful*

Information-rich sites attract heavy traffic without advertising. My own globalchange.com site has over 2.5 million different visitors a year, almost all of whom arrive from search engines or links from other people who have found the pages helpful. Make sure that navigation is easy, as well as online purchase.

8 *Offer better 'family' care*

What is the point of spending a small fortune in acquiring new customers if you are failing to keep the ones you have? It is often the people who buy your product who are most likely to be forgotten. Make sure you stay in touch. Make them feel cared for with a single point of contact where possible. Use personal knowledge, provide better aftersales service, better billing accuracy and extra attention for upset customers if things go wrong.

9 *Have greater passion*

Only sell a product or service you are passionate about, believe in and would recommend to close friends. If you aren't passionate about it, don't even think about selling it.

10 *Be more responsible*

Sell to others as you would like them to sell to members of
your own family. Only promise what you can deliver. Tell
the truth all the time.

How to waste millions of euros on marketing: use a weak
headline, confusing language, an unclear story, not enough
facts, an unconvincing benefit – and make sure the company
is hard to contact rapidly.

So, then, all marketing is a promise of a better world, and
that promise is often strengthened by linking great products
to great causes. In doing this we strengthen brand as well as
corporate image, customer loyalty and employee morale.

But, ultimately, brands and marketing are all about one
thing: customers. How can we find better ways to manage
these relationships on which the future of every business
depends?

BETTER CUSTOMER RELATIONS

'I truly believe that Tesco spends more time than anyone in retailing in listening to our customers, finding out what they want and finding a way to deliver it.'

Terry Leahy, CEO of Tesco[1]

'We insist that everything we do must focus on our customers. For some of our companies that is an important return to past values, as in the past few years we have concentrated very strongly on financial indicators and the reorganization of portfolios ... My personal experience is that companies that are very customer-focused not only tend to have a stronger position in the market, higher growth rates and better results, but their employees also identify much more with their companies.'

Michael Diekmann, Chairman of the Management Board,
Allianz[2]

We serve people because they are worth it, because what is important to them is important to us, because we get huge satisfaction out of knowing we have given pleasure or helped meet a real need – and we expect to be rewarded for doing so.

Anything else borders on prostituting our true selves;

we become mere mercenaries, hired for a tedious task that means little or nothing to us; we develop a couldn't-care-less attitude that is likely to alienate customers.

Your salespeople may be the only human contact your customers ever have with your business. How friendly and helpful they are will dramatically affect your customers, both existing and potential, who will judge your entire organization by their experience of a single individual.

Treat staff well, so that they feel appreciated and cared for. Respect their views and honour their achievements. Praise them often, encourage them when they are weary, have fun together and celebrate the good times, and they are likely to create the same kind of positive, life-enhancing culture when they are with customers.

Above all, remind them how every single thing they do makes life better for other people.

> 'The picture will depend on your other strengths and interests – a better product, a better team, a better life, or a better world – it will always be inspirational to you.'
>
> Benson Smith, author of *Discover Your Sales Strengths*[3]

Part of the family

We live in an age in which communities are changing rapidly, families can be spread in different nations and where many people can feel isolated and feel a need to belong. That's why building family or tribal groups at work and with your customers is so powerful:

- 'When I go into the store I am always greeted like an old friend.'

- 'Our team is like a family. We really support each other and take an interest in each other's lives.'
- 'Although we're a large corporation, the atmosphere is wonderful. You really feel you belong.'
- 'Jerry, the sales rep, has become a personal friend and I would trust him with my life. He really helped me out at a very difficult time last year and I'm glad to do what I can for him too.'
- 'They're all such nice people.'

For many years Currie Motors, a UK Vauxhall car dealership, ran a very successful advertising campaign on the slogan: 'Nice people to do business with'. Powerful and demanding to live up to, but great to shout about if you're sure that you are.

Working together: better than declaring war

Last-century management books are obsessed with thrashing the competition, battling to grow market share (at the expense of others), pushing others out of business, fighting to undercut prices, beating on quality, exploiting competitive advantage. All these are weak motivators for most people in business except those at the top whose job survival and huge financial rewards depend on them.

These testosterone-dominated 'war aims' are out of step with a third-millennial, feminized, emotionally-enabled world which prefers dialogue to bullying, cooperation to competition and partnership to power games. But, in any case, to a *customer* such fight-to-the-death strategies are totally irrelevant. When I go to a retail outlet I am not particularly impressed by how many of their direct competitors went out of business as a result of predatory pricing aimed at increasing market share. Nor does it do me any favours, as a *customer*, that the owner is prepared to exploit a near-monopoly position as soon as the last serious competitor has gone to the wall.

I also get no satisfaction, as a customer, from the owner's boast that his suppliers are screaming because he is late paying his bills and he is using what is rightfully their money to reduce his borrowings.

Business only survives in crowded marketplaces by making sure that it offers what people are looking for, aiming always for new standards of excellence.

Customers want competitors to cooperate, and such cooperation creates respect, appreciation and loyalty. You see it when a shop assistant recommends another store to try, or a sales rep tells you why a competing product may in fact be more suitable. But it is exactly that spirit of community that creates trust: it speaks powerfully to customers about integrity and a real interest in their needs.

Others have coined the term 'co-opetition' to express the local realities of business life. For example, in West London where I live there are clusters of antique shops, clusters of takeaways, clusters of curry houses and clusters of Chinese restaurants as well as clusters of clothes shops and so on. More partners than direct competitors, these groups of similar businesses attract communities of people with the same interests for whom that cluster is attractive as well as very convenient. Together, they become a centre of excellence and experience, and they are all the more successful for it.

Influencing the influentials

Opinions of previous customers can have a huge impact on customer relations generally. In their book *The Influentials*, Ed Keller and Jon Berry show how one person in ten can shape the opinions and choices of entire communities, cities or regions.[4] Malcolm Gladwell echoes this finding in *The Tipping Point*: once you reach critical mass things often change rapidly.[5]

Berry labels his 10 per cent as 'influentials' and notes that they tend to be community-minded and actively 'concerned' about a better future. Their opinions spread like wildfire; they are informal community leaders, responsible for starting and stopping local trends and, because they tend to be well-connected, their collective influence can spread rapidly across a region.

So what do these influential minorities think about business?

- Most of them say that business has a duty to customers, workers, community, and shareholders.
- More than 70 per cent say that business has responsibilities in:
  - product safety
  - worker safety
  - cleaning up their own water and air pollution
  - quality
  - advertising honestly
  - paying a fair share of taxes.
- Between 40 and 50 per cent add responsibilities for:
  - charging reasonable prices

- being good citizens in the communities where they operate
- paying good salaries
- providing healthcare coverage for workers
- providing jobs to people.

For decades influentials have been saying that companies should be responsible to customers first, then to the nation generally and lastly to the shareholders, but all as part of the same story. Great responsibility should be an integral part of great profitability, and one should naturally encourage the other.

> 'When you satisfy your customers, you also create jobs
> for your employees, as well as orders for your suppliers.
> Happy customers will make your business profitable and
> therefore will create happy shareholders. Happy customers
> are the key to creating true shareholder value.'
>
> Bernd Pischetsrieder, Chairman of the Board of Management,
>
> Volkswagen AG

The all-important human touch

If you want an easy way of really annoying your customers, then the best thing is to get rid of human beings and replace them with robots – starting with corporate telephone switchboards. These automated systems can make customers angry and do nothing for corporate image.

Why should I have to have to act as an unpaid telephone operator? I wouldn't mind if I finally got through to someone who understood the business, but these robotic systems are often connected (eventually) to people who spend their entire lives in cubicles taking one call every two minutes, day and night, under pressure of disciplinary action if they fail to achieve their quotas, and with low levels of senior team support.

For many large companies, the only personal contact with customers is on the phone. What is more, many phone calls to businesses are made by people who already have a problem and an element of disaffection. They have important reasons for phoning and how their calls are handled will affect their loyalty for a long time. It can be the worst possible economy to put the entire client relationship at the mercy of some robotic system. Even worse is to contract out huge sections of customer relations to people who are badly trained and who know little about the business they represent.

So, then, we have considered better ways to lead, market and manage customers – but all of this can be swept away in a moment unless we also pay attention to better public relations.

9

BETTER PUBLIC RELATIONS

It's becoming a fundamental requirement for corporations to demonstrate in the media how they help create a better future not just for shareholders, but also for customers, consumers, colleagues and communities.

And that means telling good-news stories. But the problem is that bad news can erupt unexpectedly at any time.

There's a serious, almost invisible, threat to the future success of every large corporation and it's growing rapidly. It has greater power to turn your company upside down than any other corporate challenge over the last thirty years. It can destroy your business in a week.

Like a virus it arrives unseen and lurks within. It's a thousand times more lethal to old ways of doing business than the internet or globalization. It can take out a whole network of businesses in one event. Governments can't defend against it, it's resistant to law and most CEOs are unprepared for it. No book of management strategy adequately addresses it, and most employees have never heard of it.

At the same time it can energize a neighbourhood, create

Who shot robin?

On 22 May 2004 newspaper headlines reported the slaughter of nesting birds inside Wyevale Garden Centre in Gloucestershire. A few pairs of robins were shot after the manager became fed up with alarms going off at night. The national reaction was outrage with wall-to-wall TV, radio and press damnation of the 'appalling' act.

a people-movement, inspire many nations and will change our world.

You take a call at work.

It's a journalist working on a story.

He's asking awkward questions about your business.

He seems to know a lot more than you do.

The following day the scandal is all over the *New York Times* while CNN, Fox News and CNBC are broadcasting round the clock. Your share price is already in free fall …

It doesn't matter who you are, what business you are in or the size of organization you work for. It could happen tomorrow. Companies can disappear almost without trace overnight.

Enron, WorldCom and Arthur Andersen are just three of hundreds of organizations changed forever by recent media revelations – the birth pangs of a new kind of world that wants the game played by different rules.

'You have to go the extra mile, not just because it is right, but because your survival depends on it. The rules of the

Wealthy food giant sues starving Africans

On 24 January 2003 Nestlé was forced to abandon its claim to a $6 million debt from the Ethiopian government going back to 1974. Here was a wealthy food company suing a famine-stricken nation. Attacked in the media, as well as by 30,000 e-mail campaigners and thousands who boycotted products, Nestlé settled for a smaller payment which was immediately given back to fund an aid programme.

game have changed forever. If Sarbanes-Oxley doesn't get you, the markets will.'

Clive Mather, president and CEO of Shell Canada[1]

And when that news story breaks about your own organization you will find globalization and the digital age will spread the wave of impact wider and faster than you could ever imagine. Any big story can generate over a thousand media calls a day from every nation of the world.

More than $70 billion was wiped from the value of Enron on account of a single event. Just one story involving very few individuals in a huge, well-respected and 'strong' organization like Arthur Andersen can set off an unstoppable chain reaction leading to meltdown. Tens of thousands redundant. A brand name mocked or cursed. The senior team utterly disgraced.

No other business factor has ever had such violent, awesome destructive power.

We need new ways to manage this risk.

I often ask managers to consider what are the most

damaging headlines that they can possibly imagine about their organization. Make your own list … it will describe a values bomb right under your feet just waiting to explode.

Whatever happened to trust?

'Many people think that executives no longer run their companies for the benefit of consumers, or even of their shareholders and employees, but for their personal ambition and financial gain.'

Charles Handy, author of *The Hungry Spirit*

Charles Handy's words are borne out by research, which reveals that:

- 90 per cent of Americans feel that CEOs cannot be trusted to look after the interests of their companies.[2]
- 95 per cent of British people say that senior executives are only in business for themselves.

As we have seen in Chapter 4 on leadership, trust is a scarce commodity. In many countries such as the US and UK, faith in politicians has sunk as low as confidence in the journalists who write about them. It is no surprise, then, that the reported comments of politicians are so often dismissed as political posturing at best and criminal deception at worst. Leaders of corporations are suffering the same contempt, as are their auditors and financial advisers.

In contrast doctors, teachers, religious leaders and single-issue activists are generally trusted in many societies. At least two-thirds of the public say that they trust environmental organizations and their scientific advisers to tell the truth. Physicians are the only group commanding similar respect.[3]

Lesson: form partnerships with single-issue activist groups, take their advice, enjoy their support and you will win public trust more easily.

The cost of negative media coverage

Question: if a major newspaper is running major stories every day attacking your corporation, how much would you have to spend in advertising in the same paper to counteract the damage?

Answer: it could be many hundreds of millions of dollars. The more pages of advertising you buy, appearing alongside hostile news stories, the more it looks as if you are trying to 'buy' your way out of a disgusting mess. The faster you spend, the greater can be the backlash. Therefore you would not attempt it, unless you wanted to show that you had taken prompt action on (for example) an issue of public safety such as a product recall.

Half a page of positive editorial can be more powerful than 20 pages of advertising. A half-page *hostile* editorial can be more powerful than a hundred pages of advertising. At $50,000 per page, that's $5 million wiped off the value of an advertising campaign in a single story. Coverage over ten days in ten major publications could result in more than $500 million in damages if the story is serious.

The trigger for months of unwanted attention and damaging stories about your own business may be an event in another industry altogether, as we saw with the collapse of Arthur Andersen after the troubles at Enron. Another example is where a board member is accused of misdeeds while working for another corporation: there is also likely to be some damage to the reputation of the corporation he or she is now part of.

And the larger the business, the more people take big decisions, the more inevitable it will be that someone, or some people, will do serious wrong. The more successful you are, the more you will be a target – for individual journalists, editorial teams, political lobbies or activist groups.

Compliance is dead as a defensive strategy

In every board of large corporations there is one word which comes up time and again: compliance. Are we keeping to all the rules?

But compliance as a defensive strategy is dead. Not just slightly dead – totally dead. Just keeping to all the regulations can destroy a corporation. We need to go further than compliance demands. As Clive Mather, CEO of Shell Canada, explains: 'Meticulous compliance with all the new regulations is a must, but it is not enough. We have to try harder; we have to set the highest standards in everything we do, because trust is essential in our business. In every sense, it is our business.'[4]

You can comply with every law, keep to the exact requirements of every regulation, conform to every guideline and still hit major trouble because rules and regulations keep changing in response to every new scandal or public concern. And when they do, you can be sure that you will be judged not by whether you kept to the rules of 2003 during that year, but by whether what you did then looks 'right' now. You may defend yourself by saying that everything you did was within the law. But what happens when the world moves on?

It may seem unfair to judge past actions by today's attitudes, but that is exactly what happens. In every business today you can find illegal activities that used to be approved of. Take insider trading, where an individual makes a killing on the stock market because he or she stumbled on internal secret information, shortly to be announced, that would soon alter share prices. A few years ago such trading was considered normal, clever business. Today it could put you in prison. There are numerous other examples of *yesterday's* wise actions having become *today's* folly.

Imagine that the CEO of a corporation is being interviewed live on CNN. The issue could be any one of a host of ethical issues. Let's say that today's story is about bribery and corruption and the CEO manages a German company. Until recently, bribes were tax-deductible in many countries, including Germany. However, in 1997, 34 countries signed a pledge to make such payments illegal.

Let's imagine the interview:

'Are you embarrassed by the e-mail leaks showing that you authorized secret payments to Nigerian government officials?'

'Everything we did was perfectly within German law.'

'Do you disapprove, then, of the new law making such payments illegal?'

'The new regulations are a good thing.'

'So you agree that people who pay large bribes in future should be put in prison?'

'Well … I …'

'I invite you to judge your own behaviour by your own standards. If bribery is wrong now, surely it was wrong then?'

'But times have changed …'

'Do you actually have a conscience of your own – or do you just make it all up as you go along, on the basis of what you can get away with legally?'

The CEO walks out.

We need to take the moral high ground and be cleaner than clean. That means that we have to understand exactly where these trends are going, how future scandal headlines could affect our industry, how people will react, how legislators will respond, and then set a robust framework for all we do.

Why the media ignores good news

'Ill news goes quick and far.'

Plutarch, *c.* 46–*c.* 120

It seems unfair that a corporation can have great products, quietly get on with the job and be largely ignored in the media, yet a single act by one employee can create negative headlines for months. Why should this be and what can be done to ensure greater balance?

Firemen who risked their lives rescuing people from the Twin Towers were rightly celebrated as national heroes.

Bad news sells good news

'The good news is the advertising. That's what it's all about. And the bad news – the dead guys and the crime – is to get the suckers into the tent, get up the emotional pitch to sell the advertising.'

Lewis Lapham, editor of *Harpers Magazine*, August 1995

Their heroism will never be forgotten. Generations to come will take inspiration from those stories of bravery.

And every day in our local communities there are thousands of others who make huge personal sacrifices for others.

These stories warm the heart. They are a powerful antidote to all the bad news of slayings, robberies, child abuse, cruelty and injustice. Sadly, because of the powerful attraction of sensational and shocking stories, criminals get more air time than heroes, and terrorists get more than ordinary criminals.

A story about a paedophile school teacher molesting a seven-year-old girl will always achieve far wider coverage than a story about a youth worker who has rescued sixty teenagers from heroin addiction.

I've known people turn off CNN after watching almost non-stop during catastrophic events, because they found too much TV news-watching makes them anxious or depressed. But people tend to prefer knowing bad news to knowing good news, and so shocking stories get high ratings.

Media coverage is a lottery: the news is determined by the simple fact that a certain number of newspaper pages have to be filled every single day, and a certain number of minutes of TV and radio bulletins.

Most days there's a wide choice and some days there's none. There are times when an entire edition of a newspaper can be dominated by multi-page coverage of a major story, but on other evenings a news editor may be embarrassed by what he is going to have to elevate to the front page.

Good-news stories only get big coverage on quiet days. Most get little or no coverage at all, but grateful journalists keep such material for a quieter moment.

Objective, hard-hitting comment from a senior executive on a major news story can give a positive boost to corporate profile. It is far easier to comment on a negative story about something else than it is to create a positive story of your own. However, corporations often find this kind of media role difficult. Media calls on major issues tend to be referred by the press office to the CEO, who may be busy, travelling or nervous of criticizing a competitor or the government, or of being accused of hypocrisy if a similar event was to happen inside her own corporation.

Openness, candid perspectives which clarify issues – these things are rare, and time-pressed journalists are always grateful for quiet off-the-record comments, data, background and contact details of other people they can talk to.

If you adopt such an approach to the media, your organization is likely to be high on the list as soon as a story breaks about the industry – positive or negative. And if, by some unfortunate chance, that story should be about some trouble in your own organization, you are more likely to be called early and treated sympathetically. This gives you the opportunity to turn a potential public relations disaster into a media opportunity for reconfirming your (very well-known) commitment to the highest values in your industry, your thought-leadership on hard issues and your campaigning for rigorous standards to be adopted by all. Your dismay at the disappointing or shocking news/allegations about your own corporation is likely to be reported, as well as your insistence that, if true, such a thing must never, ever happen again.

Great values strengthen the bottom line

'In a just cause, the weak will beat the strong.'

Sophocles, 495–406 BC

One of the most serious mistakes any business leader can make is to think that values are disconnected from the bottom line, that doing the right thing will only increase costs without gaining a commercial advantage.

The second greatest mistake is to think that adopting 'good practice' will save you from a severe roasting. News headlines can change public mood in hours. 'Normal' ways of doing things then become targets of intense resentment, anger and outrage.

But let us be clear: although direct benefits from strong values may be difficult to discern on the balance sheet, neglect in this area can wipe out your balance sheet altogether.

Ethics: the corporation's immune system

Strong ethics keep corporations healthy. Weak ethics make companies sick. You may not see it at first, you may not even know it's happening and you may get away with it – but it's a huge risk.

Most companies are far more serious about their 'numbers' than their 'values'. But values are the immune system of every organization. You can have the greatest profits in the world but if your corporate immune system is damaged it's only a matter of time before you'll be in deep trouble.

Just as in humans, weak immunity on its own never kills a corporation. It's the other problems which strike when your white cells (value leaders) are damaged. The human immune system is invisible, impossible to locate in one place and hard to measure. You hardly know it's there and take it for granted. The number of cells involved is tiny; their impact is infinite. Your corporate immune system is the same: hard to define, hard to locate, hard to manage and susceptible to being seriously weakened with no outward signs of trouble. Even the smallest attack, under these circumstances, can become a mortal blow.

Ethics are a challenge to measure, slippery to get hold of and it's not always obvious how strong ethics will make you money, but look what happens when that bad-news story breaks. Client confidence falls, investors wobble and the leadership is distracted, diverting its energy from growing the business. Image is wrecked together with morale. Previously reliable staff start calling in sick or work less hard. You can't recruit the best and you can't retain them either. First to jump will always be the top wealth generators. You can lose 10 per cent of your top team and 60 per cent of your real talent – and it can happen almost overnight.

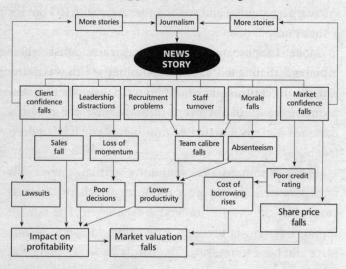

Customers are also affected: they begin to feel differently about your company, products and methods. Slogans sound hollow, products are questioned, and the company begins to run out of steam.

It's an ethical nightmare for the unwary leader, who storms ahead with an old route-map of strategic plans which worked well in the past, when what is needed is a new route-map to a successful future – and one that recognizes that even the definition of success is profoundly changing.

Shell lead on global warming
In June 2004 the new chairman of Shell voiced deep concerns

about global warming. His comments were received with dismay by corporations such as ExxonMobil which had aggressively defended the right to promote carbon consumption and had questioned whether rising CO_2 levels in the atmosphere had any long-term significance.

Shell took the moral high ground as a 'responsible global player', listening to the global community. This was a strong move. In contrast, ExxonMobil took the view that it was commercially dangerous to acknowledge the possibility that oil use could make the world a worse place. This was as short-sighted and unsustainable as a tobacco company promoting the idea that smoking is harmless.

A better approach would have been to say:

> The whole world depends on oil for energy, transport, plastics, dyes, inks, heating and a host of other important things. We work hard to locate new sources of oil and extract. But we are concerned that society's oil dependence could damage our future, if what many scientists believe about global warming turns out to be true.
>
> In any event, within a couple of generations the world's oil supplies will be very limited. That's why we are developing other ways to generate power and produce raw materials, for a more sustainable future.

When passion, enthusiasm and integrity shine through, it will always be better for your business.

The Tylenol crisis: Johnson & Johnson act fast

Prompt action in a crisis can turn a potential disaster into something that enhances reputation. In the autumn of

1982, seven people on Chicago's West Side died after swallowing Extra-Strength Tylenol capsules laced with cyanide – 1000 times the minimum to cause death. News travelled fast and caused a nationwide panic. Johnson & Johnson took immediate action, recalling 31 million bottles with a value of $100 million despite its confidence that the products had not been tampered with in their factories, warehouses or distribution networks. By acting fast and so firmly, they restored confidence in the brand and saved their reputation for integrity, honesty and the highest ethical standards.

Ten ways to make your values work for you

1 If you are proud of your values, talk about them – often. Make bold statements about how you help build a better world. Contribute to public debate.

2 Create a stronger, more enduring 'halo' effect towards your corporation and products, by paying careful attention to all marketing messages and branding.

3 Be seen as thought-leader, not just about (say) how to make a better chocolate bar, but on wider issues that concern people such as equal opportunities, sexual harassment at work, child labour, human rights or environmental damage.

4 Make sure that the media hear about the wonderful efforts you are making – whether supporting local schools, providing help to children who are partially sighted, saving lives in Uganda and so on.

5 Encourage a constant supply of good-news items by releasing employees to give time to causes they are

passionate about. Two days of extra paid leave per year per person will generate huge numbers of interesting stories which will find their way into local press and radio, website discussions as well as national media. (See Chapter 17 for more on benefits from corporate encouragement of volunteering.)

6 Don't be afraid to speak out on issues which relate to some aspect of your business or the area where you operate, when you know you speak for the majority of ordinary decent people.

7 Create high-profile partnerships with single-issue activist and not-for-profit groups on areas of mutual interest – for example, protecting the environment, women's health or animal welfare.

8 Become the first place where journalists go for immediate comment, facts, background and help in locating people to interview. Make sure that your media office is well-resourced and open 24 hours per day rather than defensive and hard to get hold of, obliging rather than restraining, seeking to serve rather than seeking to dominate a story.

9 Develop a reputation for total honesty, frankness, sharp insights, quotable quotes and reliability.

10 Show courage: don't be afraid to criticize bad practice by others in the industry or deficiencies of government. Be confident about raising difficult issues that affect your industry as a whole.

10

BETTER INNOVATION

'Innovation is the central issue in economic prosperity.'

Michael Porter

'Innovation is the specific tool of entrepreneurs, the means by which they exploit change as an opportunity for a different business or a different service. It is capable of being presented as a discipline, capable of being learned, capable of being practiced. Entrepreneurs need to search purposefully for the sources of innovation, the changes and their symptoms that indicate opportunities for successful innovation. And they need to know and to apply the principles of successful innovation.'

Peter Drucker

Better innovation means better products and services

Most organizations are full of really great ideas which never make it – for a start, most of these great ideas stay inside the minds or immediate friendship groups of the people who have them.

Kwik-Fit innovations reduce staff departures

Turnover at the call centre, based in Uddingston, Scotland, fell by nearly half from 52 per cent to 29 per cent. Employee surveys showed steady increases in staff satisfaction. All 650 staff were asked to attend workshops to generate practical ideas about improving retention and motivation. The HR director said: 'Our turnover is still higher than we would like, but our staff now feel listened to and know that their opinion counts.'[1]

The paradox of innovation

Here is a strange thing: the paradox of innovation:

- CEOs often complain about lack of innovation.
- Workers often say leaders are hostile to new ideas.

A common frustration for managers is how to find better, practical, low-cost ways of getting the job done, but a common frustration for workers is being asked to do stupid things in an inefficient and life-wasting way. As a result, workers may be labelled as obstructive and uncooperative, while management is heavily criticized by them for being out of touch, heavy-handed, arrogant and ignorant.

That's why innovation workshops are often electrifying, so long as participants are persuaded that management are committed to making their best creative ideas work and will back them with proper resources, courageous decision-making and campaigning at more senior levels.

There are few things more encouraging to a group of

people than to be asked for ideas and to see things change for the better as a direct result: to be able to say 'That was *my* idea' or 'It was *our* team that came up with that'.

Reward those whose ideas are used, honour them publicly, give them an ongoing profile, show them why their innovation has made such an improvement to many people's daily lives and, before long, you are likely to see yet more innovations.

When people have a clear vision of the future and are passionate about making it a reality, you can't *stop* the flood of innovations: great ideas, concrete solutions, practical down-to-earth immediate actions to get great results. You also get huge cooperation, rapid agreement, solid effort, readiness to change and astonishing progress.

> 'Systematic innovation consists in the purposeful and organized search for changes, and in the systematic analysis of the opportunities such changes might offer for economic or social innovation.'
>
> Peter Drucker

The only reason why people innovate is to achieve a better life in some way, so:

- Show people why it really matters.
- Convince people of your urgency.
- Promise to take all ideas seriously.
- Reward those prepared to risk failure.
- Commit yourself to making great ideas a reality.
- Celebrate successful team innovations.

How often have you heard comments like these?

If only they would do x … they would save y overnight.

I don't understand– if they had only done z it would have saved us two weeks' work.

If you're not hearing these kinds of statements, watch out. Your organization may be near perfect, or there may be trouble ahead. It may mean:

- You are too senior and too remote.
- People fall quiet the moment you walk in the room.
- You work with people who are half-dead, non-questioning robots who should have left the organization years ago.

'Mindless habitual behaviour is the enemy of innovation.'

Elizabeth Ross-Kanter

Increase productivity by at least 5 per cent at zero cost

'Nobody ever came up with a great idea all by themselves.'

Thomas Edison, 1847–1931

Great ideas can come to an individual, but are more often born within a group. Here is an exercise I did with a client recently:

Situation: You have twelve key managers for two days.
Task: Identify great ideas which are 'low-hanging fruit' or 'no-brainers' – things we just have to *DO*!
Test: Ideas which will be:

- rapid to introduce
- low-cost
- easy to do
- likely to produce an immediate increase in productivity, client satisfaction, worker morale, cost savings or other measurable advantage
- able to be agreed immediately by senior leaders.

Target: Add a minimum of 5 per cent to existing projections for revenue/profit.

We started with over a hundred really great ideas that emerged from a three-day senior leaders' conference for 70 people a few months previously. Wonderful suggestions had been faithfully captured on flipcharts by small groups, with the usual promise that all would be looked at.

How many times have you heard that?

And we know exactly what usually happens after a conference, workshop or other internal event. At best, an e-mail is later circulated with a mass of detail which is deleted as semi-junk by most of those who attended and is ignored by those who really count. At worst, the flipcharts are folded into a corner and are thrown out when the conference administrator leaves for another job.

But, on this occasion, the team were totally galvanized. For a start, their own two-day thinking process was taking place just a couple of doors away in the same hotel from a three-day global board meeting. They knew that on Day 3 they would be summoned to present suggestions for practical immediate action. And they also knew that the needs were urgent.

That group presented their executive board with seventeen different proposals, of which sixteen were approved in full, without qualification, there and then and became part of group strategy, with line management allocation at executive board member level.

Innovation levels are so appallingly low in many organizations that you are likely to generate major potential savings in less than an hour if you have the right people and the right stimulus.

Recently, with another client (a global bank) an innovation workshop was split into four teams and given less than ten minutes to generate a new significant new idea. They were asked to:

- choose a real problem which was hard to solve
- present to the group
- brainstorm (flipchart) possible solutions
- ask themselves whether there was an unusual approach that could be developed
- consider how to take it further.

In a very short time one of the groups came up with an immediate proposal which they all reckoned would cost less than $100,000 per year to implement and would save at least $2.5 million and possibly $5 million each year in software development costs, and perhaps up to 20 per cent in project development time, on software projects inside the corporation.

This demonstrates that great ideas which save millions of dollars can be found rapidly if you have the right people and prepare them in the right way with a strong enough vision of a better future. The secret is …

- Give people space.
- Allocate time as a team.
- Encourage wild and unusual thinking.
- Think the 'unthinkable'.
- Be slow to criticize an early idea.
- Use every suggestion as a learning opportunity.
- Expect answers to come from unusual approaches
  – they often do.
- Have fun!!

> 'It is better to have enough ideas for some of them to be
> wrong, than to be always right by having no ideas at all.'
>
> Edward de Bono

Another idea is to trim your business and product lines
by using the building a better world test. Cut away some of
what you take for granted every day, in order to focus on
growth. Remember:

- Some products are not worth making.
- Some business is not worth having.
- Believe in every single thing you do.

All children innovate

> 'If you want to be more creative, stay in part a child, with
> the creativity and invention that characterizes children
> before they are deformed by adult society.'
>
> Jean Piaget, 1896–1980

Find me an active young child who is not constantly inno-
vating – experimenting, exploring, pushing, pulling, trying,

succeeding and often failing, with a curiosity about everything and everyone.

Imagination, the world of fantasy, is where innovation happens. Here, we see possibilities, unlimited by the rigid confines of today's reality.

> 'When I examine myself and my methods of thought, I come to the conclusion that the gift of fantasy has meant more to me than my talent for absorbing positive knowledge.'
>
> Albert Einstein, 1879–1955

And then as they get older most children learn to conform: not to be different, to be the same, to be part of the crowd. They copy others' accents, dress in similar clothes and, slowly but surely, their natural innovation starts to die.

What has all this to do with innovation in business? Make sure people feel as comfortable as a young child when they take steps to be creative for you.

Creative innovation: breaking the pain barrier

The key to rapid innovation is suspending critical judgement at an early stage. So often we get too serious and rational about the problems while we are just dreaming about a solution.

Remember, as Albert Einstein said, 'If at first the idea is not absurd, then there is no hope for it'. Others agree:

> 'Every act of creation is first an act of destruction.'
>
> Picasso, 1881–1973

'All great discoveries are made by men whose feelings run ahead of their thinking.'

C.H. Parkhurst

'Creativity comes by breaking the rules, by saying that you're in love with the anarchist.'

Anita Roddick

'Daring ideas are like chessmen moved forward; they may be beaten, but they may start a winning game.'

Johann Wolfgang von Goethe, 1749–1832

So, what can we learn from all this? Always allow free brainstorming of ideas as you search for a better answer. Allow feelings to run beyond logic, use intuition before analysis, put anarchy before order, without judging either ideas or individuals, and you will generate radical ideas as raw material for further creative thought.

'Innovation by definition will not be accepted at first. It takes repeated attempts, endless demonstrations, monotonous rehearsals before innovation can be accepted and internalized by an organization. This requires courageous patience.'

Warren Bennis

'Nearly every man who develops an idea works it up to the point where it looks impossible, and then he gets discouraged. That's not the place to become discouraged.'

Thomas Edison, 1847–1931

Finally, the greatest aid to innovation is to *write it down*. Great thoughts have a habit of flying straight into and then straight out of the mind.

Great need encourages high risk

The greater the future danger, the greater the risks we are prepared to take to avoid it. I was recently giving a seminar in a room which was seven floors up and looked out over a roof-top garden. I asked the group what we would do if both fire exits were blocked with rubble after an explosion. In a few seconds we had all agreed how we would get down. Every table in the room was covered with table cloths. We would tear them down the middle into narrower strips, tie them firmly together until we had enough length to reach the ground, secure one end to a metal bar on the roof and use it to climb down one at a time.

Risky? Yes.

Danger of falling? Sure.

Would we do it? Just try to stop us!

Just see who would still be waiting at the top with flames pouring out of the windows.

Lesson: make sure people sense danger if you want them to innovate fast.

Why adults stop innovating

I have worked for organizations in which the senior leaders are feared rather than respected, mistakes result in punishment, managers have long memories and people keep ideas to themselves. People are often held back because they:

- don't understand the bigger picture
- think that the benefit from the idea is likely to be small
- worry about failure and blame
- think that they might even lose their job.

And there's another issue that holds individuals, teams and entire business units back. Who cares?

- Does it really matter?
- Why bother?
- Why should I?
- Someone else may have already thought of it.
- It may involve me in more work.

Most organizations actively resist innovation even when they claim to want it. Yet, in some organizations it seems that the sun is always shining. Their mission is clear, and people know why their work is really important. They are encouraged and rewarded: courage and willingness to make mistakes are both welcomed. In these organizations you find CEOs promising to respond to every e-mailed idea from anyone at any level. Anyone whose idea is used is regarded as a hero and is honoured in every way.

> 'If you're not failing every now and again, it's a sign you're not doing anything very innovative.'
>
> Woody Allen

Great ideas are alive

> 'Never before in history has innovation offered promise of so much to so many in so short a time.'
>
> Bill Gates

Once you have seen something, you can never unsee it. When you see how something creates a better future, you are changed.

'Once a new idea springs into existence, it cannot be unthought. There is a sense of immortality in a new idea.'

Edward de Bono

You can 'know' but still be blind. Revelation is more than data. Seeing is more than intellectual understanding.

'The real voyage of discovery consists not in seeking new landscapes, but in having new eyes.'

Marcel Proust, 1871–1922

'Creativity is just having enough dots to connect.'

Steve Jobs, CEO of Apple and Pixar

In summary, when people are driven by clear vision, with a strong sense of purpose and gripped by urgency, they will tend to innovate rapidly, when also convinced that new ideas will be valued, however strange they may at first appear.

But a key issue is the quality of your people ...

11

BETTER PEOPLE

- 'We're having problems recruiting enough high calibre people.'
- 'Some of our very best people are leaving.'
- 'Reducing staff turnover is a major board priority.'

Companies can radically improve profit margins by doing more to attract and retain highly talented people. The future of every corporation is determined by relatively few. Performance can be more than doubled if you persuade your best people to stay a year or two longer.

- The most talented bankers are twice as productive as their average colleagues.
- The top 25 per cent of software developers are worth five times the average developer.
- The top 25 per cent of sales teams are worth fourteen times the average sales team.[1]

Old-style incentives don't work the way they used to – if they did, staff turnover would not be such a problem. Winning the war for talent is a survival issue.[2] Your greatest asset in future will not be products, but people: their ideas, initiative, memory and experience. Highly motivated, gifted people are the ultimate self-renewing resource.[3] Their intellectual capital will shape your future more than investment in plant, processes, product development and marketing.

Eighty-seven per cent of human resource directors say retention is a prime concern.[4] Those who leave take with them their understanding of clients, products, the company and those who work for it, as well as their network of relationships with customers, suppliers and so on.

It can take years for a new recruit to build up the same depth of understanding, friendship and trust. People buy from people and, when someone moves on to a competitor, clients may follow.

Organizations can lose top people faster than they recruit, train and integrate. The faster that revolving door spins, the sooner these companies face serious instability.

Keep your best people and grow faster

All these are reasons why reducing staff turnover (or encouraging valued people to stay) is one of the simplest and most effective ways to grow a business. Large organizations can save hundreds of millions of dollars this way.

Vacancies are costly. They paralyse teams, hold back progress, waste time and effort, and are demoralizing. Some 85 per cent of UK companies have problems finding the right people[5] and 77 per cent have trouble retaining the talent they have.[6] About one-third of jobs advertised fail to attract applicants. Seven out of ten of those that do apply are unsuitable because they don't have relevant skills or experience.[7]

It has been calculated that a national clothing chain must

sell 3,000 pairs of $35 trousers to cover the cost of replacing one senior salesperson who quits, including recruiting, training and lost productivity.

Losing front-line workers can cost a business nearly half their salaries, rising to 1.8 times their salaries for professional associates and 2.4 times their salaries for managers.[8] The cost of replacing a typical white-collar middle manager can be more than $100,000. For a large corporation, the loss of a single senior executive may reduce turnover by millions of dollars. When stakes are this high it is very important to know why people are leaving. Exit interviews are an essential part of people management; 62 per cent of companies carry them out on the majority of their employees who leave.[9]

The damage caused by high staff turnover can be even greater for small to medium-sized companies where teams are smaller and the departure of a single key worker can be devastating.

Consider the following scenario. The head of a sales team of three leaves a small software company. One of the remaining two is junior; the other is a recent recruit. The business owner is forced to take on the role, while also trying to recruit and oversee the business at the same time. The impact could be enough to precipitate closure.

'There is a drive today, in people of various ages, cultures, and professions to find the meaning of life, to have relationships based on something unchangeable, and to struggle to do the right thing. Organizations that help people do these things – or, as a minimum, don't place obstacles in the way – will be the ones that will attract and retain the best

Staff turnover penalties: why losing key people costs so much

- Advertising the post.
- Interviewing new applicants.
- Training new member of a team.
- Loss of productivity while person prepares to leave.
- Loss of client or internal relationships.
- Loss of specialist understanding about the business.
- Zero productivity during unfilled vacancy.
- Low productivity while new recruit gets up to full speed.

and the brightest and most enthusiastic in the twenty-first century.'

James R. Lucas, author of *The Passionate Organization*[10]

The talent famine

If you do lose key people, there's already a shortage in many countries of skilled people to replace them, and it's going to be even harder in future. The numbers of young people entering college, doing MBAs and going into lower levels of management are going to fall significantly.

That's because fewer babies were born in many countries around fifteen to twenty-five years ago. Too few people are climbing promotion ladders. If you haven't trained up enough talent of your own, you'll have to attract it from someone else.

Put the famine of young adults and continued economic growth together and you're facing a combined shortfall of at least 15 per cent in the young executives age group compared to today in some parts of the world.

Employer branding

As a result of all this, corporations are paying closer attention to how they are perceived in the job market and listening more to what people *really* want from work.

Image and reputation are paramount when attracting new job applications. Make sure that those who work elsewhere are in awe of those you hire, admire your care, envy your training, crave your values and identify with your passion. Make sure that your teams are among the best, most fun, most interesting, challenging and fulfilling work environments in the world.

Public perception of occupations really matters

If you want to recruit great people, start working on their friends and families. Make sure they strongly approve of what you do. It's a well known fact that people want to be respected in their careers by those who mean most to them.

Criticism of the company you work for can come from unexpected places and have immediate results. A participant in a business school seminar told me how his seven-year-old daughter had been shocked by a television programme about children working in the textiles industry. She confronted her parents, both of whom worked in clothing companies, and neither could give her easy answers about conditions in many garment factories. As a direct result, both her parents changed careers completely – her mother joining a fair trade organization.

Employer of choice

Many organizations are making great efforts to become 'employer of choice'. They want to be top of the list for aspiring graduates, MBA students or senior executives looking for jobs. Here are some examples of how corporations are explaining this commitment:

- Unilever: 'Investing in employee recruitment, training and development programmes that position Unilever as employer of choice.'
- A&P: 'A&P is one of the fastest growing food chains in North America and on its way to becoming employer of choice.'
- Barclays: 'Being an employer of choice, we understand that in great companies, motivated employees provide excellent service and satisfied customers.'
- Queensland government: 'We want to be first on the list when young people go looking for jobs.'

Some jobs are harder to recruit for than others – and that's nothing to do with the challenge, pay, bonus structure or quality of management, all of which may be world-class. It's related to differences in *mission*, and whether people think that your mission is important. Just look at the prestige value of different jobs: *business* comes *bottom* in the UK, and some industries are rated very low indeed.

Public disapproval of business managers and leaders is just a symptom of a wider affliction: the total failure of most business leaders to demonstrate why their products or

> **Prestige of occupations**
>
> The figures below show the percentage of people who say that a job has 'very great prestige'. Prestige is linked to motivation – approval from others that the job is worthwhile[11]
>
> | | |
> |---|---|
> | Doctor | 61% |
> | Teacher | 54% |
> | Scientist | 53% |
> | Lawyer | 18% |
> | Banker | 16% |
> | Business | 12% |

services are necessary for the well-being of our world. This is a serious problem. How can you hope to create strong, well-motivated business units when it is clear that many people think that business is often incompatible with doing anything worthwhile?

Doctors, teachers and scientists don't tend to enter into the debate: their mission and value to society are clear (so long as the scientist is ethically minded). Surveys show that lawyers, bankers and business managers are held in quite low esteem – and this will be even more the case if their work is connected in any way with tobacco or arms industries, oppressive regimes or other 'suspect' interests.

Surveys also show that people want to be known and remembered primarily for doing good.[12] They do not want to be remembered as selfish, or for selling their souls to employers they don't respect or even positively disapprove of, in return for financial gain.

> **Six things to keep in mind**
>
> Focus on your dream
> Remember who you influence
> Remember honor and duty
> Keep good role models in front of you
> Get your daily surge of positive reading and listening
> Just do it!
>
> Dexter Yager

Most people hope that others will recall their *lives* as ones that enriched others and made the world, at least in some small way, a better place. They would prefer their epitaph to be: 'A faithful friend' or 'A beloved wife and mother', rather than 'A great money-maker'.

> 'The purpose of human life is to serve, and show compassion and the will to help others.'
>
> Albert Schweitzer, 1875–1965

So, if this is true of how we would like to be known or remembered *personally*, what would you like your *business* to be famous for? What would you like your *team* to be widely known for? The answers to these questions lead us to better ways to recruit and retain.

Better ways to recruit and retain

What sort of things do you do at the moment to recruit the very best people? What are you offering?

HR directors tend to give the same answers:

- Great salary
- Bonus
- Share options
- Challenging job
- Private healthcare

- Career prospects
- Generous vacation allowance
- Great team
- Training
- Chance to travel

Their basic lists vary little – for one reason. These items are precisely what any manager would dream up after reading late twentieth-century theories of psychology and motivation, which focus almost entirely on naked self-interest.

Appealing to 'self' tends to mean things like generous remuneration packages and the promise of an interesting, challenging and enjoyable job – with perhaps a token interest in work–life balance. But, as we have seen in Chapter 1, this list is rarely enough to satisfy an individual for long.

According to Charles Woodruffe,[13] job satisfaction means:

- a sense of achievement
- a sense of being respected and appreciated
- a sense of autonomy
- a need for balance between work and private life
- a sense of fun in a good working environment.

Surveys show a significant mismatch between promises in job adverts, and what actually encourages people to commit with enthusiasm and passion for a long period of time.

To put it another way, people usually join for 'hard' reasons but often leave or choose to stay for 'soft' reasons. This means that the incentives you offer someone to *join* may be totally different from the package of incentives you need to make the same person *stay*.

On recruitment, hard facts score highest: pay, conditions, company reputation, job description and an impression gained at interview of what the job will actually be like.

People applying for a job may have inside intelligence from someone they know, but still cannot quite know what they are getting into before taking up the post. After a couple of years inside the organization everything's become very different. Ask them how the job's going and they could still be giving you the answer three hours later.

People often *stay on* with an organization for soft reasons: they like the team, they have great friends at work, they like the atmosphere, they think their job makes a real difference and is worthwhile, they are respected and appreciated, and their boss is fair and easy to work with. Equally, they *leave* for 'soft' reasons, too: they might object to the atmosphere in the team or to how decisions are made, or feel misunderstood and unappreciated, or stifled, or unhappy at the way in which others have been treated. People usually move on for more than a simple offer of more money or promotion.

The trouble is that 'hard' motivators can be put together quickly. It's just a matter of throwing more money at the problem. In contrast, 'soft' motivators can be difficult to sort out – for example, changing a male-oriented or difficult office culture. Many bosses use 'hard' motivators to try to retain restless workers, totally failing to recognize that higher pay and other tangibles are unlikely to retain someone whose *heart* has moved on.

How people feel about work

Positive	*Negative*
Money/perks	Bad pay/perks/feeling exploited
Personal status/title/prestige	Poor job status/title/low image
Good stepping stone/learning	Learning nothing new
Understand me	No interest in me personally
Treat me well/own space	Treated like a commodity/bullying
Give something important to the team/others	Can't see impact of my contribution on the rest of the team
Friendship/sociability	Emotional distance
Achievable targets	Impossible expectations
Trust me/believe in me/like me	Feel people don't trust/believe in me
Stability and security	Instability/insecurity
Change is under control	Change out of control
Reasonable hours/weekends	Very long hours/lost weekends
FUN!	BURDEN!

There's far more to motivation than money and perks. So much more to inspiring people than a stack of things designed to appeal to self-interest such as a faster car, grander job title, better promotion prospects or a bigger bonus. If only it were that easy.

Conversely, the good news is that although you may not be able to compete on hard factors such as the highest salaries on offer, or the most exciting career path, or being the most dynamic and well-known organization, you may still be able to hang on to a very strong and highly motivated team, once you've managed to get them to join.

You may hear people talking of the wonderful crowd they work with, the great atmosphere, their understanding boss, the positive working environment, and why they have turned down many major offers out of loyalty to a special group of people they have grown to be part of. Creating the right culture is the secret of holding on to your key employees.

The best believe in what they are doing

Remember that every worker is in essence a volunteer. You may think you have some rights over their time because you are buying hours of their day, but the *reality* is almost always different.

Motivation is a battle for the heart, not just an appeal to the mind. Passion is always an expression of the human soul. It cannot be contrived, imitated, manipulated or constrained. As Bill Pollard, Chairman of ServiceMaster, has remarked:

> Many people think that power comes from ownership. In a sense that is true. You can buy people's time and presence at a given place. But you cannot buy enthusiasm, initiative or loyalty. You cannot buy devotion of the hearts and minds and souls of people ... Ownership of results does not start with stock ownership. It begins with dignity, pride of accomplishment and recognition of a job well done.[14]

Every corporation needs people who love to work together, enjoy being part of successful teams, are deeply fulfilled by doing something satisfying and important, and are totally committed to the vision.

> 'Choose a job you love and you will never have to work a day in your life.'
>
> Confucius, 551–479 BC

Human beings are free spirits who cannot be controlled for long without tyranny and fear. Many managers fall into the unconscious trap of working in this negative way at least some of the time. They may favour strict line-management hierarchies, tough management 'stretch-targets', close supervision, endless reporting requirements, harsh performance reviews, veiled threats, career-blocking, punishment for poor results (every bonus scheme can also be viewed as a punishment scheme once people come to depend on a bonus as part of their regular income).

Such tactics may work quite well in a recession, with those who fear unemployment, or for those under financial pressure who depend on a big bonus. But none of these strategies is likely to make people feel wanted, appreciated, honoured, valued, significant or important. None of them adds to the positive passions people feel when they roll out of bed in the morning and get ready to go to work.

People do what they want – paid or not

Paid or not, people tend mainly to do what they want. It is human nature to concentrate on tasks we want to do, believe are necessary or important, and enjoy. Sure, there are things every job requires which can be difficult, challenging or even unpleasant (such as making a friend redundant) but, for best results, jobs always have to be balanced by strong positive enjoyment or fulfilment in other areas.

Management is the art of constructively channelling this dynamic energy in order to achieve your own goals.

'What I know is, is that if you do work that you love, and the work fulfills you, the rest will come.'

Oprah Winfrey

Passion comes from purpose not pressure

Talented people can always get work somewhere else – and maybe get better paid if they do so. Some may already be so wealthy that they don't need to work for you in any case.

Your fellow workers will be the first to promote your company to friends as a great place to work, and the first to jump ship if things look bad. They are willing partners, choosing to be part of your team, and their ongoing commitment will depend on their changing feelings about life, and their circumstances.

Of course, we need clear management targets, challenging and inspiring goals, accurate and real-time monitoring of the right metrics, proper performance reviews, rewards and sanctions. But they only become fully effective *after* every person knows how important they are in helping create a better future.

Helping people do what they are best at

One powerful way of achieving commitment and engagement is to ensure that people are able to do what they do best every day. A Gallup workplace survey of 1.3 million people over more than a decade shows that the majority of people only spend, at the most, an hour or two each day doing what comes most naturally to them.[15] That means that the rest of the time they are doing something which they don't feel particularly good at.

Enthusiasm means:

E nergy for change
N ew opportunities
T argets that matter
H eartfelt commitment
U rgency
S acrifice is worthwhile
I nspiration to achieve
A ction with purpose
S olutions that work
M otivation

This factor is strongly linked to morale, productivity, retention and staff turnover. Those who spend most or all of their time playing to their strengths usually have high commitment and passion for their jobs.

Despite this, a mere 20 per cent of employees in large organizations have the chance to do what they do best every day. These fortunate individuals are:

- 50 per cent less likely to leave.
- 38 per cent more likely to be more productive.
- 44 per cent more likely to have high customer satisfaction scores.[16]

Managers usually respond to skills deficits by offering extra training, rather than by moving people around into other roles where they are playing more to their strengths. But training rarely brings performance up to the standard of those whose main skill is in that same area.

ServiceMaster: cleaning to create a better world

ServiceMaster is a rapidly growing service organization providing, among other things, a wide range of support to schools, hospitals and other institutions. Under C. William Pollard, author of *The Soul of the Firm*, they found a way of motivating people to do the most menial and simple tasks with passion and total commitment.

Many of their workers are people with few educational qualifications or prospects when they join. They are trained, given a smart uniform and taught the importance of doing what they do, and how they help every day to create a better kind of world. Take the example of a janitor in a hospital who is required, every hour, to clean wash basins, urinals and flush toilets. This is the kind of story I have heard:

'You are a healthcare worker, and a vital member of our hospital team: your job is to keep the place beautifully clean, keep people well and prevent cross-infection of sick and vulnerable people. When sick people come in here and they see how clean and pleasant it is, it gives them pleasure, raises their spirits and helps them along. Some even come in here to have a chat with each other. What you do is really important in this hospital!'

In addition, the corporation offers great opportunities to study. The message is: 'We train you because we believe in you, and we are totally committed to your future.' The whole experience is life-enhancing, rather than degrading and demeaning, which helps explain why the quality of what they deliver is so high – reflecting their four corporate values: 'To honour God in all we do, help people develop, pursue excellence and grow profitably.' As Bill Pollard says, 'People want to work for a cause – not just for a living.'[17]

We can easily waste huge amounts of great talent this way: when we ask people to do things they are less good at, they are unable to really shine. We can also undermine their self-confidence by pushing them continually into areas where they are unlikely to excel, setting them up perhaps for failure and humiliation.

Gallup research shows that training energy is usually more profitably invested in fine-tuning existing talent so that performance becomes outstanding.

Predicting high performance

Can we predict which employees will be most successful? From 1995 to 2001 more than 3 million employees were interviewed by Gallup from more than 300,000 different business units in hundreds of organizations. The results were added to data from 10 million customers, plus interviews with 200,000 managers, and a further 2 million talent-fit/role-success interviews.

The results of this combined study are important: they show that, in most corporations, only 20–30 per cent of employees are 'engaged' in their work – that is, feel personally committed – yet this small proportion of people contribute most of the profits.[18]

The surveys established this result by looking at the productivity and profitability of different business units and relating these changing factors to fluctuating scores for average levels of staff motivation, talent-fit and a number of other factors. Profitability was strongly correlated with the average level of 'engagement' of team members in the priorities of the business.

The research confirmed the importance of 'emotional compensation': 'Stretching themselves to make a difference comes naturally when employees see that what they do has a profound impact.' It's impossible to get the best out of people unless they see how they contribute to a better future.

And people like building a better world together. This is a team emotion. One of the strongest correlations with individual productivity and commitment was whether or not the person being interviewed had a best friend at work. If you do have a best friend who is a colleague, the chances of you being fully engaged in fulfilling the mission rise by 54 per cent. Not having a best friend at work reduces the chances of passionate engagement to almost zero.

So what do we learn from all this? Passion at work is usually a group emotion, and highest performance is almost always generated by groups of friends working closely together in a common cause. If you want to boost output, make sure your mission is inspiring, your objectives are clear and agreed – but invest also in relationships.

Emotional economics: a missing factor

Emotional economics is now being used as a leading indicator of growth and profitability in a growing number of corporations. Gallup have developed a battery of twelve key questions which provide an indicator of the degree of engagement.

Business units in the top half of engagement are on average:

- 86 per cent more likely to have high sales and customer satisfaction scores
- 70 per cent more likely to have low staff turnover
- 70 per cent more likely to show higher productivity
- 44 per cent more likely to be more profitable
- 74 per cent more likely to have low accident rates.

Engaged employees are more likely to:

- use their talents every day
- give high performance
- show innovation and efficiency
- support others around them
- commit emotionally to the task ahead
- have high energy and enthusiasm
- look for new ways to add value
- feel great about the team, group and company.

They are also fifteen times more likely to recommend the company as a place to work, three times more likely to be happy with their reward packages and three times more likely to spend their entire careers at the same company than actively disengaged people.

In contrast, those who don't feel engaged are often a destructive and negative force. They are likely to:

- do the minimum
- have a low level of commitment
- avoid taking risks
- have no sense of purpose
- lack enthusiasm
- spread negative views.

Those who are actively disengaged are likely to account for most days off sick, the most accidents, the highest employee turnover, the lowest productivity and to be responsible for a significant loss of customers.

In many organizations the impact of this actively disaffected group can cancel out the entire impact of the high performers, and surveys show that 30 per cent of such a negative group still plan to be with the same company in a year's time.

It has been estimated that lost productivity attributed to disengaged people can be as high as a third of the entire salary bill, and that the total cost of non-engagement to the US economy could be up to $363 billion per year – more than the federal budget for education or defence.

You can make huge savings once you connect with passion. Gallup has data on many corporations where engagement levels were low before the introduction of new policies to improve the level of commitment. In one hospital, a small increase or decrease in annual engagement scores was strongly correlated with revenues per person admitted to the hospital for treatment. A software company saw its employee turnover halve as the proportion of its staff that were highly engaged rose from 7 per cent to 36 per cent in twelve months, saving them, by their own estimates, around $250 million of costs. (See pages 209–10 for the Q12 system on which these studies on engagement were based.)

All this is background to a new model of motivation ...

12

BETTER MOTIVATION

'I haven't scratched the surface yet of my real purpose for being here.'

Michael Jackson, singer

'Pleasure in the job puts perfection in the work.'

Aristotle, 380–322 BC

We have seen that there is a serious *motivation gap* between what people feel passionate about *outside* work and what their bosses want them to feel passionate about *at* work. This is a potent cause of staff turnover, low morale, low productivity and a host of other problems threatening the future success of all large businesses.

We have also seen how this motivation gap is growing, despite billions of dollars spent on intense efforts to solve the crisis – training, seminars, coaching, books and research, almost entirely based on old self-obsessed models of human behaviour. Hence we've seen a huge 'motivation' industry grow up around such things as self-realization, self-development, self-fulfilment, self-awareness, self-regard, self-respect and self-actualization.

We urgently need to find a different way of motivating

people – one that captures all the passions they have and connects with what's really important in their lives. We need a new model that fits more closely with how we live, think and feel.

Four circles of human motivation

We can think of our lives as four circles, or dimensions of human experience. I call them the four circles of the human heart, or of motivation.

Self-motivation

> 'The greatest use of life is to spend it on something that will outlast it.'
>
> William James, psychiatrist, 1842–1910

Self is the inner circle, the core of our being. Self is very important, but most people like to feel that they contribute positively to other people's lives and recognize that they derive fulfilment from others. (See pages 25–29 for more on self-orientated motivation.)

Every physician knows how easily a man or woman can

slip into deep depression once they become convinced that they are of no real importance to anyone else. People need to feel needed – as well as loved. Of course, depression can itself make people blind to the morale-boosting contribution they make to others, thus feeding a downward spiral of anguish and despair. The result is death of spirit. Life stops having meaning. What is the point of getting out of bed – if only to eat, drink, or satisfy other basic instincts?

> 'A man who becomes conscious of the responsibilities he bears towards a human being who affectionately waits for him, or to an unfinished work, will never be able to throw away his life. He knows the "why" for his existence, and will be able to bear almost any "how".'[1]
>
> Viktor Frankl

It is not enough to be loved. It is not enough to be appreciated. There is a sense in which the human spirit only comes alive when we are convinced we make a difference to other people's lives. This is not only a basic rule of humanity but is also vital to understanding motivation at work – and is an element that is hardly represented in any of the usual lists of recruitment and retention factors. It's the reason why volunteering is so popular across America, Europe and most other parts of the world (see Chapters 1 and 17).

> 'Life's most important and urgent question is this: what are you doing for others?'
>
> Martin Luther King, 1929–68

This same desire to make a difference in other people's lives is also an important reason why work–life balance has become so important; indeed, discussions about work–life balance are usually about being able to spend more time with those we are close to.

Family motivation

The second circle of the human heart is about family, however you define that to be – our inner group of special people and friends. Many organizations suffer from 'family blindness', which damages morale, increases staff turnover, reduces commitment and makes recruitment more difficult.

Many people have told me how angry, hurt and upset they are by the failure of their employers to see how important their family and friends are to them. They feel torn, guilty and traumatized. Surely, they say, there has to be a better way than selling your soul and your close relationships for a loaf of bread and a fast-track career? Is business success worth family failure?

Yet others tell heart-warming stories of bosses who take the time and trouble to understand home situations and do all in their power to shape jobs in a family-supportive way, while also making sure that those for whom such things are less important are also well rewarded with their own privileges and opportunities. Such bosses usually command immense loyalty and respect, and deliver great results, so long as they are first-class leaders in other important areas as well.

However, there is more to successful 'family' policies

Family, friends and motivation at work

We are whole people and cannot be sliced into work-bytes. What happens at work affects our home life and our home life affects us at work. Relationships matter.

Positive organizations
- take families seriously
- recognize that many couples have two careers between them that need to be taken into account
- are passionate about child welfare
- are flexible around ebbs and flows of home life
- are open to home-working
- are sensitive about the travel burden
- recognize obligations to parents and friends
- are inclusive of family
- encourage friendships at work

Negative organizations
- do not recognize the existence or welfare of partners/children/parents/friends
- actively discriminate against anyone who seems to have family ties which might conflict with corporate agendas
- encourage functional relationships at work only
- don't recognize that single people also have very important relationships which need to be considered

than setting up a nursery. Indeed, such efforts can backfire if they mean that people with no children feel they are being treated unfairly. And whatever we do must be culturally sensitive, adapted to each local situation, and not everyone has a family.

Many people find 'family' at work, which is why so many people enjoy going to work, why relationships at work are often close, why many romances start at work, and why redundancy or retirement can be so painful. In an age when many traditional family relationships have broken down, these 'work families' are becoming more important and powerful. They add stability and loyalty, but can be destructive if exclusive, as with an office affair.

Community motivation

Self and family/friends are powerful motivators, but a two-dimensional self–family model of the human heart is still, however, incomplete. For a start, it fails to explain a curious fact: as we have seen, people are often far more motivated to work for *nothing*, if it interests them, than if they are paid a huge sum of *money*.

If you seek true passion and undying devotion to your cause in people who work for you, then you need to look more widely than mere self-interest or concern for family.

Community and motivation at work

Positive organizations	*Negative organizations*
* invest in community support	* break up communities by their actions – for example, by mass lay-offs
* are the social glue holding community together	
* make a long-term commitment to the local area	* make huge rapid geographical shifts in investment
* care for the marginalized	
* are service providers – either directly through their job output or by assisting others	* make no direct or indirect contribution to the community

The third circle of the human heart is about community. We've seen how the majority of executives in many countries give so many hours to worthy causes (or would like to), outside of self-interest, or family and friends. In almost all cases, these gifts of time are for the wider community, the larger neighbourhood, societies, organizations, activities, clubs, churches, synagogues or other local religious groups. In some cases there may be a benefit to the individual – for example, as a member of the same society or club or group – but in many volunteering examples there is none. (See Chapter 17 for more on this passion for community.)

World motivation

The self–family–community model of motivation is still incomplete. One vital aspect – one of the greatest roots of raw passion today when it comes to campaigning for change or working to make a difference – is completely missing: a concern for the wider good of all, for humanity and the future of the world – the fourth circle of the human heart. We see its importance in the donations people make to literally hundreds of thousands of not-for-profit organizations, aiming to improve something somewhere, far away from local community, town, city or even the nation itself – and in the extraordinary wave of solidarity and compassion that swept around the world after the tsunami that caused such destruction and killed so many people at the end of 2004.

The environment, rainforests, protection of endangered species, global warming, human rights, racial equality,

World and motivation at work

Positive organizations	Negative organizations
■ have a sense of global responsibility	■ have no interest in global issues
■ care about the environment	■ do not care about environmental damage
■ care about social justice	■ have no interest in social justice

disaster relief in far-away places, the future of the Palestinians, Israelis, Iraqi people and so on – these are expressions of deep concern for the wider world. And this concern is one further step removed from self-interest, or concerns for personal relationships or the wider community.

It's one reason why people either feel proud to work for an organization or so embarrassed that they will avoid the topic of work with people they meet. It's not a question of whether an executive is part of an activist campaign movement or whether they have some religious or philosophical objection to a business such as arms manufacture or human cloning. It's more a case of whether they

UN global compact

Since 2000, 1,700 corporations have signed a new UN global charter embracing human rights, better labour conditions and stronger environmental standards. In addition, twenty financial institutions have pledged to factor social and environmental practices into equity valuations.[2]

are prepared to actively defend the company they work for when with their friends, whether their children will be proud or ashamed of what they do, and whether it's the kind of business that sits comfortably with their own values.

This fourth dimension, or 'world motivation', is a powerful force. Just look at the way consumers boycott companies who seem to be polluting the planet or employing children in developing countries as virtual slave labour in terrible conditions.

Companies wised up to world motivation a long time ago. You'll have a hard time trying to find an annual report of a major corporation that doesn't talk about environmental policies. But that was the case for many years before they were legally required to do so in the UK and other countries.

World motivation is far more than a phrase in an annual report for shareholders. Workers and consumers also share these concerns, and business leaders are taking action together.

Your life-target

'The most important thing in motivation is goal setting. You should always have a goal.'

Francie Larrieu Smith, US Olympic 10,000 metre runner and
volunteer for the Susan Kikomen Breast Cancer Foundation

When we place all four circles of the human heart together, they form a target shape. Every one of us is different. The shape of your life-target is different from mine – and it will go on changing for each of us as we journey through different stages in life. Our own target areas, aspirations, dreams and concerns are as varied as they are complex.

People often talk about work–life balance but, as a concept, it's limited. We are talking here about *total* balance, life–life balance: the relative importance to us of self, family, community and world, and ensuring the pattern of day-to-day life reflects our own broader life-goals.

And when you join together with others who share parts of your own life-target you can be sure that great things will happen.

Most people grow 'outwards' as they get older. Indeed you could say that responsible adulthood or citizenship occurs when a person comes to understand their responsibility in all four dimensions. An important part of parenting is helping a child respect not only family but the wider community and beyond.

Different life-targets and what they mean

Here is the life target of a one-day-old delightful baby, or of a 30-year-old monster of an adult – both have only one thing in mind:

Here is someone else, who is far more concerned about the environment, more than about the quality of their personal relationships or their local community, but who places a high priority on personal satisfaction:

Here is the life-target of another person who, at this stage of his or her life, has significant family and community motivation:

So, what does your own life-target look like?

The four corners

We can redraw these four dimensions as corners – four corners of the human heart, each with separate, but closely related, drives, competing for attention, joined at the centre but sometimes pulling us in different directions.

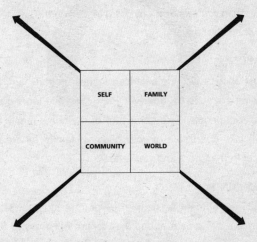

These four corners solve many questions and enable us to find practical solutions. We will see later how the four corners can be used in motivation mapping, helping match people with jobs, as a tool in change management, and why they give us a new perspective on how to influence those around us and make things happen – how to harness the passions people have.

Each of these different corners can be a powerful motivator or driver at different times, in different ways in different people. As we will see, it's rare for one to operate without any influence whatsoever from one or more of the others.

SELF

We all want a better life for ourselves and spend time and energy pursuing personal goals, interests and pleasures. Self-interest is the dominant motivator for most people. Give me exactly what I want, better quality than I ever imagined, faster than you ever thought possible, and on the best terms anywhere in the world.

FAMILY

Angst about work–life balance reminds us that 'family' is very important to us, however you define that inner group of special people. Take good care of my home family and I will take good care of your business family. Ignore this corner in the future and you're toast!

COMMUNITY

Huge commitment by people to volunteering shows that many are passionate about the welfare of others in their community, or about community issues. Prove you're a great corporate citizen. Make me proud to work for you. Make me proud to own your brand.

WORLD

Protecting the environment or endangered species, caring for the planet, human rights: responding to far-away disasters or humanitarian crises; wider issues express popular concern for the good of humanity as a whole and future life on earth. Show me why the world is a better place because I buy your products. Show me how my job directly improves the future of humankind.

Motivation is constantly changing

Motivation is never constant; it is constantly changing. Recently, in New York, I was in a meeting with a publisher who confessed that his motivation for talking about new books had suddenly fallen because his wife had just rung him from Boston to say she had been taken into hospital. Motivation can change in a flash, as one corner overtakes another.

Each corner operates at a different level. They are *not* equally important nor directly comparable. It all depends on the industry and the stage in life, or culture, of the individual. In addition the relative importance of each is likely to change over time in the minds of consumers, media and workforce.

But before we look at matching motivation to jobs, we need to dig deeper into one of the greatest workplace issues today: a better work–life balance.

13

BETTER BALANCE: WORK–LIFE OR LIFE–LIFE?

'Most of what people really want in life – love, friendship, respect, family, standing, fund – is not priced and does not pass through the market.'

Gregg Easterbrook, author of *The Progress Paradox*[1]

As we have seen, everywhere you look, people are talking about getting a life, finding a balance between work and home. The very phrase 'work–life balance' sums up the whole problem, because it tells us that people think that *work* is the opposite of meaningful *life*. We should be talking about life–life balance.

Every time a company talks about new policies under the heading of work–life balance, there's a risk of making matters worse by encouraging this dual-think, which is, at its root, very negative about work.

But it's all just the tip of a huge iceberg, a sign of a far greater force for change which every business needs to understand. This issue of balance is so central to workplace thinking that we need to take a closer look.

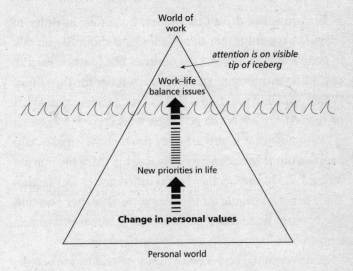

Many of us are turning our backs on work-obsessed culture as part of a bigger rethink about the whole of life. The purpose of making money, for most people, is to do something better. People work to get money, which they spend in the hope of an improved, happier kind of life. But money often fails to deliver. Look at the sky-high suicide rates in wealthy nations, compared to developing countries. There is a weak correlation between a country's income and how satisfied citizens feel with life.[2] In wealthy, industrialized nations, economic growth does not guarantee improved morale.[3]

The secret of happiness

If only the secret of personal happiness was as simple as getting wealthy and spending more.

Of course, people who are hungry or who lack the basics

of life are easily driven by money, but often in order to provide basic things for others they care about. If you talk to people on low incomes in countries like India or Poland, you'll find a common passion to earn more for the family. What happens if my child is sick and needs treatment? What happens if my father can no longer work?

We know that if you are very poor, money makes you happier, but if you are reasonably well off, extra income has little effect. In the US there is no difference in satisfaction levels between people on incomes of $20,000 per year and $80,000 per year.[4] Those with highest incomes in Switzerland are less happy than those in the tier below.

A survey of the *Forbes* list of the most wealthy 100 people, each with a net worth of more than $100 million, found hardly any difference in personal happiness compared to a sample of people chosen at random from a telephone book. And it is not difficult to find very wealthy people who are miserable.[5]

We know that those who experience tragedies, such as losing a loved one or their sight, may be unhappy for a year or two but, after that, they usually regain their usual level of happiness. The opposite is true for those who gain a sudden increase in wealth: for a short time their happiness rises and then falls to normal – or even below.[6]

'The one question politicians are too afraid to answer: if people aren't getting any happier as they get richer, why do we continue to trash the planet and turn people into consumptive zombies in pursuit of economic growth?'

Jonathon Porritt, chairman of the UK government's
Sustainability Commission, and former director of
Friends of the Earth[7]

More can be less: do we really think that people with 1,000 TV channels actually enjoy life more than those with 100? It could be the opposite. Too many choices can increase the stress of decision-making.[8]

Happiness is correlated with such things as strong relationships, a stable marriage, many friends and belonging to a religious group or having faith. Having an extrovert personality and an enjoyable job and living in a stable democracy are also factors positively linked with happiness.[9]

It is vitally important to understand these facts not only in finding ways to motivate people, but also in designing products and services, since a valued service or product is one that is likely to make those who pay for it happy.

Here is another paradox: those most obsessed with achieving happiness rarely seem to find it in their personal lives. The more they struggle to find contentment and self-fulfilment, the more elusive it seems to become. John Kay, a former professor at London Business School and Oxford University, calls it the obliquity principle, and it also applies to companies: those that aggressively pursue profit to the exclusion of all else are unlikely to be successful. An indirect approach may be the best means of achieving some goals.[10]

> 'We act as though comfort and luxury were the chief requirements of life, when all that we need to make us happy is something to be enthusiastic about.'
>
> Charles Kingsley, 1819–75

Anxious in the East, stressed in the West

Wealth and worry often go hand-in-hand. Stress-related

disorders have risen dramatically and are now the commonest reason for medical consultation, despite huge gains in personal spending power, every conceivable labour-saving gadget and a boom in leisure technology.

Anxiety disorders are now the most common mental illnesses in the US with 19.1 million (13.3 per cent) of 18–54 year olds affected. Anxiety disorders cost the United States more than \$42 billion per year – even more than cancer treatment.[11] And the higher you are on the corporate ladder, the higher the incidence of serious mental afflictions: 49 per cent of the highest achievers in the world have been diagnosed with one or more psychiatric disorders.[12]

Even though the US is the wealthiest nation in the world, one in every 10,000 Americans kill themselves each year. Suicide is the eighth most common cause of death and accounts for 1.3 per cent of all who die each month. That's one reason US spending on antidepressants jumped 21 per cent in 2000 alone. But it's not just America which is gripped by this psycho-epidemic: if current trends continue, by 2020 depression will be the second largest cause of disability worldwide, after heart disease.[13]

> 'Even more people today have the means to live but no meaning to live for.'
>
> Viktor Frankl, author of *Man's Search for Meaning*

There's a new addition to the Japanese vocabulary, *karoshi*, meaning death by overwork. Close to one hundred Japanese workers commit suicide *every day*: the suicide rate for 50–59 year olds in Japan is 68.9 per 100,000, one of the highest rates in the world.[14]

We all want enough to live comfortably, but the definition of comfort in wealthy nations seems to soar ever higher into the stratosphere, forcing us to work ever harder to attain a 'basic' standard of living that previous generations would have felt was extremely luxurious.

This false illusion of wealth-induced happiness is hitting home amongst affluent executives, many of whom are downsizing rapidly. And that's a challenge for corporations which are struggling to keep their best people with ever-larger bonuses and share options.

Michael Dell, CEO of Dell Computers, said recently:

> You get to a point where a certain percentage of the people have made so much money that it's not even other jobs in the company that excite them. You've got to think about what really motivates people, what gets them excited and you need compelling and exciting projects that keep those folks engaged. You've got to be kind of loving them and paying a lot of attention to them. Being part of something interesting and exciting that has impact is much more important to them.[15]

We end up sacrificing *relationships* for *things*. But which will be more important to *you* in the years to come? When your working life has long ceased, in the long retirement years ahead?

Time to get a life

Half of all Americans feel that society puts too much emphasis on work and not enough on leisure. That's almost *double* what it was twelve years earlier. It's much

the same in Europe, Australia, Japan and other industrialized nations.

In other words, the gap between personal and working
worlds is widening. As a result, half of all business managers
are seriously thinking about working fewer hours for less
money. Seven out of ten Americans today are less willing to
work hard to get ahead.[16]

Most workers report that long hours have negative effects
on their job performance, including making mistakes (63
per cent), taking longer to get things done (73 per cent), or
performing less well generally (74 per cent).[17]

Over a quarter of respondents say that long hours
have made them physically ill, with 26 per cent saying that
overwork has caused them mental ill-health, has added to
stress or made them depressed.[18]

Of those who work more than 48 hours per week, 68 per
cent say that it damages leisure and hobby time, as well as
vacations; indeed, 56 per cent of UK senior managers check
into work by phone or e-mail when on holiday.[19]

Personal pain affects both work and home

Of those UK managers earning more than £60,000 per year,
33 per cent have sacrificed family life for career.[20] More than
four in ten (45 per cent) blame long hours for straining their
relationships and, sadly, 11 per cent are convinced that their
hard work helped break up their marriages.[21]

When you allow for the fact that not all workers in
these polls were married, the figures suggest that employers are helping to destroy perhaps one marriage in seven.
The hidden emotional toll is even worse: for every marriage

> **Taking a long vacation?**
>
> *Average days leave each year in the US*
> After one year   9.6
> After two years   13.8
> After ten years   16.9[22]

that falls to pieces, another three will weather the storm, at great personal cost, not only to spouses juggling family and work, but to their partners and of course, perhaps most of all, to their children. It is hardly surprising, then, that half of all married couples, with at least one job between them, say that their relationships are suffering from excessive work demands. Despite working over 48 hours per week, the other half (47 per cent) believe that they have struck the right balance between work and the rest of life.[23] But it is likely to remain an issue when considering job moves or promotion.

Promotion or a life?

Many managers find themselves working harder than they want for more money than they need. For example, 38 per cent of BT managers said they would gladly turn down promotion to have more time at home.[24] But think about it: what's the point of recruiting great people you can't promote, who don't want responsibility, and would rather leave than climb your career ladder?

Although the number of managers working six days a week has halved to one in ten in just three years,[25] it remains the case that:

- 72 per cent of managers are criticized by family or friends for overwork[26]
- 33 per cent of managers say companies don't do enough to help workers find a balanced life[27]
- 40 per cent of Americans say one parent should be at home at least part-time.[28]

More than half of 6,000 managers in another survey said they wanted to work four days per week, for longer each day. They're fed up with trying to juggle excessive family and work commitments and hope that ring-fencing their jobs into fewer days will improve their personal lives.[29] In yet another study, 10,000 US, British and Japanese managers said that striving for work–life balance has now become their first or second career priority.[30]

Fifteen years ago, executives attending leadership training at Ashridge Business School said that their top career motivator was to acquire technical and functional skills related to their jobs. Today their number one priority is to achieve a better, more balanced lifestyle, while also being successful.

As we have seen, talented people have more options, tend to be more fickle and leave more quickly if dissatisfied. They also tend to be better informed, well networked and more aware of other opportunities.

So what are all these people going to *do* with all this extra time and energy when they *get* a life – when they find the balance they seek? Where will all that talent go?

A survey of 1,000 Americans who took part in an online goal-setting system revealed a big shift from 'hard' business goals to 'soft' personal goals:

- achieving physical or spiritual well-being (32 per cent)
- financial concerns (19 per cent)
- relationships (15 per cent)
- personal or professional development (12 per cent)
- work or career concerns (10 per cent)
- service to others – (7 per cent).[31]

Ultimately, relationships are usually our most treasured possessions, whether we are billionaires or poverty-stricken.

Home truths in Berlin

In many ways, Mark's (not his real name) story is typical of the revolution. He began with an ambitious work-based dream, but the reality shook him.

I had flown to Berlin to lead a seminar on global trends for 30 senior bankers from around the world. The day was drawing to a close. I was talking about personal values and how in a rapidly changing, turbulent world it's even more important to know what they are. At this point, Mark put up his hand and began to speak.

'I sure wish I wasn't here,' he said. 'Wish I was back in New York.'

Sensing the suppressed emotion in his faltering, quiet voice, all eyes turned towards him. The room fell absolutely silent. Most of the other participants had never met him before.

Mark paused for a while, eyes watering, face cast down on his hands. He could hardly speak without breaking down. He'd flown in yesterday, having left his 13-year-old son Larry at home in floods of tears, after a row about his maths grade. Mark travels all the time, works long hours and brings work home.

He'd only just got back from another trip and was about to leave again for two weeks on a training programme. The limo was waiting, he had a flight to catch, and as he was about to leave – why is it so often these things crop up *now*? – it emerged that there were big problems with Larry's work.

There was a brief and animated discussion. Larry just hates doing his maths. Mark told him it was important. Without it, Larry would never make it, never go to college, and never be able to get a decent job.

But his son Larry wasn't buying this story: 'I don't care.'

Mark pressed on, taking a reasonable but firm tone with his son. 'You just have to push through. And it's worth it. Look how successful I've been with the bank – and all because I worked hard at maths.'

But at this point his son burst into tears and cried out in anguish: 'I *hate* your job, Dad! I'd rather sweep the streets than do what you do! If *that's* what maths is for, then I never want to do maths again … I *see* what the job's doing to *Mum* … And I *know* what the job's doing to *me* – and I hate it.'

Mark was dumbstruck, didn't have a word to say. He was taken aback by the emotional force of his son's outburst and the sudden revelation about his parenting and his marriage. And the limo was waiting. There was no time for a family conference, for making up, for listening, for understanding …

Mark is a highly successful banker with everything going for him. He enjoys the challenge of the job and the recognition he receives. It's everything he always wanted and hoped for. But, at that moment, he was in a personal crisis. His dream of corporate success had brought with it a personal nightmare.

A few hours earlier, before his talk with Larry, everything was going fine. But now he wasn't so sure: his world in question, values in doubt, his success challenged. His son's words rang true. Rapid promotion, outward success and an intensely enjoyable job had distracted him from other things that, fundamentally, were far, far more important to him.

Mark was a million times more passionate about his own son's future than the profit margin of the bank, or the commissions his team earned last year.

I speak at many executive events and, afterwards, people just like Mark come and talk to me – some experiencing tensions at home, some with marriages completely fallen to bits, some only having limited contact with children on the other side of the world, and maybe other problems in their current relationships.

Please don't misunderstand me: I'm not saying that long working hours are the only killer of successful relationships, but time after time these people say that pressure at work was, or is, a significant factor. And the result is often long-lasting personal pain, sometimes affecting more than one generation.

Not long ago employers were all telling their workers that there was no such thing as a career and short-term contracts would be the norm. Now the argument has backfired: employers are applying the same logic to companies they work for. Now it's *people* who don't want a career with an employer:[32]

> I want to do something worthwhile. I want to put something back. It's depressing as hell thinking this is all I've done with my life. This job is all I've amounted to. Making some money for somebody else. Hardly any time to spend with my kids. Whenever I come home and listen to them I find they've changed so much and I've missed it all again. No more!

> I actually turned down a partnership in the firm. Can you believe it? All my adult life I went on thinking this opportunity would be everything. But, once I had my wits about me, I actually turned down the partnership because I realized it meant I would have absolutely no life outside work. I really would go insane, you know.

> Last year I spent six entire months away from home travelling. It's hurting the people I love … last weekend I realized that I'd become a stranger to my own children … Despite what they're telling you in that boardroom, don't believe it, shareholder value is not the centre of my existence.

Job flexibility keeps people committed

> 'Nobody motivates today's workers. If it doesn't come from within, it doesn't come at all.'
>
> Herman Cain, author of *Leadership is Common Sense*

I have lost count of the number of people who have confided in me that they dare not even talk about their hope to have children some day, in case it damages their career prospects. It upsets me, since I know how important 'family' is for many of these people. All too often, senior executives are fearful to let their bosses into the secret that everyone else knows, which is that they are going to have a baby soon and would like to talk about maternity leave. And as for any suggestion that they would like to come back part-time …

Anyone who has children will agree that a first child is a huge life-event, and that young children are usually a major focus of thought, planning and pleasure.

When a couple have been trying for a long time to have a child and have just received a positive test result, their next e-mails are likely to be about that rather than the workplace operational review, and when a toddler is acutely sick in hospital, a mother or father may be physically at work, but their mind and heart are likely to be elsewhere.

Flexible work options should be simple, well-marketed and built on trust. The reality is that despite the hype, those with flexible jobs often get sidelined away from the real action, despite the fact that part-timers are often more highly motivated and hard-working than their colleagues.

'There is more to life than increasing its speed.'

Mahatma Gandhi, 1869–1948

The 'family' key to better business success

Strengthening family life must be a major priority for any company that is interested in retaining the strongest possible workforce.

Companies which help their staff members juggle home

> **Flexible working adds to profits**
>
> Asda (one of the four big UK supermarket groups) believes that flexible working was linked to a £4 million reduction in the cost of absence, as well as better retention and recruitment. Options include: 'shift swaps' for personal reasons; 'store swaps' for students who study in one place and go home in the holidays; 'grandparents' leave' for older workers; leave for new mothers and fathers; school-starter schemes; spring holidays for older workers (the so-called 'Benidorm leave'); and elder care. Asda also encouraged short-term flexibility such as juggling work hours, changing rosters or reducing working weeks.[33]

and work lives are rewarded with 'significant' levels of improved performance according to research by the Joseph Rowntree Foundation. Performance is enhanced by extra parental leave, help with childcare, flexible working, job-sharing and allowing employees to work from home.[34]

Heroic sacrifices every day

It is not enough to pay large salaries without understanding why people need to work, what they intend to do with the money, and what they wish they were doing instead of working for you.

As every HR director knows, for many people, the primary reason for working so hard is to provide more for their children. Every day, millions of parents choose to have less so that their children can have more. Mothers give their children the best food and save their own scarce spending money to buy them new shoes. Most parents are passionate about their children having the best. Parents are a significant driving force behind, for example, the billions spent in the UK and Europe on organic food – a market that is growing rapidly in most developed countries.

> 'All of us want a better more peaceful world for our children.'
>
> Fave Crosby, psychologist[35]

That's why corporations need to be so deeply involved in children's lives. It's where the hearts of many workers lie. That means more than a nursery, or an after-school club, or allowing flexible working hours. For a start, are you sure that providing professional childcare is *really* always in the best interests of children or family well-being?

Pressures on dual-income parents

We need to listen very carefully to what working mothers of young children are actually saying. Surveys show a consistent pattern: given the choice, most mothers with small children prefer to be at home or to work short, flexible hours – although they are often profoundly grateful for subsidized high-quality childcare facilities at work. A survey of 2,000 mothers with part-time or full-time jobs outside the home found that only one in five wants to be a career woman and six out of ten would quit the rat-race tomorrow if they could, in order to spend more time with their children.[36]

Most full-time 'working' mothers of young children feel worn out from juggling career pressures with the investment they want to make into their own children's lives. Seventy-five per cent say that they are not living the life they were expecting, and that the pressures are affecting their social lives as well as their enjoyment of sex.

Another survey found that only 2 per cent of women about to give birth want to go back to work full-time. Of those who do, 66 per cent go back for the money and 88 per cent want subsidized childcare or a nursery but only 8 per cent of companies provide it.[37] Most believe that work is ageing them prematurely and complain they feel stressed most of the time.[38]

> 'Giving gives life not only to others but to you yourself.'
>
> Sean Covey[39]

Pressures to give extra time to children can be greatest at the beginning and end of the school day, during school holidays and when children are ill. Parents of teenagers also feel pressures when their children are rapidly developing into adulthood and are no longer willing to communicate 'on-demand' during momentary mid-week gaps between office hours and domestic duties.

If you look at new recruits to industry from graduate entry programmes you will often find the majority are women, and that they are clearly outperforming their male colleagues, yet women are progressively outnumbered at more senior levels. So where do all these exceptionally talented women go? This is a corporate scandal. Many of the most capable members of the workforce are being eliminated through low-level discrimination, hostility to their values, imposition of practical difficulties and other obstacles. All-male boards are likely to have members who are only there because more talented women opted out somewhere along the line.

Family-centred men also find similar career blocks are applied in subtle ways. For a start, many men are part of two-income households. Partners also have their own career pressures. Whose job will win in the relocation stakes? Some children are also more mobile than others, depending largely on age. We need to take a more holistic view of workers in families.

'Family' people: the glue holding organizations together

In our globalized world we urgently need leaders with well-developed emotional and social skills, able to build relationships across many thousands of miles, supported primarily by electronic channels. We need leaders who create warmth: family-builders, relationship managers.

Those with strong family lives, long-lasting local friendships and community commitments are likely to be glue holding teams together. These are the people who remember clients' names and family details; they are people on whom the future of your business could depend and yet are difficult to promote because they insist on having a life outside the office.

The very people we most need in international offices are, by the nature of their circumstances, resistant to frequent air travel and multiple relocations. In contrast, many of those you send around the world may be those for whom relationships are less important and less suited to holding large networks together over large distances.

Family-friendly companies recognize that it is not enough to look at employee downtime through international travel – lost productivity due to being unaccessible or unable to work while waiting in customs, waiting for luggage, travelling and so on. They also need to pay attention to the impact on all their family relationships – which includes their parents, as well as their children. The window of total freedom between the end of child-rearing and new responsibilities for elderly parents is often relatively small. This can lead to a profound reassessment of work priorities.

Retirement age is history

Retirement should happen when you want to stop work and can afford to do so. As simple as that. The idea of a fixed retirement age is becoming an absurd nonsense.

My grandmother continued working as a physician doing part-time insurance medical examinations until she was 83. She died over a decade later. She was unusual, but there will be many like her in the future. In the US there are already over 70,000 people who are more than 100 years old, and that number will double over the next six to ten years. Every four years the Japanese government adds another year to its projections of women's life expectancy.

Each stage of life is lengthening: we live in an age in which many young men and women only settle down in stable relationships with family commitments when they are in their mid- to late thirties, having spent the previous decade and a half enjoying freedom and taking one degree or training programme after another.

Many 65 year-olds are still passionate about wanting to work – even if only part-time – and often have a financial need to do so. When they retire, this age-group often substitute paid work, for which they are no longer eligible, for a wide variety of unpaid jobs.

But older people often make wonderful employees: more reliable, more dependable, more likely to get out of bed in the morning, more experienced in life, more sensitive to the needs of older customers, and often a source of practical ways to solve management problems.

So what does all this mean for employers?

1 Understand that each worker has a family, their own inner group – people they care far more about than your business objectives.
2 Make sure you know about what's going on at home, what the pressures are.
3 Think about ways in which you could help make work easier, more fun, more fulfilling for them.
4 Make sure they know that, as far as you are concerned, children must come first. While you expect every effort to make suitable child care arrangements, you recognize that things sometimes don't work out, there may be a crisis, a home carer may become sick, two children may be off school today, a husband or wife may be travelling or in hospital.
5 When there's a problem at home, gladly and rapidly release stressed-out carers to go and sort things out for as long as they need.
6 Encourage portable computers, the use of mobile

phones and flexible home-working, trusting that most urgent tasks will be completed on time, and that you will be amply rewarded by dedication, loyalty, passion, commitment and gratitude. After all, next time it may be your turn to call in a big favour.

7 If the employee is in a two-career household, make sure your discussions reflect that. Offer career-planning meetings with both, not just with the person you employ.

8 Discuss these kinds of issues openly and make sure those who have no children or elderly dependants also feel valued and appreciated and give them the same kind of flexibility (and favours) you give to others in different circumstances.

Many bosses are scared that such relaxed attitudes will erode office discipline, lead to abuse, resentment and lost productivity. The key to it all is having a well-motivated team in the first place, who are enthusiastically committed to achieving tough targets, for something they believe will be worth all their efforts.

So, we have explored a new model for motivation and the importance of life–life balance. How can we better match jobs to people's passions?

MOTIVATION MATCHING: JOINING BUSINESS AND PERSONAL GOALS

If you want the best from people, match the job you are asking them to do with what they feel is important. Most organizations assess the suitability of job applicants on their past experience, qualifications, references and perhaps even their psychological profile. But none of these things tells you whether the person being interviewed is going to be 'turned on' by what they are going to be asked to do.

Some companies make a superficial stab at the process with questions like 'How would you feel working for a tobacco company?' or, perhaps, 'I see you have been working as a volunteer for Friends of the Earth for many years. Are your friends going to be happy about you working for a large oil company?'

Motivational matching has received almost zero attention in the past, except in careers advice, but will be a key part of successful organization building in future. Talent matching is well understood and, as we have seen from the Gallup research (see pages 161–5), critically important.

Talent + Motivation = Big Results

Organizations can start by using combined talent/motivation

assessments to help select the right people for different jobs. However, what happens when you just can't find talented, high-calibre people with the motivation you want for the job? Expect motivational matching to encourage the rapid shaping of jobs, cultures and practices to attract the very best.

How does motivation matching work?

First, you score motivators and talent requirements of a set of job vacancies. Second, you score motivators and talents of those available. Finally, you match the two together.

Different motivation patterns

There is no such thing as right or wrong motivation when it comes to building organizations. The key to is match individual motivation to the nature of the job and, if necessary, pay attention to the whole context of the job, and make the job itself a better motivator.

People differ enormously, and each individual has his or her own motivational profile which can be measured, either subjectively by the individual or objectively by external evaluation using quantitative tools. Individual motivation can change dramatically over time – for example, after the birth of a first child or after a mid-life crisis.

In the same way, job motivators vary enormously, even within the same section of the same organization, depending perhaps on the team leader's management style.

Five-star motivation

The five potential motivators are shown below as five points of a circle or a star, based on the four circles of the human heart (see Chapter 12) with a fifth dimension for the client or customer. To illustrate how varied individual motivations can be in particular jobs, the five points have been scored for a number of different people. Different scores may be obtained from different people doing the same jobs for the same organization.

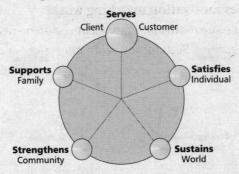

Tom is a cleaner; he hates the work but does it to support a young family. In the evenings he earns extra in a bar. 'It's just a job,' he says.

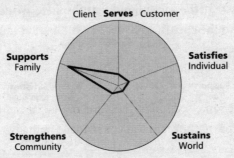

Hazel is a social worker who feels passionately about child welfare and the care of the elderly. She is deeply satisfied on a personal level because she works in a very supportive team, although she is poorly paid. She feels that the job not only helps individuals, but also strengthens the community, and it helps support her family. She is highly motivated and has been in the department for over six years.

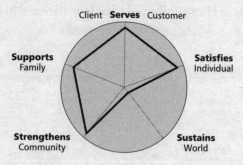

Marcus is a private banker, working with a small number of exceptionally wealthy people whom he regards as long-term friends. In fact, their loyalty to him is greater than their loyalty to his bank. He likes how the company treats people and feels that the same family atmosphere works its way through to the clients.

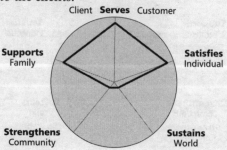

Sarah is a journalist who prides herself on delving deeply into difficult 'public interest' stories. She has no real commitment to the newspaper or her boss, and pursues her own agendas as far as she can. She is satisfied personally by researching and writing, feels that she contributes something important to the community as a whole, but admits that the terrible deadlines and weekend working are very disruptive for her family, and that their standard of living is lower than it would be if she did another job.

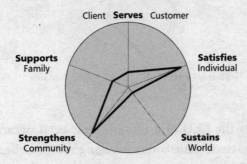

Harris is a militant single-issue activist, interested in the environment. Everything in his life is oriented around this.

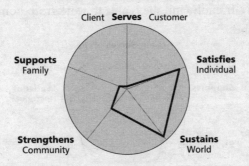

George runs a small corner shop. Three generations live above the shop and work in it during the day, all helping from seven in the morning to eleven at night. He is constantly tired and finds the shop a burden. However, it is a family business; he knows he provides a service and believes that small shops like his are important for the local community.

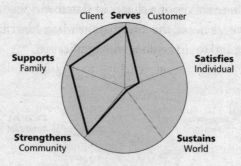

Susan is the CEO of a non-governmental organization active in developing countries. She has an excellent team, enjoys the work, knows that she helps make a difference to thousands of lives, is strengthening community both in the area served and also in the areas giving support, and feels she is helping build a better and more just world. The job is family-friendly, and she is able to work from home when she wishes.

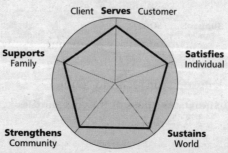

Motivational audit – for people, jobs and organizations

You can carry out a simple motivational audit by asking those in your team what their most powerful motivations are at work, and the reasons why they think people might be motivated to join them. This can be done using either a free-text response survey or a cluster of statements with scores.

You can then use the information when advertising job vacancies and in discussions with applicants.

A useful motivation matching tool can be built on the Q12 system devised by Gallup (see pages 164–7).[1] Positive scoring of the ten Gallup statements below is strongly correlated with personal engagement, team performance, profitability, morale, low staff turnover and high commitment to corporate objectives:

1 I know what is expected of me at work.
2 I have the materials and equipment I need to do my work.
3 At work I have the opportunity to do what I do best every day.
4 In the last seven days I have received recognition or praise for doing good work.
5 My supervisor, or someone at work, seems to care about me as a person.
6 There is someone at work who encourages my development.
7 At work my opinion seems to count.
8 The mission or purpose of my company makes me feel that my job is important.

9 My associates or fellow employees are committed to doing quality work.
10 I have a best friend at work.

Motivation matching adds weight to Question 8 about the purpose or mission of the organization, and whether the person feels that he or she is contributing to a worthwhile cause. It is in this area that we see the greatest potential for harnessing the common passions people have for, say, volunteering in the community to the passions we hope they will have for what the organization is also trying to achieve.

The following are examples of motivation matching questions.

Those inside corporation

1 How important do you think the mission of this corporation is?
2 Do you think that what we do as a team contributes significantly to other people's lives?
3 What is the contribution we make?
4 What makes you want to come to work each day?
5 In what ways do you feel personally fulfilled in working here?
6 What do we offer people who are looking for a strong sense of purpose in what they do at work?

Those being interviewed

1 What are you most passionate about outside of work and family?

2   What kinds of things would you choose to spend your time doing if you were retired?

3   Do you give time to help organizations or others outside of your family and close friends – or would you if you had more time? If so, what is it about these situations that is important to you?

4   What kinds of tasks and jobs do you feel are most important in life?

5   How important is it to you to feel there is a purpose in what you do?

6   Do you think that what we do in this organization is important and, if so, why?

So, then, we have explored leadership, team building and motivating people more effectively. We now need to turn to one of the greatest challenges in any business: managing change for the better.

15

MANAGING CHANGE FOR THE BETTER

'We have seen more change in the past five years than in the previous 150.'

E. Mervyn Davies, CEO, Standard Chartered[1]

'All my experience suggests that individuals will eagerly embrace change when given a chance to have a voice in inventing the future of their company ... to create a unique and exciting future in which they can share.'

Gary Hamel, chairman of Strategos[2]

Every year billions of dollars are wasted trying to make people change the way in which they work. Resistance to change is a number one killer of healthy corporations. Boards may spend days, weeks or months approving a battle plan and executive teams may work hard to flesh out the details, often running up huge consultancy bills in the process, but all too often the result is disappointing: little or nothing seems to happen, even though the underlying threats are growing more serious.

So why is change management such a huge money-spinner for management consultants – and such a huge source of angst for business leaders?

The reason is simple: people don't want to change. That is because they don't see the point or, even if they do, they are all too often convinced that the end result will not be worth the effort, for them.

> 'Only the wisest and stupidest of men never change.'
>
> Confucius, 551–479 BC

However, if approached differently, change management can be rapid, easy, relatively painless and effective. The secret is to win people over as enthusiastic drivers of business transformation. Radical change can happen rapidly without a change management programme when everyone sees the crisis, knows what to do and believes that there is hope for the future.

Instant change management

> 'Change starts when someone sees the next step.'
>
> William Drayton, president, Bank of the United States, 1840–41

Here is a fact: if a major incident affects a corporate head-quarters, you do not need a change management programme to:

- get large numbers of people to suspend everything they are working on
- get them all to leave the building rapidly
- get them working hard on a major programme to restore full operational efficiency in a temporary building up the road.

Why is this so easy? Because the problem is clear and

demands an urgent response. Failure to act fast and efficiently could have disastrous consequences. Failure to recover rapidly could mean major losses and some people losing their jobs.

Using our building a better world model: it's obviously a far better world for all to get out as fast as possible, and it's a better world for all to rebuild rapidly and operate very flexibly in the meantime.

So, then, if you are trying to change an organization, here are some fundamental questions, which many senior managers fail to answer properly before embarking on major restructuring or other disruptions:

- Why is this change so necessary?
- Who will benefit from all the effort?
- Have you fully accounted for hidden costs such as lost morale and increased staff turnover?
- Do you really believe it is of the utmost importance yourself – or is it something you feel has been imposed by others, whether shareholders, analysts, an out-of-touch board, a short-sighted boss or whatever?
- Are you certain the change is going to end with you and the organization in the right place?

Change management can only succeed if people have a vision of where they are going – and that vision has to be accurate.

Past decades are littered with the debris of failed corporations that had the wrong products, wrong services or were unable to compete because of archaic structures, out-of-date systems and bad decisions. But making things happen differently inside a big organization is a huge challenge. In fact, it takes so long that large companies have to start adapting many years before they expect the future to arrive. And the personal cost can be huge.

What happened to work?

The trouble is that, regardless of level of ambition, those of us who work for a living have never had to work so hard, under such difficult conditions, for such uncertain rewards.

Many managers are feeling battered and bruised. Hit by one event after another, there's little time to regroup or reflect, and leading can be a lonely business. Profit warnings, share price pressures, painful lay-offs and great geopolitical uncertainties can sweep away even the most comprehensive strategies – and that's despite outstanding management over many years.

The corporate world is in constant flux: 9,265 US corporations changed status in a single year, merging assets of $1.4 trillion. Over half a million Americans are made redundant *every week* in bad times, and then as many new jobs may be created just as rapidly a few months later. Today's scale of corporate destruction and re-creation is truly unprecedented.

At current rates of merger there will soon be a relatively small number of global 'holding' companies controlling a far larger proportion of commercial activity in America and Europe. Of course, this pace is unsustainable and, before long, we will see a frenetic number of demergers as super-corporations realize that being bigger can have drawbacks for shareholders, consumers or workers. But demergers also bring big changes and stress.

Hundreds of thousands of individuals have gone to work one day for one company, to find the next day they are working for another.

Management chaos from endless reorganizations

Often, these mergers create chaos in management, confusion in products or services and great uncertainties for people. Such changes can be traumatic. When you merge two cultures, two tribes, two families, two histories, what do you get? Huge potential problems.

The dotcom boom is estimated to have attracted more than $30 billion of investment into startups in a single year, much of which was lost. Once again, the fall-out was huge for many individuals, who found themselves jobless and with their career prospects damaged. Some of them lost their life savings.

In 2001, 1,492,129 American businesses filed for bankruptcy – an all-time record. Most of them were small or family-owned – typical of 98 per cent of all businesses in the US, employing 60 per cent of the workforce and responsible for 66 per cent of all new jobs despite the impact of mergers and the creation of super-corporations.

Massive stock market crashes around the world in the autumn of 2001 also resulted in shockwaves, felt in tens of thousands of small to medium-sized businesses dependent on larger corporations for their existence.

Enron's stock market value was $90 billion before it collapsed in late 2001.

We have also seen sudden and catastrophic currency crises in nations such as Mexico, Turkey, Indonesia and Thailand, with rapid falls in value of up to 75 per cent. Assets have been destroyed, loans recalled and businesses closed.

Familiar household names disappear overnight as a result of rebranding, takeovers, market pressures. Factories open, close and move – all within months. Landmark buildings are destroyed and new ones built. Boom times also produce huge adjustments for people, with constant reshaping of jobs and teams to accommodate growth, coupled with immense work pressures and strains on personal life.

Weary of change – yet more change to come

> 'Man has a limited biological capacity for change. When this capacity is overwhelmed – the capacity is in future shock.'
>
> Alvin Toffler, author of Futureshock

This all adds up to a world of chaotic instability. Yet within this shaky, unstable world, boardrooms are frustrated with *how long* it takes to make major changes. By the time a corporation has managed change, the world has changed again, new values have risen to the forefront, and the company is in need of change, yet again.

And the people affected, the mass of ordinary workers, are, quite simply, getting worn out. With all these job changes, people tend to lose any strong sense of loyalty to and emotional bonding with their employers.

Constant rapid change at work is de-enervating, demotivating, depressing, especially when the benefits of change are unclear. It breaks up stable teams, weakens meaningful work relationships and destroys many previous efforts. Just ask people who have been through three major mergers in three years.

Thriving on chaos no more

> 'Humankind has two basic and equally important strong needs: stability and change.'
>
> Tom Peters[3]

In his best-selling book *Thriving on Chaos*, Tom Peters suggested that the winners of tomorrow would deal proactively with chaos, as a source of market advantage, not a problem to be ignored.

Today, we have come to see things rather differently. Chaos can be unhealthy. To many people, our modern world seems to be shaped by random forces over which we have little or no control. And every day, as the world changes, it can feel like a more meaningless place.

It is true, as Tom Peters reminds us, that managers and organizations need to be supple, flexible, rapidly adaptive and ready for constant radical change. However, it all comes at a high personal price.

Vision: the most powerful motivator for change

> 'Change involves the politics of the community. In a world in which people have staked out territorial claims for themselves around roles, resources, and psychological investments, why would anyone want to co-operate with

changes that reduce their status and influence? ... Even when customers will benefit and money will be saved, turf wars prevent change from happening.'

Nigel Nicholson, author of Managing the Human Animal[1]

It's easy to move people when they're captivated by hope for a better future (whatever that may be for them), and are very frustrated with the current situation. By contrast, people who are very satisfied with the current situation and feel negative about what is proposed are impossible to change and energy-consuming to manage.

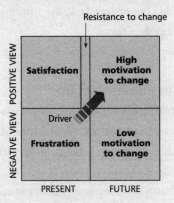

The trouble is that what companies claim will result in a better world is often light years away from what workers feel is likely to be a better world for them personally. The result: zero motivation to change.

Tell me this: the latest restructuring is better for *who* exactly? The company answer is usually that it is better for customers who get better services and products at ever lower costs, and also for shareholders who get better returns. But workers can get lost along the way.

What large corporations need for change is an unstoppable people-movement for radical action. And the main driver for such a movement is a rapidly spreading conviction that the crisis is real and that the proposed changes are right, are most likely to bring the best outcome for most people and, most importantly, are likely to have a positive result for key individuals.

> 'Employees have to be convinced that what you are doing is leading to the right kind of development for the firm. They have to feel in safe hands – that the firm's leader is really caring for the prospects of the institution, and by extension, for each of them.'
>
> Rolf Breuer, Chairman, Supervisory Board, Deutsche Bank[5]

The mysterious power of groups

Humans are complex creatures, and many aspects of our collective nature remain mysteries. What happens, for example, in the concert hall between a gifted violin player and her audience? Why is it that live concert performances have a different dimension for the players than a studio recording? How is it that you or I can walk into a crowded room where everyone is silent and, within a couple of seconds, detect the general mood and the emotional energy?

And one of the greatest mysteries is the personality of groups. Groups are very special creations. They quickly develop their own character which can be enduring. We need to understand what groups are about, to find better ways to change them.

Any group creates its own culture. Take a group of ten

men and women. Over the next decade every single member could be replaced twice over and yet, if any of the founders of the group was to visit ten years later, they might well find much that is familiar and derives from the group's first days together. This is true of clubs, churches, associations, not-for-profit organizations and business groups of all sizes.

Now, of course, we would expect a certain degree of this if, for example, the group is still writing software for financial services clients or providing community services for young people. But I am talking about the more subtle differences between one such group and another: it could be whether the group tends to socialize in the evenings or includes spouses and partners in big decisions, or is very creative, or very ordered and precise, whether everyone works strictly to a time clock at the start and end of the day or whether they use flexitime, or whether they wear suits or t-shirts and scruffy jeans.

Groups have a life of their own

Groups are 'alive' in the sense of having a living identity of their own that is distinct from, and goes beyond, the individuals within it. It is almost a spiritual thing, just as elusive when it comes to formal analysis as the strange magic that is wrought upon an audience by a world-class performer. There is an invisible, but significant, added dimension – a force operating on another level altogether.

This added factor can affect buildings, even when empty. Places have atmospheres as well as associations. They connect with memories in our past and with our imagination, as well as with our subconscious associations.

That's why office relocations are sometimes effective in assisting change. Take two organizations and merge them together. The smaller is shoe-horned into the existing offices of the larger with all kinds of territorial feelings, in addition to cultural insecurities. Then the two are relocated as one, and the two workforces become less easily definable.

Group culture is a particularly big issue in not-for-profit organizations and religious groups. When there is no written contract, no pay, no terms and conditions of service, no formal beginning or end to the working relationship, no enforceable objectives, no reward system and no line management, the power of groups is especially great. It dictates what people want to do together, how they did things in the past and the way they do things around here.

Leading groups can be difficult because we imagine, perhaps, that we have a certain authority and, with it, a liberty to make changes. But, in practice, the hidden power of the group can be stronger than the leadership. You see this hidden power when someone who was relatively open to a particular course of action, or who was used to doing things in a certain way, joins a group with a different culture. Within a few months you may find that the person's own perspectives and preferences have changed. So long as they identify strongly with that particular group of people, they may be inclined to 'go with the flow'.

You may find that everyone in that group is being held collectively to a particular course of action, not by each other (because if they were on their own they would choose differently) but by the invisible power of the group itself – this combination of past and present, of culture and previous ways of doing things.

These are all reasons why leading a group in a new direction requires far more investment of time and energy than many people realize, and another reason why so-called 'change management programmes' are often unsuccessful.

Changing group behaviour requires a high level of personal passion and integrity, a compelling vision of a better future and a convincing and clearly understood strategy about how to get there.

In *Seven Habits of Highly Effective People*[6] Stephen Covey talks about the principle of win-win. That means taking care to try to understand each step from other people's point of view. It's one of the most powerful ways to reduce conflict, reach consensus and make things happen in groups.

Discover and address hidden loyalties

Groups often express strong loyalties to, for example, the values of the founder of an organization or a previous leader, even if retired, distant or dead. They may express loyalties to a national team, in the case of a foreign takeover. They may be deeply loyal to a set of foundational principles that first drew them into the business.

Hidden influences need to be identified, honoured, respected, talked over and incorporated into any changes that are proposed. If those influences are to be overlaid by others, or set aside in some way, then you need to show why. Group members need to know that the group's heritage and values are appreciated and important.

They also need to know why following the old way will

result in trouble and why the new direction is the right way forward. They need to see, touch and feel some of the realities of this better world – to have an early sense that it really will be for the best.

It has often been said that people don't tend to think in meetings. The real change of mind and heart tends to happen beforehand, and the real work of persuasion therefore happens outside a meeting room, especially in the case of those whose opinion carries most weight. It is also the case that meetings allow those who are uncertain to get a collective feel for where others want to go. Meetings allow those who do not have strong feelings on an issue to fall into line behind those who do.

Fight fewer battles

Many workers are thoroughly cynical when it comes to yet another reorganization. They have long memories. They know that change management programmes often get overtaken by events – markets change, investors move on, competitors move in, or a merger or acquisition makes it irrelevant so they have to start all over again.

Many senior executives in large corporations have been through several reorganizations in the past few years, and rarely do you find people who would defend the rightness of all those major changes. Many are weary, fed up, hardened veterans of fickle, badly thought-out and poorly implemented changes.

Successful change management means fighting fewer battles, changing less to make more happen. As every battle commander knows, only some hills are worth dying for. A central role of effective leadership is knowing which they are, and seizing them with minimum casualties.

Give persuasive reasons to change

> 'You need to motivate people; to share the vision from the management team down to the shop floor. You also need to convince people that is where we want to go, and convince them of the need to change. And you only achieve that by spending a lot of time communicating and listening.'
>
> John Goossens, former CEO, Belgacom[7]

We have seen in an earlier chapter how few people get turned on by the idea of adding shareholder value, or increasing the bottom line, except as a way of increasing their own pay package.

Although it is true that all such things can ultimately affect every person in the organization, the one person who is most exposed, of course, is the CEO, and one can't help but suspect that at the heart of many of these drives for change is a key anxiety in the CEO's own mind about staying at the helm or being able to depart with honour. But leadership of major change has to be based on far more.

> A vision needs to be an imaginative picture of where the company will be and why that positioning will be a transforming event not just for the company but for its customers and its other constituencies ... When I hear CEOs explain where they want to take their companies, there is an element of personal passion, almost as if the leader and the vision were one.
>
> Jeffrey Garten[8]

Smart managers enthuse others to go in a particular direction, because they have got hold of that same vision for themselves. It is now their agenda, their calling, their vision, their drive, their ambition!

People-movements change the world

In 1987 I found myself, as a cancer physician, on an AIDS ward in the centre of London, advising colleagues on how to make the last weeks, days and hours of those dying of AIDS more bearable and comfortable. It was a harrowing episode, and I will never forget what happened. That visit led directly to the formation of a people-movement, ACET, which continues to grow rapidly with the aim of saving lives and caring for those affected by HIV.

ACET stands for AIDS Care Education and Training and, today, you will find the movement in Russia, Ukraine, Slovakia, the Czech Republic, the UK, Thailand, Zimbabwe, South Africa, India, Nigeria and other nations. It grows without formal global leadership, or a central organization, yet it has distributed over a million pieces of literature, over 200,000 free books, cared for thousands of sick or dying people, supported more than 1,000 AIDS orphans in their African villages and educated over a million young people face-to-face.

There is nothing particularly unusual or remarkable about the ACET story – there are a hundred other stories like it – but it happens to be one I have had the privilege to have been involved in for more than seventeen years.

How it happened

I was so shocked to see how badly people were dying with AIDS in London hospitals, and how reluctant hospice teams were to get involved, that I started a new not-for-profit organization. Our aims were simple: first, to provide practical help so that men, women and children sick with AIDS could spend as much of their lives in their own homes as possible, and if they wished, die there surrounded by their own family and friends; second, to reach young people at risk of HIV with a life-saving message that they could relate to and help them find healthy ways of living.

As these thoughts were developing I was asked to write my first book, *The Truth about AIDS*, which contained a challenge to churches and to governments to take effective action.

The organization grew fast, and everywhere I went to speak about AIDS people came up offering their time, finance – even their own homes. Their responses were profoundly moving.

We began national care and prevention programmes in the UK in 1988 and international programmes began in countries such as Uganda and Romania two years later.

By the mid- to late 1990s it was clear already that a large number of other not-for-profit groups had started, taking their inspiration from some of the work of ACET. At the same time, we made all the different country operations independent, with full control over every aspect of their affairs. Almost all grew more strongly as a result. Passion and autonomy are a powerful combination.

Today, new country operations are being started on a

regular basis in places I have never visited, started by people I have never met, without any central planning or control.

Katarina phoned our home from Heathrow airport.

'Hello,' she said. 'I am Katarina from ACET Croatia.'

'I didn't know there was an ACET Croatia,' I replied.

'I friend of Milan and Tómas', she explained – and it all made instant sense.

In the mid-1990s one of a hundred of our English schools educators had gone to the Czech Republic where he had trained and inspired a drug rehabilitation worker called Tómas to continue his embryonic work. Stuart moved on to New Zealand and Tómas developed a Czech schools programme which now reaches the majority of teenagers across the country. Milan from Slovakia came to see what was happening and took the vision from Tómas back to his own country. Milan, in turn, now has his own national team of volunteer schools workers, who are working in 60 per cent of all high schools in Slovakia. Others then began to develop similar work in Croatia, Slovenia, Russia and Ukraine.

These programmes have been largely self-funded, yet are driven by the same infectious passion and vision that we had back in 1988.

They are unstoppable.

If all the other ACET initiatives around the world closed down, the momentum in the former Soviet bloc countries is likely to continue to grow and flourish, and similar things are happening in other parts of the world.

Yes, change is often difficult and can be costly, but when people are connected to the passions they have, change happens with or without a change management programme.

So if your vision is clear, your cause is powerful and your strategy right, you won't be able to stop change from happening all around you. You may even find that you yourself become one of the chief resisters of change – many leaders find it uncomfortable feeling a little out of control.

Win the moral argument

This is an extremely important principle. It's the reason why, in the corporate world, there is often failure to get consensus on codes of practice or standards of behaviour.

Failure to win hearts and minds has serious consequences. Those who try to manipulate, bully or intimidate people into following a stupid regulation or process will find they create a million paths of resistance – a grassroots campaign that results in destruction of leadership. It's the same with all laws and systems of justice.

If you want change, a powerful way to achieve it is to win the moral argument. Every sensible law, regulation, code of conduct or procedure is an instrument whose total aim is to build a better world. Every court case hangs or falls on this issue.

Laws, rules, regulations, and policies are completely unenforceable unless citizens are convinced that these rules do indeed result in a better way. If they are not, the police don't arrest and prosecutions are not brought, and, if they are, juries fail to convict – even when the evidence against the defendant is overwhelming.

Winning the argument is a more subtle process than you may think. It's not a matter of going out and telling people they'll get a bonus if they comply with company policy.

Let's take the example of a large organization which has just merged with an even larger one. Those fortunate enough to have secure jobs are told they will get a big reward if they drive a savage, ruthless, rapid restructuring with mass redundancies. Managers then find they have low-level rebellion on their hands, with silent obstruction at every level.

What went wrong?

The answer is that the managers forgot that people work for people, not for organizations. Most individuals worth employing are not prepared to build a better world for themselves at the expense of their friends. Often it's not *what* happens, but the *way* it's done that builds a better or worse world in people's minds.

But when did you last hear friendship being talked about as a key factor in making decisions in large organizations? This is typical of the terrible mess organizations get into by applying psychological theories from previous centuries to a third-millennial workforce.

> 'An effective corporate culture is increasingly a source of competitive advantage, which is why we pay such enormous attention to our corporate values; teamwork, respect, integrity and professionalism.'
>
> Dolf van den Brink, board member, ABN AMRO[9]

New technology and change

Technology should make our lives easier, more enjoyable and more fun. It should help get things done faster, give better results and reduce stress. But in reality, we often have to work harder, longer and faster, or are frustrated by unreliable, confusing systems which are poorly designed, are introduced without proper consultation and are vulnerable to bugs, viruses and network crashes.

Middle managers may be reluctant to cooperate with new systems which threaten their jobs. Take the example of a bank manager, who has been told that new technology means her branch will close. At the very end, having helped with design, sold the changes to her customers, facilitated the process of winding down the branch, what happens? She discovers in an e-mail that her job is over.

Technology is supposed to improve quality of life but often doesn't seem to. It's no good telling your staff that they are more productive using e-mail, if the result is five times as many messages to deal with. Nor is it any good telling them that a new screen will ease eye fatigue, or new chairs will help backache, when they are now almost chained to their desks all day.

Constant messaging may be great for managers but can undermine leadership and relationships. Recently, I was asked to facilitate a discussion on global trends with a team of fifteen people from around the world who were used to meeting every couple of months. As each person entered the room, almost without a word, by force of habit, they sat at their long board table, opened a lap-top and plugged in power plus ethernet cable. For almost half an hour before the meeting began, each member of the team tapped away answering mail – sometimes from each other.

Other companies have given Blackberrys or other wireless devices to all their executives, and every meeting is punctuated by people reaching into their pockets – just to be sure that they are not missing some vital mail.

But constant communication can become tiresome and destructive of personal life; it can also rob leaders of space for reflection as well as for quality decision-making. By making ourselves hyper-available we can dishonour those who work for us, by discouraging them from thinking for themselves. A powerful sign of trust is telling people that they need to communicate *less* frequently, rather than more.

So, then, new technology can be a recipe for disaster, building a worse world when it should be building a better one. It often does build a better world, but the issue remains, is it building a better world for *you*?

16

BETTER STRATEGY

'Nobody really knows what strategy is.'

Editorial in *The Economist*[1]

'Within both business and academic circles it would be quite miraculous if you could identify two people who shared the same definition of strategy.'

Michael Cusumano and Costas Markides[2]

'Anyone who claims to be a strategist should be intensely embarrassed by the fact that the strategy industry doesn't have a theory of strategy creation! It doesn't know where bold, new, value-creating strategies come from ... There's no foundation to the strategy discipline.'

Gary Hamel[3]

Business strategy is the battle-plan for a better future. It underpins the success of companies and shapes their progress. Many corporations talk about strategic goals, usually aligned to faster and more profitable growth – but such goals and targets must not be confused with the battle-plan itself. Goals and targets are merely practical steps along the way to a better life.

By definition, you cannot have an effective business

strategy without clear, accurate vision, and that is often a major challenge.

You can have powerful strategy with perfect management, yet by the time vision is reality, the world has often moved on and made such efforts irrelevant. That's why forecasting is so important: we need to build as accurate a picture as possible about the kinds of trends we can expect.

The death of shareholder value as the primary goal

However, there is an additional and even more pressing challenge. You can have the greatest strategy in the world but what's the point if no one *cares*? Strategies only matter if the end result matters. And, too often, that is where business leaders lose the plot altogether. It is not enough to say that the end result will be a stronger business, greater profit or higher share price. Consider what the following people have to say:

> My business school in America was wrong, I am now convinced. The purpose of business is not to make money full stop. To say that profit is a means to another end and not an end in itself is not a semantic quibble: it is a serious moral point.
>
> Charles Handy, author of *The Age of Reason*

> The idea of taking from a foreign investment and giving nothing back to the community is history.
>
> Michael Bonsignore, former CEO of Honeywell[4]

> Putting profits after people and products was magical at Ford.
>
> Don Petersen, former CEO of Ford[5]

Many strategies fail because they have been built around objectives which don't create passion, because the end point *has* no point to those who have to make it happen. Many corporations have failed to understand this basic need for strategic purpose.

Shareholder value is a weak foundation on which to base business strategy, even if such value has a rational basis and can be reliably measured – both of which are questionable. We often see irrational market pricing, and there is an ongoing debate about how much intellectual capital, goodwill, brand equity and so on are really worth. As Lawrence Weinbach, Chairman of Unisys, says:

> I look at shareholder value as a result of several things. To me, if you take care of your people and your people then take care of your customers, your shareholders win. The vision of the company is to increase shareholder value and what I tell everyone here is, shareholder value is the result of the three-legged stool. If we get it right with customers, employees, reputation – then shareholders win. I'm very mindful of shareholder value but I don't look at it as the single reason why I'm in business. I think of it as a result of what we've been able to accomplish.[6]

Shareholder value is a dangerous strategic goal to aim at in isolation. A strategy that aims merely to protect or enhance shareholder value is invalid by definition since, as we have seen, strategy is the battle-plan for a better future and must be built on vision. So where's the vision? The idea of 'wealthier shareholders' is uninspiring to most, except to those who have huge share options, and is too general to provide specific direction.

Shareholder value cannot invent products, nor promote initiative and innovation, nor inspire efficiency. Speeches about shareholder value are useless at creating vision, direction, purpose or sense of mission. By definition shareholder value cannot drive a business forward. Research shows that long-term success is linked to two convictions: the absolute necessity of profits and a purpose beyond maximizing shareholder wealth.[7] As Michael Diekmann, Chairman of the Board of Management at Allianz, explains:

> If you measure a company's success only in terms of its financial results, your position can be very strong in the short term. But, in the long term you may lose sight of your corporate strategy.[8]

Shareholder value *on its own* is a morally bankrupt, narrow idea that has become a mindless, last-century business mantra, chanted in unison as a strategic goal by senior executives around the world, despite the fact that those same executives reject it as a personal goal in their own lives. There's more to life than today's share price. It is morally bankrupt because the only obligation in such a business philosophy is to owners, which means that duties to customers, staff, community and environment have no importance whatsoever unless they have an impact on the owners' wealth.

Some object vigorously. They defend their intense, exclusive focus on shareholder value by arguing that board members have strictly defined, legally binding duties to protect shareholder interests in every possible way (without breaking other laws). Their hands are tied by the owners, they say. But owners are changing all the time. The average privately owned share in the US changes hands every few weeks or months, and institutions are also buying and selling on a daily basis.

Despite these attempts to hide behind the argument of legal requirements, such share-obsessed corporations have been condemned as foolish at best, and downright evil at worst – often by some of the very owners they say they represent, as well as by some of their own customers, workers and those in the wider community.

Our society has come to see that a strategy to build *shareholder value*, without a clear mission based on robust *ethical values*, is a complete nonsense. In fact, it has proved one of the fastest and most efficient ways of destroying an entire global business.

In any case, shareholder value is a useless component of vision as well as a useless motivator. Who on earth (except the owner of a large corporation) wakes up in the morning and thinks: 'What a great day – let's go and make some extra shareholder value, let's make some more dividends and make the share price soar'?

> 'Our aim is to continue developing our corporate responsibility programmes innovatively and to the mutual benefit of Prudential and society as a whole.'
>
> Jonathan Bloomer, CEO of Prudential[9]

'As a business firm, we want to excel at generating profits, creating value for our shareholders. If we don't want to play by these rules, we don't belong in the ballgame. But we also believe that the business firm can be a community to help shape human character and moral behavior and to be involved in developing people as the soul of the firm. The measure of success of a leader in our firm cannot be limited to the value of our shares or the profit we produce. More importantly, it must relate to the people we work with and seek to serve.'

C. William Pollard, former Chairman of ServiceMaster[10]

Life is very tough for CEOs and chairmen of publicly listed companies. In *Having Their Cake*[11] Don Young and Pat Scott argue powerfully that extreme short-termism in investment decisions is in danger of systematically destroying many large corporations. CEOs and chairmen are being forced to dance to the ever-changing tune of fund managers, analysts, media pundits, bankers and stockbrokers, to the point where they are often distracted from longer-term challenges of the business.

In contrast Warren Buffet's highly profitable investments over three decades with Berkshire Hathaway have been built on long-term ownership of shares in companies with sound fundamentals. 'Our favourite holding period is forever.'

The need for strategic purpose

'Strategy is not the consequence of planning but the opposite: its starting point.'

Henry Mintzberg, author of *Managers not MBAs*

What we need is strategic purpose. Such things as 'beating

the competition with lower prices' or 'increasing market share through better selling' or 'growing by acquisition' are *not* strategies in themselves; they are merely steps forward to a greater future. But steps to what *ultimate* purpose for employees? What *is* that greater future about?

As we have seen, workplace motivation is falling. People want more meaningful jobs, targets, goals and personal objectives, and large share options, although enticing, are no substitute for a more 'worthy' agenda.

Many employees are no longer prepared to half-kill themselves to 'push competitors out of business'; they remain unconvinced that such 'success' will make them happier and more fulfilled, or the world a better place. Yes, it may protect their jobs, or increase their bonus, but only at the expense of their families and other things that matter to them. And extra financial rewards are particularly useless motivators for talented people who may, in any case, soon be recruited elsewhere on better terms.

I am a free-market capitalist. I believe in the principle of a lightly regulated market economy and the power of economic growth to deliver prosperity, health and education to both the poorest and the wealthiest nations. But we must recognize that a major challenge exists when it comes to personal motivation, just as we recognize the need for government support and legal protection for those who are vulnerable.

Free-market dogma assures us that fighting to the death will mean higher efficiency, lower prices and better-quality products; this means (in theory) we will all eventually enjoy a better life (despite the pain of 'structural adjustment'). But capitalist theory is uninspiring to the ordinary individual and can leave many in the gutter for prolonged periods along the way. People's *feelings* about work and business are far more complex.

Many business leaders talk as though their employees are naturally loyal to their company and will lay down their private lives in order to help the company grow even faster. Why should they? These leaders forget that 'jobs-for-life' have long ceased to exist and that fast-growing successful corporations often make large-scale redundancies as technologies improve or markets change. They also ignore the fact that many of their best people are constantly moving around from one corporation to another in the same field. It is absurd to expect them to swear total life-commitment to destroying a competitor, for which they may still feel deep affection, where they have good memories and good friends, and in which they may hope for another job in the future.

So how do we develop strategic purpose? How do we connect strategy with worthwhile aims?

Developing strategic purpose

'Strategy involves tough choices on three dimensions: which customers to focus on, which products to offer and which activities to perform.'

Costas Markides, co-author of
Strategic Thinking for the Next Economy

Business schools often teach strategy by looking at success stories to see how strategy developed and was implemented. The trouble is that it's always easier with hindsight. The reality is often different: strategy formation is an untidy, complex and elusive process, which combines analysis of the market, the competition and internal strengths and capacity with hunch, intuition and a host of other factors – including the personalities and preferences of business leaders.

However, one thing is certain: strategy must be built on vision. Strong vision can result in strong strategy, but poor vision makes effective strategy impossible.

Vision + Strategy → Strategic Purpose

Some argue that it happens the other way round: keep flexible to take opportunities as they come, and build your vision around that. But if the business is only opportunistic, without any driving principle, it can devalue vision to little more than being a flexible and profitable company – hardly enough, as we have seen, to provoke widespread passion and commitment. Either way, you land up in the same place:

Opportunity → Vision + Strategy → Strategic Purpose

For example, a drug company says: 'Our strategy is to grow sales of paediatric asthma drugs by 10 per cent a year and increase our margins while cutting prices.' This has zero strategic purpose. It may work for an analysts' meeting, but not inside the corporation.

Alternatively, the company could say: 'Every year thousands of children die suddenly from asthma. Clinical trials show that our drugs are amongst the best. Our aim is that at least 10 per cent more children with asthma are able to get these drugs each year, as a result of new promotion, lower prices and greater efficiency – and to spend more on developing even better drugs for the future. We believe that lives will be saved as a direct result.'

Which strategy conveys vision?

Strategy *must* engage those we work with, or it will be little more than ink, paper or wasted computer space. Strategy has to connect today's reality with a compelling story about how we are going to change the world, and why we are going to do so.

Good or great strategy – built to last better?

Jim Collins is the author of two influential books on strategies for long-term business success: *Built to Last* and *Good to Great*.[12] Both books are based on research into carefully matched corporations, some of which succeeded and others that didn't. One of his main conclusions is that passion is a central feature of all companies that went from 'good' to 'great'. Strategy, he concludes, should be directed towards those things we feel passionate about: passion for products, passion for services or for what the company stands for.

Companies 'built to last' – that is, having several decades of significant success – were all visionary companies; they were highly idealistic as well as highly profitable. Hewlett Packard, Merck and Co., Sony, Johnson and Johnson, Boeing and Ford are all examples of big vision corporations, driven by a sense of calling.

> 'A visionary company doesn't simply balance between idealism and profitability. It seeks to be highly idealistic AND highly profitable.'
>
> Jim Collins

Core ideology must never change

Core ideology, says Collins, must never change, which is why so many of these organizations have tended to promote internal people rather than risk confusing the vision by bringing in loads of outsiders. However, Collins ignores the power of infectious enthusiasm.

History shows that passion – which, as we have seen, is the basis of strong, effective leadership and of people-movements – can be caught so long as the cause itself is sufficiently worthwhile. If the cause is weak and subtle, then you may indeed be far safer to recruit insiders who have managed (finally) to work out what the mission is all about.

Stick to the knitting – stick to your values

Tom Peters is well known for his challenge to 'stick to the knitting'. He meant 'stick to core competences and skills', but we can apply it here as a call to keep to foundational values and remain true to the original vision, honouring basic principles.

> 'You don't have to be angry to right a wrong to work toward a better world.'
>
> Wayne W. Dyer, author of *10 Secrets for Success and Inner Peace*[13]

Big Hairy Audacious Goals are always the same

Jim Collins talks about Big Hairy Audacious Goals (BHAGs) which engage people, grab them in the gut, and are often linked to cult-like values, like a religion. But he failed to identify a universal vision, passion or driver.

Yet, a single root passion is there, to be found in every

chapter of *Built to Last* staring us in the face, in all these successful companies, and one which is very familiar to us, the inescapable call: the mission to create a better world.

> 'The core of our efforts is focused on making the world
> a better place by extending and enhancing the lives of
> millions of people through the highest-quality products.'
>
> Peter R. Dolan, CEO of Bristol Myers-Squibb

Strategies to merge social and financial goals

Harvard Business School professor Lynn Sharp Paine argues in *Value Shift* that companies can no longer achieve superior performance without merging social and financial goals. Her research shows that, before Enron's scandal broke, many considered the corporation to have strong values, so, clearly, values themselves are not enough unless the value-system is enterprise-wide. And that means top-to-bottom change.[14]

Her review of 95 academic studies of the relationship between corporate financial performance and social performance found that 55 indicated a positive correlation, eighteen a mixed picture and only four a negative picture.

Developing better strategy

There are at least ten different schools of strategy formation: a fit between internal strengths/weaknesses and external threats/opportunities; a formal planning process; an analytical discipline based on military strategy; entrepreneurial vision; cognitive road maps; emergent, learning processes; a social process; contingency planning; responses to the environment; transformation; and so on.

These different approaches all contain useful elements, but taken to extremes they pull in many different directions.

Discussions about strategy are also bedevilled by jargon: best-product position, customer solution, competitive advantage, system lock-in, customer targeting, aggregate metrics, scenario planning, strategic innovation are just a few examples. How do we sort out the confusion?

Costas Markides, Professor of Strategic Leadership at London Business School, has described the who, what and how at the heart and soul of strategy:[15]

- Who should the company target as customers?
- What products and services should the company offer a targeted customer?
- How can the company do this efficiently?

Gary Hamel describes five conditions for developing strategy:

1 New voices – young people, newcomers, those at the edge of the organization.
2 New conversations – debates that cross all departmental and geographical boundaries.
3 New passions – encouraging people to explore widely.
4 New perspectives – searching constantly to see themselves, customers, competitors and the wider world through new pairs of glasses.
5 New experiments – small, low-risk projects as learning environments, where new competencies can be developed in case they are needed.

If the team environment is right to develop new strategy,

then innovation in this area will surely follow, and all the lessons we have seen in the earlier chapter on innovation apply here too, all built on the primary requirement to engage people personally in the process. Powerful new strategies will then begin to emerge and develop into maturity.

In a rapidly changing world, every successful strategy must have flexibility and responsiveness at its heart, enabling corporations to be leading innovators or fast followers in new areas. That means monitoring what really matters and paying close attention to early indicators of possible significant change. It also means rapid decision-making.

But these are far more likely in organizations where a high proportion of managers are competent, clear about vision, totally passionate about the cause, driven by a strong sense of urgency, worried about complacency and aware of the seductive nature of their previous success. And all of *that* depends on the quality of senior leadership as we discussed in Chapter 3.

Thus we find that it is useless and dangerous to try to develop business strategy in isolation from defining mission, paying attention to leadership and team dynamics, and encouraging innovation, change management and personal motivation. But when all these elements come together, strategy will be sound, the battle-plan will be rapidly carried out, the organization will be transformed, and the ultimate vision will become a powerful and morale-boosting reality.

LESSONS FROM NOT-FOR-PROFIT ORGANIZATIONS

Nine out of ten people will volunteer if asked: the huge boom in volunteering and community involvement is evidence of that. Every corporation has important lessons to learn from the passionate commitment of millions of people to voluntary organizations and causes.

We need to understand why people give time, why the desire to make a difference is such an important part of our lives and why it's so ignored by most workplace incentive schemes.

Volunteering is a window into the passions of the soul; 86 per cent of volunteers give help because of compassion for those in need.[1]

'We must become the change we want to see.'

Mahatma Gandhi, 1869–1948

Paying for the privilege of being allowed to work

When I was the CEO of an international aid and development agency, I was constantly amazed at what people offered to do, without any financial reward whatsoever, and also what people were willing to do even when the financial rewards were tiny. Since many were also making financial gifts or paying their own expenses, they were effectively paying us for the privilege of being allowed to work, rather than the other way round.

Most of our best team members were volunteers first, until their roles grew so much that we could no longer afford to give them the time they needed for their 'day jobs'. And, later, when times were tough, some of those same people went back to working as volunteers, earning a living doing other jobs in addition.

> 'We make a living by what we get, we make a life by what we give.'
>
> Winston Churchill, 1874–1965

I'm still involved in the work in places like Uganda, India, Russia and Thailand and see people make similar sacrifices every day. If companies could get just 25 per cent of that same kind of commitment, most would find their productivity soar overnight. What's the secret?

It's not enough just to be a not-for-profit organization. There are tens of thousands of people in such organizations who also feel as disconnected from any worthwhile cause in their daily work as most of their colleagues who work for corporations.

It's easy to dismiss this compassionate impulse as something superficial, unusual or irrelevant to the serious business of motivating people at work, but you cannot ignore it without writing off a significant element of national life.

Take, for example, the enormous charitable sector in America today. There are 1.6 million charities, constituting one of the most vibrant, dynamic, rapidly growing and extraordinary parts of the economy, playing a central role in the lives of over 150 million ordinary people. It's a similar story in Europe and many other parts of the world.

> 'It's easy to make a buck. It's a lot tougher to make a difference.'
>
> Tom Brokaw, former TV presenter and author

Boom time for volunteering

As we have seen, 73 per cent of British adults give their time voluntarily each year; the figure is as high as 83 per cent in Scotland. Between 1991 and 1999 the average number of hours a year given per person in the UK rose from 140 to 210.[2]

In Ireland 33 per cent of the population give a total of up to 1,000 hours a year to voluntary organizations, contributing the equivalent of 660 million euros to the economy.[3] In France 25 per cent of adults give an average of 270 hours a year, valued at 76 billion euros, and there are 880,000 not-for-profit organizations in the country.[4] These Irish and French figures do not include informal volunteering. In Belgium, 20 per cent of the population give an average of 250 hours a year to organizations, equivalent to around 200,000 full-time jobs, and the number of not-for-profit groups has increased eightfold in the last 30 years.[5] Across the European Union as a whole, between 5 and 20 per cent of the population contribute between 1 and 6 per cent to the GDP by giving time formally,[6] to which should be added a countless hundred million acts of kindness and practical help which never get measured.

'Volunteering: Doing more than you have to because you want to, in a cause you consider good.'

Ivan Scheier, author of *When Everyone's a Volunteer*

American citizens give over 200 hours a year each to the community – more than 20 billion hours a year, worth at least $437 billion or around 3.7 per cent of GDP, if you value each hour at the official government rate of $21.83 an hour (2003). That's equivalent to almost one-fifth of the Federal budget ($2,319 billion in 2004).

The total value of 'doing good' in purely financial terms is more than 5 per cent of the US economy, if you include gifts of both money and time. That's greater than the direct contribution of the entire motor vehicle industry to GDP and larger than that of the US telecom industry.

Seventy per cent of 102 million American households give money to charity – an average of $1,000 a year or 2 per cent of their income, over $70 billion of donations every year.

All these figures relate only to a single twelve-month period. If you widen the timeframe you find the great majority of adults in most countries have given time in the more distant past, or will in the future. And wealthier people in their middle years are most generous with their time – which is why straw polls of senior executives give such impressive results when you ask who is giving time to a cause they believe in or to help other people.

Remember that, for every person who actually volun-teers time or gives money, there are perhaps five others who are sympathetic to that cause, have given to it in previous

Volunteering in America

- 58 per cent volunteered for a church, charity, or other community group in 1997 – up from 44 per cent in 1984. Half did so regularly.[7]
- 59 per cent volunteered at least once in 1997 – up from 53 per cent in 1994.[8]
- 59 per cent were involved in community activities in 1997, 49 per cent working for others for no pay.[9]
- Volunteers outnumber those involved in established civic organizations by more than two to one.[10]
- The number of volunteers rose from 80 to 93 million between 1987 and 1995 with an average commitment of 200 hours a year.[11]
- 83 per cent volunteered at least once a month for at least one of a series of civic activities.[12]
- 58 per cent of teenagers worked for others for no pay in 1998.[13]
- 28 million senior volunteers gave 5 billion hours in 1998; 51 per cent of seniors gave more than four hours a week. The peak age of these volunteers was 55–64. The value of their gift was $71.2 billion to no-profits and causes.[14]

Figures in Canada are lower: 25 per cent give their time formally.[15]

years, will do so in future, or are 'with them in spirit'. That's a huge popular movement: millions of ordinary people acting from their hearts, rather than being organized by government or driven by commercial promotions, without formal leadership and without national structures.

'You don't get out of life what you want. You get out of life
what you are.'

John F. Roedel, President, CNCTool.com

The fact is that the desire to do good, to make a difference, is a vital force in our society, part of the air we
breathe.

More than that, we expect the people we work for, or the
companies we employ, to do good as well, every day in every
way. That's why corporate ethics is such a big issue.

Arthur Andersen's collapse after allegations that they
shredded Enron papers has been just one of hundreds of
recent examples of the public demand for goodness. Yet,
because conventional management theory cannot easily or
adequately explain this urge to do good, it ignores it, except
in pure commercial terms such as winning consumer confidence, or image-building.

Why?

Because as we have seen, the whole of corporate life has
been built on a foundation that is now out of date and out
of step with the public mood. The curious thing is this:
despite the overwhelming commitment of the majority of
their workforce, the volunteering spirit is largely ignored or
misunderstood by companies.

Companies worldwide are beginning to wake up: 81 per
cent of multinationals now connect volunteering to their
business strategy – even if in a very small way – compared
to only 31 per cent a decade ago.

As part of this common cause, many corporations now
release their people – including those most valuable to them

Corporate volunteering benefits

- Leverage grant dollars.
- Helps with recruitment.
- Demonstrates a stable commitment to community, even in lean times when leveraging extra value from cash donations.
- Encourages teamwork.
- Develops leadership.
- Gives employees new skills.

– to work in the community for days or even months at a stretch. It helps morale, improves skills, increases loyalty, raises profile, encourages recruitment, builds their brand, and does something very worthwhile – all for a modest cost.

In the UK 1.5 million workers give almost two working weeks a year in formal volunteer schemes supported by their employers, with a value of £1.1 billion.[16] For example, more than 33 per cent of Westpac employees volunteer a total of 500,000 hours a year to the community, with company backing. Similar schemes are widely used in other nations; for example, Ford Australia gives every worker two days off a year for volunteering.

In the US 52 per cent of large companies now include commitment to community as part of their mission statements. The companies involved say that corporate volunteering creates better communities and improves their public image; 97 per cent say that it also improves teamwork;[17] 70 per cent say that it improves public relations; and 57 per cent believe it improves employee commitment.

Every corporation has vital lessons to learn from the best not-for-profit organizations, which have many of the same vision-characteristics as profit-making corporations, but without the complication of needing to return equity or pay dividends to owners. But, once we set aside this important distinction, we find that they are very similar in other ways. For example, both may reward employee performance; both may be incorporated as corporations; both may raise capital (whether as interest-bearing loans or on a speculative share-value basis); both may sell products and services; both are required to generate a surplus on activities and to run their affairs prudently; both are required to provide products and services which offer good value for money, and make differences to people's lives.

In addition, both are also affected by changing conditions, changes in how consumers think and feel and changes in the competition – yes, not-for-profit organizations have competitors just as aggressive at times as profit-organizations.

Similarly, both are most effective when they connect passion with their organizational objectives; when their strategies are clearly going to deliver outcomes that most people consider important.

In some respects, great companies are like effective single-issue non-government organizations (NGOs) run on a not-for-profit basis. Many have successfully copied some of the primary characteristics of the best not-for-profit organizations. Just how similar some of these organizations are can be demonstrated by not-for-profit organizations that become owner-organizations and vice versa. There are many examples of the former, especially in banking, such as building societies in the UK or credit unions in the US. But we can also find examples where owners have given their entire organization to a charitable foundation. One such occurrence is Andrews Estate Agents in the UK which was given, on the owner's death, to a charity. Over fifty years later, it continues as a significant force in starting new not-for-profit initiatives – providing, for example, the start-up funding for ACET (see page 226).

This estate agent's business is still operating on a profit-making basis, just like any other, but all the dividends become charitable gifts. This improves morale and has provided a very special working environment.

Many corporations encourage NGO activity. For example, ServiceMaster has a 'We serve' day every year, whereby each employee spends at least a day in the field, and many are also encouraged to do volunteer work.

The Hope HIV story

A friend of mine, Phil Wall, was deeply affected by the plight of AIDS orphans on a trip to southern Africa and set about raising more than £1.5 million for a new organiza-tion he founded, called Hope HIV. As a fundraising exercise, he decided to give away £10 notes to tens of thousands of young people, with no strings attached. In a single month, with the help of friends, who shared the risk, he gave away more than £50,000. No records were kept, but with every note he gave a leaflet explaining about the AIDS crisis and challenged them to use the £10 to raise much more. Many took the challenge to become mini venture-philanthropists and raised the first million rapidly through thousands of imaginative money-generating schemes.

Phil then had another idea: many corporations spend (or waste?) a lot of money on activities like paintballing competitions or other experiences designed to help team-building, leadership development and build morale. Phil ran a workshop for several teams of executives and challenged them with the story of the teenagers.

He gave a five-figure sum to each group and gave them a time limit to raise the most money. The winning team would fly to southern Africa and see for themselves what was being done to help these children. The exercise ran over several months and was hugely successful:

- It built morale.
- It gave teams something worthwhile to work on which was outside 'work'.
- It was fun.
- It involved many other people.
- It generated a 'feel-good' effect.
- It created a better future for children in great need.
- It improved team awareness of other countries and cultures.

Of course, many NGOs are badly run, and others become entangled with all kinds of conflicts between passionate, well-meaning people who have their own agendas and feel they have a moral right to be heard because they are giving time. NGOs can be the best and the worst places to work, but overall the lessons are clear:

1 Define your cause.
2 Be clear and focused.
3 Stick to a single issue that matters.
4 Build your case on moral rightness.
5 Appeal to the heart.
6 Concentrate on major need.
7 Channel passion into practical response.
8 Deliver measurable results.
9 Keep the costs of overheads very low.
10 Keep a sense of perspective and fun.

Volunteers can be easy to find, rewarding to work with, but hard to manage. If someone is giving generously of their own time, they may not be open to doing so at someone else's convenience: 'I will do this my own way.' The normal workplace obligations are reversed. In business, a manager can lean on staff on the basis that they have an obligation to the firm as a result of being paid. But a volunteer manager has obligations to his or her team who are in effect paying the organization by giving time – and maybe money too: 'You owe me; I owe you nothing.'

Power and control can be difficult issues: volunteers may not take to being bossed about in any way, and may want to come and go as they please. They may have a low threshold for not following through on commitments – 'After all, I am doing you a huge favour.'

And then there is the further complication when volunteers become staff. An organization grows and reaches the point where volunteers are not enough to drive the organization. But at what rate do you reward someone who until now has gladly worked for nothing for ten hours a week, when you now want to contract them formally for twenty? Are you going to pay them the market rate per hour for twenty hours, or only for ten?

But these dilemmas only serve to highlight the huge contrast between the typical business world and the voluntary sector, and why business managers often fail to get people to do a full day's work, even on high salaries.

We need something of the volunteer spirit in every organization. Any business that fails to generate some kind of willingness to 'go the extra mile' is at risk of grinding to a halt. When passion fades and people lose touch with what it's all for, productivity falls, absenteeism rises and profits vaporize.

18

BETTER WAYS TO INVEST

So-called ethical investment funds are one of the fastest-growing areas of financial services, overtaking conventional unit trusts. In the UK alone there are now over 50 such funds with more than £4 billion under management. In the US the figure is over $13 billion – with more than 40 mutual funds operating some kind of positive or negative screening.

Another $3 billion is invested in socially targeted ways such as community investment banks. Although this is still only a tiny fraction of the $8 trillion under management, many pension funds are switching to some kind of investment screening. Investment fund managers are recognizing that a complete range of product offerings must include an ethical fund.

Ethical funds tend to invest more heavily in smaller companies which can mean greater growth, but also greater risk, and performance has been variable with some excellent returns and others less favourable.

Some companies are going to find it hard to get people to buy their shares. Investors are increasingly aware that they can invest according to ethical criteria and are asking independent financial advisers to recommend such options.

The Ethical Trading Initiative

The Ethical Trading Initiative is an alliance of companies, NGOs and trade unions committed to working together to implement good labour practice. The code contains the following provisions:

- no forced labour
- freedom of association and the right to collective bargaining
- safe and hygienic working conditions
- no child labour
- living wages to be paid
- no excessive working hours
- no discrimination
- regular employment to be provided
- no harsh or inhumane treatment.

In July 2000 a new Pensions Act in the UK required investment managers to state what social, environmental and ethical guidelines they were using in deciding what shares to buy and sell. France, Sweden, Germany, the Netherlands and Switzerland also have pension investment laws, while the rest of the EU is likely to follow soon.

This area of business is so big now that stock exchanges are starting to list companies which their advisers consider ethical in a separate ethical or 'doing good' index such as the FTSE4Good and the Dow Jones Sustainability World Indexes, which exclude companies whose ethics don't match new expectations. And many large investment funds are offering packages which guarantee that every investment is

An example of long-term ethical behaviour

The Co-operative Bank has always had a strong ethical stance, constantly consulting with customers on a wide range of issues. At times the organization looks more like a non-government organization (NGO) than a bank.

More than nine out of ten customers approve of its ethical policy. Its market share increased with the promotion of the policy through cinema, poster and direct mail marketing. Over ten years, following a fresh ethical initiative, the bank has reported record profits, making it one of Europe's fastest growing banks. Twenty-eight per cent of its new customers say that the bank's ethics are a key factor in their opening an account.[1]

ethically sound. The Paris Bourse has also insisted on companies providing clear information in their annual reports about their social and environmental policies.

There were howls of protest from some companies who found themselves excluded from the new ethical elite, because they realized how damaging it would be to their brand as a whole. One of these was the major UK food retailer Tesco, which was horrified to find that it had been excluded from the FTSE4Good index, fearing that this could wipe millions off sales as well as damage its share price. After all, consumers were bound to ask what dark and terrible secrets there were which disqualified it from inclusion. Tesco lobbied hard. The objections were listed and countered in detail one-by-one. The company made heroic efforts to appear cleaner than clean – and was added to the index.

But all investments in future will tend to be 'ethical' since the noose is tightening around the neck of corporations that pollute, discriminate, allow sexual harassment, exaggerate product claims, fail to honour promises, deceive shareholders, are cruel to animals, are dishonest or fall short in other areas.

And as we have seen many times, it is hard to connect with passion in consumers or workers, if you are clearly acting in unethical ways.

19

BUSINESS VALUES – THE ULTIMATE TEST

'The price of greatness is responsibility.'

Winston Churchill, 1874–1965

'A well run business must have high and consistent standards of ethics.'

Richard Branson, Chairman, Virgin Group

'It is not that humans have become any more greedy than in generations past, but that avenues to express greed have grown so enormously.'

Alan Greenspan, Director of the Federal Reserve

'Defining the purpose of the corporation as exclusively economic is a deadly oversimplification, which allows overemphasis on self-interest at the expense of consideration of others.'

Kenneth Andrews, former editor of *Harvard Business Review* and professor at Harvard Business School

We have seen in Chapter 9 that ethics are the immune system of every corporation when it comes to protecting brand and corporate image. But where do strong ethics come from?

The purpose of *business* is a better *world* and profit is the reward for making it so. The promise to *customers* is a better *life*. And this promise, to be meaningful, must have a connection with human happiness. Good business means more than profit: it means making a genuine contribution to well-being or contentment.[1]

Bad profit means making money out of selling a false hope – products or services which do not really make people any happier or more fulfilled than they were before, or which make some people happy at many other people's expense.

Corporations that are passionate about purpose, deliver on promise and focus on process (provision of proven products and services for profit) are likely to be rewarded with long-term success – so long as they also pay attention to one other factor.

One vital element is still missing; hence all the attention given recently to single-issue activism, consumer campaigns, corporate values, social responsibility, corporate governance and mission statements. We have already touched on many of these things in earlier chapters on leadership, marketing, advertising, change management, the war for talent, motivation and strategy.

> 'Capitalism is the astounding belief that the most wickedest of men will do the most wickedest of things for the greatest good of everyone.'
>
> John Maynard Keynes, 1883–1946

Although Keynes had his tongue in cheek in this famous quote, he was, at the same time, making a serious point:

capitalism does not always deliver on the business promise of a better future.

History has demonstrated that 'market forces' are unstable, erratic, violent, dispassionate, blind to human suffering, insensitive to tragedy and deaf to cries of injustice, tyranny and environmental destruction. In growing recognition of this problem, business ethics are now attracting huge media attention, which in the current climate can be far more damaging to profits and customer relationships than winning or losing a legal battle. Public opinion often changes long before regulations and the legal process, and can be a powerful warning to corporations to clean up their act.

As Harvard professor Lynn Sharp Paine has pointed out, society cannot survive if its most influential and widely established players (corporations) are exempt from the normal expectations of moral and considerate behaviour.

> 'People talk about ethics in business but the real issue is ethics in life.'
>
> William Pollard, Chairman, ServiceMaster

A recent study has concluded that two out of three of America's largest corporations have been involved in illegal activities of various kinds during the last ten years.[2] The corporate scandals we have seen are likely to be only a tiny fraction of the number that have taken place. And we can also be sure that, for every breach of the law, there are many more that belong to the twilight area between what is criminal in one or more countries and what most people would endorse as morally right.

It is hardly surprising, then, that 70 per cent of chief executives say that corporate and social responsibility is (now) an essential issue for their business. They know that the world has changed and that companies which run on a narrowly defined shareholder-value philosophy are likely to hit a crisis. And 89 per cent of marketing directors say that business should be involved in addressing social issues of the day – because they can't sell otherwise.

But what should those business ethics be based on, and how should that be expressed in community action?

Business for Social Responsibility (BSR) is just one of many new groups which are helping drive changes in corporate values: a 'global organization that helps member companies achieve success in ways that respect ethical values, people, communities and the environment'. Member organizations (more than 700) include Levi Strauss, AT&T, Chiquita Brands, Agilent Technologies, Ford Motor Company, Gap, Fedex, Hallmark, Starbucks, Nike, Reebok, Hasbro, Coca-Cola, Wal-Mart, Monsanto, Philip Morris and McDonald's. The turnover of the combined membership is more than $2 trillion, and the companies, together, employ over 6 million people.[3]

> 'I believe business has a social responsibility. In the communities where you work you ought to help create an environment where you can develop and attract the kind of people you need.'
>
> Lawrence Weinbach, Chairman of Unisys[4]

Many organizations have tried to define their own codes of conduct. Huge efforts have been spent spelling out what should or should not be done, how people should behave and what their wider responsibilities should be. At the same time, business schools have made attempts to adjust old-style MBA programmes and executive training.

It is hard to get business leaders to write about business ethics, and many business schools find the topic one of the most challenging to teach. Ethical questions are often highly complex, specific to a particular culture, country, decade, business or industry, and there can be a great danger in generalizations. Yet these challenges have to be faced. It is no longer appropriate for corporations to set out general statements about compliance with regulations or commonly accepted practice.

But where do we draw the line between right and wrong, ethical and immoral? The lazy response is to hide behind the law, deferring all ethical questions to politicians: 'If it's legal, it must be all right.' Laws, though, vary between countries, which is very confusing for a law-obsessed global corporation. Are we saying that a particular action is morally right in Poland but not in Spain? Getting corporations to obey laws is certainly a major challenge. In any case, activist campaigners, representing some 28,000 non-government groups worldwide, often go far beyond law in their demands, and have had great success in changing corporate policy.

The lesson of history is that every negative media story about a corporation has the potential to develop into a single-issue campaign, and every single-issue has the potential to become a government regulation. So laws usually lag behind consumer pressure.

A prime example is the debate over obesity. On current

HSBC hands cleaners a rise

HSBC has awarded cleaners at its London headquarters a 28 per cent pay rise, following pressure from 'living wage' campaigners. The deal followed a similar move by Barclays who agreed to pay cleaners £6 per hour, plus sick leave and holiday pay. Cleaners addressed shareholders at HSBC's AGM to explain the hardship they faced. An HSBC spokesman later said that corporate social responsibility was important for the organization.[5]

trends, 250 million people will have type II diabetes by 2023 (because they are overweight): and 30 per cent of American newborns are expected to develop the disease during their lives – many as children. Diabetes already affects 25 per cent of those over 60. The health cost in the US alone is likely to grow to $100 billion per year – as a result of diabetes-linked blindness, heart disease, strokes, kidney failure and a host of other major problems.

But whose fault is it if someone eats too much? Twenty years ago the finger would have been pointed almost entirely at the individual. But in today's culture the blame is laid firmly at the door of food manufacturers and retailers. You can sell foods such as French fries and burgers and boast of natural ingredients, yet still be in deep trouble, as McDonald's continues to find. Before government regulations changed, the corporation acted rapidly with many alterations in menus, portion size, salt content and salad variety, responding to customer behaviour and a declining market, as well as challenges to its image.

At the same time, McDonald's has continued to embrace a growing range of socially responsible initiatives, ranging from supporting 100,000 families with very sick or dying children who stay in Ronald McDonald houses, to biodegradable packaging. None of this will be enough to stop activist pressures, but it is typical of the kinds of decisions being made by many corporations that go far beyond legal requirement.

> 'Managers would be mistaken to regard legal compliance as an adequate means for addressing the full range of ethical issues that arise every day. "If it's legal it's ethical" is a frequently heard slogan. But conduct that is lawful may be highly problematic from an ethical point of view.'
>
> Lynn Sharp Paine, professor at Harvard Business School[6]

If strict legal compliance cannot keep a corporation ethically sound, what can?

Many organizations talk about benchmarking against so-called best practice, but best practice is not enough either: it merely implies conformity with informal guidelines or accepted ways of doing things. 'Best practice' is usually associated with 'operational excellence' more than morality, and the two can be in direct conflict – for example, in a manufacturing facility that copies 'best practice' to reduce costs, but also poisons the water supply.

> 'Living well and beautifully and justly are all one thing.'
>
> Socrates, 469–399 BC

Benchmarking is useless from the ethical point of view, because all it does is encourage corporations to copy each

other's 'benchmark' or ways of working – a foolish and hazardous course, unless we are sure the example is ethical in
the first place.

Corporations often hide behind benchmarking, by
arguing that they followed 'widely accepted practice', but this
is cowardly and amounts to abdication of moral responsibility. There are too many examples in history of collective
madness or moral blindness.

Corporations have also tended to defend themselves by
saying that they are not responsible for a particular problem.
A recent example was a campaign against Coca-Cola by
AIDS activists who thought that the company should be
educating and giving free antiviral drugs not only to their
own employees, but also to those of their bottlers and suppliers. Although Coca-Cola had no organizational *responsibility* for these other organizations, they accepted that they
had the *ability* to help, using their networks of business relationships.[7]

The next stage of the Coca-Cola activist campaign was
to force through a resolution at the annual general meeting,
calling the company to review the economic impact of the
HIV/AIDS pandemic in Africa on its operations. This was
driven by the Adorers, Catholic members of the influential
Interfaith Centre on Corporate Responsibility, which now
represents 275 faith-based organizations with a combined
investment portfolio of $110 billion.[8] Many more corpora-
tions are going to be subjected to these kinds of pressures
to prove how they are contributing to a better kind of
society.

'Relational and ethical dimensions are vital in building and sustaining a successful business.'

Michael Schluter, President, The Relationships Foundation

We can see from all this that we urgently need a simple ethical test for all corporate activity, which works in every culture and every time zone and will continue to provide safe guidance for executives in future. We need a widely applicable moral value, against which *all* decisions can be measured: an easy-to-grasp, universal principle of business action, which provides a practical reference point for those faced by ethical dilemmas.

'Cultural relativism is morally blind. For relativists, nothing is sacred and nothing is wrong. For absolutists, many things that are different are wrong. Neither extreme illuminates the real world of business decision making. The answer lies somewhere between.'

Thomas Donaldson, Professor of Legal Studies,

Wharton University

'People want their company to be a good citizen. They want it to show true concern for the world, for the environment. They want it to have a social conscience.'

Jorma Ollila, CEO of Nokia[9]

Efforts have been made to create a universal guide to business ethics. For example, in her *Harvard Business Review* article 'Ethics without the Sermon', Laura Nash suggests that twelve questions be asked about the ethics of business decisions:[10]

1 Have you defined the problem accurately?
2 How would you define the problem if you stood on the other side of the fence?
3 How did this situation occur in the first place?
4 To whom and to what do you give your loyalty as a person and a member of this organization?
5 What is your intention in making this decision?
6 How does this intention compare with the probable results?
7 Whom could your decision injure?
8 Can you discuss the problem with the affected parties before you make the decision?
9 Are you confident that your position will be as valid over a long period of time as it seems now?
10 Could you disclose, without a qualm, your decision or action of your boss, your CEO, the board of directors, your family, society as a whole?
11 What is the symbolic potential of your action if understood? If misunderstood?
12 Under what conditions would you allow exceptions to stand?

Thomas Donaldson proposes three principles:

1 Have respect for core human values which determine the absolute moral threshold for all business activities – for example, right to health, economic advancement and improved standard of living.
2 The golden rule recognized in all major religions and ethical traditions – treat others as you would like to be treated yourself.

3   Have respect for local traditions: the belief that
    context matters when deciding what is right and what
    is wrong.

But Nash's twelve questions and Donaldson's three principles can be reduced almost entirely into a central core ethic
for all business decisions. Donaldson's golden rule, in fact,
summarizes most things, once one spells out what it actually
means: treat others as you would like to be treated.

Or put another way perhaps more relevant to corporate
activity: behave as you would like others to behave.

Treat customers, workers, shareholders, communities,
nations, competitors and business partners as you would
hope to be treated if you were in their place.

Serve as you would be served

This principle of *reciprocity* is based on timeless truths
expressed by Jesus Christ and many others, including Confucius, and rephrased in a thousand ways:

- Do as you would be done by.
- Do unto others as you wish them to do unto you.
- What you do not wish done to you, do not do to
  others.

Some further questions:

- Is this how I would like to be treated?
- Is this how I would like my own family to be treated?

The principle of reciprocity applies in practical ways to all
we do:

The universal code of business practice

- Serve as you would be served (the principle of reciprocity).
- Set good examples in all you do (the principle of reproduceability).

- Lead as you would like to be led.
- Advertise as you would like others to advertise.
- Honour commitments as you would like others to honour theirs.
- Do business as you hope all business will be done.
- Trade as you wish others would trade.
- Buy as you would wish others to buy.
- Sell as you would wish others to sell.
- Work as you would wish others to work.
- Pay bills as you would wish to be paid.

Set good examples in all you do

The principle of reproduceability poses a second ethical test. If everyone else acted in a similar way, would it be a good thing?

- Is this how you would like others to behave?
- Does this set an example worth following?
- Is this a great example for others?
- What would happen if many other corporations behaved like this?
- Are we setting an example in cultural sensitivity?
- Is our example sustainable in the long term?

These two principles together form a rule of business against which all activity can be measured: run your business as others should be run, setting a good example in all things.

When we serve as we would be served and aim to set good examples in all we do, we not only act in ways that others are likely to regard as ethical, but also enhance corporate reputation, brand image, customer relationships and workplace morale, as well as strengthening the fundamentals of the business.

As Jeffrey Hollender points out in his excellent book *What Matters Most*,[11] the most powerful argument in favour of action on ethics today is often a negative one: preventing future risk. But only corporations who pursue corporate ethics and social responsibility out of real conviction are likely to succeed in the longer term. Only true conviction will solve the crisis of purpose at work that we saw so clearly in Chapter 1. And only true conviction will earn the respect of consumers, who remain deeply sceptical about the true motives for corporate largesse.

> 'Investing in the future by helping to strengthen the neighborhoods where we live and work is an important core value at Mazda. After all, we can only make a brighter tomorrow by taking constructive actions today. Our belief in a better future remains as strong as ever.'
>
> James J. O'Sullivan, CEO of Mazda (USA)

Unchanging values in a changing world

> 'Morality transcends not only markets but cultural boundaries too.'
>
> Robert Solomon

But do these two principles of 'doing as we would be done by' and 'being a good example' really work in all cultures? Standards and expectations vary, and the yardstick needs to be applied with care.

Take, for example, the stresses and strains arising from the growing inequality between the wealthiest and poorest nations – perhaps the greatest moral challenge of our generation. If the poorest and most marginalized 300 million people in Africa were already as politicized and radical as many Islamic groups in the Middle East, there is little doubt that we would now be experiencing a very turbulent new chapter in human history.

> 'How can we create a better world without tackling evils such as hunger and violence first?'
>
> Eckhart Tolle[12]

For many hundreds of millions of people, daily life has got worse over the past twenty years, despite huge earnings in some countries from oil or minerals, plus large amounts of development assistance. Two factors in this are AIDS and civil wars.

The combined assets of the world's top three billionaires exceed the combined GDP of all the least developed countries, where over 600 million people live. Just one-fifth of those alive today consume almost nine-tenths of the world's goods and services – hardly surprising when you realize that two-thirds of the world's population lives on less than $2,000 a year, and most Africans earn less than $1 a day.

DeBeers, the diamond mining corporation, told a London gathering of executives that it costs around $1 billion to create a new mine. Based on the daily wages of workers in the area, for the same cost you could employ 100,000 local workers for 30 years. That's people power parity: measuring costs not in dollars but in multiples of a daily wage.

Expect mood and fashion swings in wealthy nations to clash with the aspirations of poorer nations, resulting in resentment, conflict and added pressures for mass migration.

We need to be careful not to impose a set of current Western values, which are the product of 150 years of industrialization, on nations which are just emerging from rural subsistence living. Sustainability – the ability to meet the needs of today's world without destroying the quality of life of future generations – will be a dominant issue. Another key issue will be so-called 'full-cost accounting'. The principle here is that consumers (not the whole of society) are asked to bear the total cost of the processes used in the products they buy – for example, a charge towards dealing with the pollution that a manufacturing process is creating.

Full-cost accounting can have shocking consequences – even in the research stage. Ray Anderson is President of one of the world's largest carpet companies, Interface. He asked for figures showing how much raw material his company used each year, and found out that in 1995 his factories and suppliers extracted from the earth 1.2 billion pounds of material to make $800 million of products, and that a third of this was oil-based. Ten years later, the corporation had introduced recycling of worn carpet tiles, reduced landfill use, reduced packaging, reduced emissions of gas and heat and begun generating solar power. In a decade it saved more than $250 million.[13]

Our world faces huge challenges in managing the future in a way that preserves our children's inheritance, whether by conserving wild fish stocks, allocating scarce fresh water supplies, meeting increased power consumption without serious long-term damage either from carbon dioxide levels or from radioactivity and so on. These kinds of issue will increasingly affect how people think and feel about their own lives, the communities they live in, the products they buy, the shares they hold, the governments they elect and the causes they support.

Oil and mineral extraction: ethical challenges

If fundamental problems of injustice and corruption are not resolved, the extraction of oil or minerals could become almost impossible due to terrorist targeting of uniquely vulnerable and costly infrastructure. Quite simply, some companies will go out of business.

Ten per cent of all Shell's profits come from Nigeria, the sixth largest crude oil producer in world. A single barrel of oil buys a local labourer for more than a month. Mineral resources comprise 25–90 per cent of exports in Botswana, Ghana, Guinea, Liberia, Senegal, Mauritania, Namibia, Niger, Central Africa Republic, Sierra Leone, Congo, Zambia and Zimbabwe. In theory the economies of these countries should be roaring ahead, but the reverse is largely true.

A 2003 World Bank study described the curse of extracting wealth on the poorest nations: countries with greatest income from mining/extraction are usually those with lower economic growth, more corrupt and oppressive regimes and greater contrast between wealthy and poor.[14] They are also more likely to suffer from wars and ethnic violence. There can be a coalition of interests between a wealthy and well-armed ruling elite and a multinational looking for stable conditions for long-term extraction.

Mineral wealth also causes local currency to become valuable, so small business exporters can't sell and go out of business, making the country as a whole even more dependent on extraction.

What is the answer? Identify multinational profits by nation, so that it is easier to justify ploughing back some profits into the relevant communities. Make sure that such community funding is totally transparent at every level, with community involvement, health and education infrastructure, encouragement of small enterprises, support for human rights and no forced resettlement without proper compensation.

The age of the very special child
Child labour is an example of a very controversial issue. Some of the poorer nations are being severely judged for acting in a way that would have been completely legal in developed nations at a similar stage in their economic development.

Child labour was abolished in countries like Britain only around 150 years ago. Developed nations now live in an acutely child-sensitive age, partly because many parents in these countries are having fewer children and often later in life. Children have become a special symbol of innocence and purity in a worrying world. It's all part of a natural desire to create the best kind of life for children, without pain, suffering, unhappiness, violence, emotional abuse, seduction or rape.

At least that's the idea ...

Every time a young child is discovered in India working in a factory making products for Western markets, the same thing happens. The company gets into big trouble, and the children often descend into mortal danger. Over 50 million children in India depend for their daily existence on whatever they can get by begging, selling or working. If they don't work in some way they starve, and if they starve they're soon dead or suffering from severe ill health. So every child in India is a working child, unless completely supported by parents. Over 100 million families in India are so poor that a child has to earn his or her own food. Everyone from the age of five has to help – whether harvesting crops, carrying water, making a fire, or sitting on the pavement selling flour. And then there are the runaways. And the orphans. And the outcasts ...

My wife and I have visited a railway station in Mumbai which is home to hundreds of children, aged three to fifteen. Twenty to thirty new children arrive every day, each a runaway from home. One girl had given birth three times alone on the roof of one of the platforms – aged thirteen, fourteen and fifteen.

Girls of ten to twelve get picked up on the streets within hours by older boys, who offer affection and a meal. Within a week, many of these vulnerable young girls are on a one-way ticket to almost certain death. Recruited as commercial sex workers, they are forced to have unprotected sex up to ten times a night. It's only a matter of time before they get HIV.

Building a better world for children is a noble ideal but, if we are not careful, we can find that blind pursuit of Western ideology can kill the very children we want to protect.

So how do we apply our universal code in such a situation?

Treating others as we would like to be treated may at the very least lead us to find small ways to make a big difference, by helping to feed those who work for very little compared to western wages, right through to setting up some kind of a work-skills programme with food and shelter at night.

Setting an example worth following leads us to be very sensitive to local situations, resistant to knee-jerk moralism and misplaced charity, but actively investing back into the impoverished communities from which our workers and customers come.

Quite often there is a disconnection, for historic reasons, between where the business operates and where community donations end up. So, for example, a large US multinational may have offices in most of the poorest nations, and major revenue from some of them, yet the entire donations policy may be to support community projects in American cities. Expect this to change, and as it does, corporations will discover how much good they can do with a small budget in countries where teachers, for example, can be employed for less than $60 a month.

Community development develops markets

> 'The real source of market promise is not the wealthy few in the developing world, or even the emerging middle-income consumers. It is the billions of aspiring poor who are joining the market economy for the first time.'
>
> Professor C.K. Prahalad, University of Michigan
> Business School

Can poverty be eradicated through profit-making enterprise? China's spectacular economic growth has lifted more people out of absolute poverty in a decade than would have been the case if the entire global spending on development programmes had been used in China alone. Hundreds of thousands of new business ventures have started and have delivered significant, rapid community benefit in a sustainable way. We see the same pattern being repeated across India and many other emerging economies. Most of these businesses are family-based micro-enterprises.

But what about global corporations, which are often criticized for exploiting those in the poorest nations? Can multinationals find markets of sufficient size and value to help develop these economies in a positive way while also making a reasonable return at the same time?

As Professor C.K. Prahalad describes in his ground-breaking book *The Fortune at the Bottom of the Pyramid*, the two-thirds of the world earning less than $3 a day represent a vast market with significant collective buying power.[15] That is one reason why revenue growth has been so rapid for multinationals with the right products for poorer nations: Avon Cosmetics, for example, has seen annual growth rates of up to 70 per cent in Russia.

Another example is Hindustan Lever (Unilever in India) which introduced candy made from fruit juice and sugar for a penny. The new candy became the fastest-growing item in their product range, with an estimated sales potential of $200 million a year. The company has had similar success with low-priced detergent and iodized salt.[16]

Slum-dwellers pay larger proportions of income on basics like food. Water can cost up to a hundred times more than elsewhere, and food 20–30 per cent extra. These communities are also in the market for telephone calls and Internet access based in kiosks, as well as for mobile phones. Because they do not own property, a higher proportion of their wealth is invested in mobile assets such as TV sets and jewellery. But credit is always hard to come by. Local money-changers may be charging 10–15 per cent per day, or as much as 2,000 per cent a year.

As a result, not-for-profit micro-banking has flourished, offering small loans to groups of around fourteen women who act as security for each other. Typical repayment rates are around 99.5 per cent within twelve months, and major defaults are almost unknown.

Investing in micro-banking, education, health and

infrastructure is a sound policy from the corporate point of view, as the cost is low and the outcome in general terms is the rapid development of future markets. At the same time, corporations can make worthwhile profits.

Why Milton Friedman's views look so outdated

> 'So the question is, do corporate executives, provided they stay within the law, have responsibilities in their business activities other than to make as much money for their stockholders as possible? And my answer to that is, no they do not.'
>
> Milton Friedman

Born in 1912, Milton Friedman is one of the world's most influential economists; he was awarded the 1976 Nobel Memorial Prize for economic science. In his 1962 book *Capitalism and Freedom*, he argued that the aim of business should be to protect and enhance the interests of the owners and that other priorities are misplaced:

> There is one and only one social responsibility of business – to use its resources and engage in activities designed to increase its profits so long as it stays within the rules of the game, which is to say, engages in open and free competition without deception or fraud.[17]

Entire generations of business managers have been raised on such a doctrine. Some have gone further even than Friedman: for example, Elaine Sternberg in her controversial book *Just Business* wrote: 'business organizations that seek anything but long-term owner value are guilty not of socialism but of *theft*.[18] But as we have seen, in today's operating environment, these kinds of approaches are likely to damage the very wealth one seeks to protect. A board that fails to meet community expectations could be seen as negligent in its duty to shareholders, if they damage the reputation of the corporation as a result. To some it may seem odd that such narrow interpretations of business duty should still be taken seriously, but they are, in the US more than Europe perhaps.

'Saying the purpose of business is to make money is akin to saying the purpose of life is to eat.'

Professor Theodore Levitt, Harvard Business School

'These times will not allow companies to remain aloof and prosperous while the surrounding communities decline and decay.'

Jack Welch, when CEO of General Electric

'It is not enough simply to say that we are charged with maximising profits in a competitive world … We have to do all the usual business school stuff. We have to ensure that our strategies are competitive and deliver profitable growth, or the business dies. But any business school model is vacuous if it is not set in the context of real-world experience. So what do we need to do? My answer is this. We have to make sure that we are sustainably competitive and profitable by: one, managing our people in all their diversity; two, managing our resources internationally; and three, discharging our corporate social responsibilities to the full.'

Stephen Green, Group CEO of HSBC[19]

Well-directed community support can improve corporate image, consumer loyalty, product attractiveness, morale, workplace productivity and the size of local markets. Indeed, strategic philanthropy can provide such strong business advantages that some argue that it hardly deserves to be called philanthropy.

One justification of the Friedman approach is the idea that giving is no more effective when done corporately than when it is by people, so there is no moral logic to it: reward your shareholders and let them decide themselves how much to donate. But this argument fails to acknowledge that corporate donations can have far greater impact than numerous acts of individual generosity, grouped together in a donation of identical size.

Larger corporations can encourage changes in law, local practices and government action – for example, by offering conditional support for national programmes. Business can also encourage staff largesse with donation-matching schemes, volunteer release programmes or gifts in kind of services or products.

This multiplying effect has been created by Pfizer over the last few years. The corporation has an excellent treatment for trachoma – a common cause of blindness in the poorest parts of the world. It made a decision to attack the problem on a massive scale. Pfizer not only donated drugs, but also worked in close partnership with the Edna McConnell Clark Foundation and the World Health Organization to distribute therapy and set up clinics.

In twelve months alone the incidence of trachoma fell by 50 per cent in target populations of Morocco and Tanzania.

With support from Bill and Belinda Gates and the British government, the programme has grown to treat more than 30 million people.

Cisco also knows the power of strategic philanthropy. The corporation created networking academies: training centres and virtual training environments designed to produce a rapid increase in the number of people who can set up and repair computer networks – vital to a corporation which sells them.

When it comes to social engagement, 59 per cent of Americans prefer companies to be active on a local rather than a national (26 per cent) or global (9 per cent) basis, placing priority on the quality of education, youth programmes and the environment. People prefer specific programmes with tangible results;[20] moreover, 56 per cent of global companies have not reduced their social responsibility programme spending during the recession, and 4 per cent have actually increased their spending.[21]

The Young Presidents' Organization

'A civilization flourishes when people plant trees under which they will never sit.'

Greek proverb

What do you do with your life when you are already more successful than you dared dream when you started out? When all your financial needs are met – and more? When your children have possibly more than is good for them? When the business is continuing to grow, and your wealth is continuing to increase?

The answer is that building a better world becomes even more important, in its widest sense. The almost universal spirit of community volunteering which, as we have seen, engages such a large proportion of most societies becomes even more significant.

YPO – or the Young Presidents' Organization – is a global movement of around 9,000 business leaders. Qualifications for membership include owning or running a business with a certain level of assets or turnover and employee numbers, and to be under the age of 50. The combined turnover of all the YPO business interests is several trillion dollars a year. Each local group of members is organized into a chapter, which arranges its own social and educational programme, as well as encouraging members to participate in regional and international gatherings.

But one of the most striking things about the movement is the common desire to make a difference: to use business success to make important things happen in the wider community.

Alex Cappello has been a powerful champion of this growing desire, leading as international chairman, passionate about building a better kind of future for individual business owners, their families and wider communities. He explains:

> In YPO, we challenge each other to embrace the responsibilities of leadership – to reach out across borders, cultures, religions and political divides to create an environment of trust and prosperity. It is so important for each of us to have a positive impact on the world in which we live, by

giving, mentoring, supporting and making a difference in our neighborhoods, our cities, our countries and in the world.

A wide range of initiatives has grown out of these networks of friendships, ranging from projects supporting local charities, to a tireless group of YPOers who build homes for poor families in Mexico, to global events where members thank their local hosts by offering sizeable contributions to the communities.

Recently, a group of YPOers who attended an executive education programme in California donated more than a million dollars to support micro-lending projects in the most desperate regions of Africa. And none has had a more profound impact than YPO's Peace Action Network, which successfully connected members from Israel and Palestine; and was the inspiration behind a significant India-Pakistan meeting, where more than a hundred members from India crossed the Wagah border into the welcome arms of their Pakistan hosts and fellow YPOers.

For many YPO members, the organization has become a cause of its own, and they find that being an active player can be more rewarding than running the business which made it all possible.

'It is such an honor to call these extraordinary men and women my peers and my friends – people going above and beyond their own personal and professional needs to make a difference in the world around them.'

The competitive advantage of corporate philanthropy

Michael Porter is perhaps the world's leading authority on competitive advantage. With Mark Kramer, managing director and co-founder of the Foundation Strategy Group, he has argued that corporate philanthropy can be a powerful tool.

Porter's five steps to identify context-focused philanthropy investments are as follows:[22]

1 Examine competitive context in each territory.
2 Review the existing donations pattern.
3 Assess existing and potential giving in light of advantage.
4 Seek possible collective action/clustering.
5 Evaluate results – for example, sponsorship of sports event in brand awareness, using mailing list of organizer/club and so on.

Porter dislikes the term 'strategic philanthropy', which is often loosely used. He feels that cause-related marketing (see pages 102–8) is not really philanthropy at all, because of the obvious commercial benefits. But this is hair-splitting: the end result is still a very different relationship between community and corporation from that which Friedman proposed.

Foundations may not be the answer

Many large corporations have set up charitable foundations, but donor benefits have often been disappointing – they would probably fail the strategic philanthropy test.

The first major foundations in the US were the General Education Board established by John D. Rockefeller in 1902 and the Carnegie Foundation in 1911.

The first in the UK was the Leverhulme Trust Fund in 1915. William Hesketh Lever was born in 1851 and started the Lancashire business which became Leverhulme Brothers. The ruling passion of his life was not money or power, but the desire to increase human well-being by substituting the profitable for the valueless. He left part of his wealth to the trust on his death in 1924.

These charitable bodies are usually independent, and strongly resist pressure from founding companies to make donations that could help their business. It is unfortunate that corporations can find that they are attacked for lack of philanthropy, despite generous gifts of capital or shares in the past. For example, the Wellcome Foundation was set up on the death of Sir Henry Wellcome in 1936. The corporation he founded was later swallowed up into GlaxoWellcome and then GlaxoSmithKline, which has been attacked for high-priced anti-AIDS therapies, despite the fact that the Wellcome Foundation continues to make huge donations to AIDS research.

The Wellcome Foundation and GSK are totally independent, and there is perhaps no reason why GSK should get any credit for Wellcome actions. But consider how different the effect might have been if the company's owners had chosen to give capital away gradually year by year until the present day, rather than as a single major endowment.

Motorola code of conduct – bribery

Motorola's code of conduct: 'We will always act with constant respect for people and uncompromising integrity.' Its code of conduct on bribery states that 'funds and assets of Motorola shall not be used directly or indirectly for illegal payments of any kind' and spells this out as 'the payment of a bribe to a public official or the kick-back of funds to an employee of a customer …'. Codes of conduct need to be specific – for example, 'Employees of Motorola will respect the laws, customs and traditions of each country in which they operate, but will at the same time engage in no course of conduct which, even if legal, could be deemed to be in violation of the accepted business ethics of Motorola or the laws of the United States relating to business ethics …'

Bribes as an example of varying culture and standards

Whose ethics and whose values? Some differences in culture have been described as conflicts of relative development: situations where it might be helpful to ask what kind of decisions we would have made in our own country at a similar stage of economic progress. Examples include wage levels, safety standards – and bribery.

Is it right for a large ship, contaminated with asbestos, to be stripped and refitted in a developing country using dangerous processes which would be widely condemned if carried out in a European or American port? Is it right to pay these workers less than 10 per cent of what Europeans would be paid? And is it right if the contract was only won after providing a generous holiday in the Bahamas to an official and his family?

Until recently, bribes or other irregular financial inducements were tax-deductible expenses in countries like Germany. The definition of corruption used to be 'use of public profit for private gain', but many have broadened the definition to 'use of entrusted powers for private benefit'.

Embezzlement, nepotism, bribery, extortion, interest peddling, fraud and other irregular benefits – these all challenge development, undermine democracy and government, distort the legal process and weaken leadership (because a bribe wins power). In corrupt countries people are promoted by who they know rather than by what they know.

Corruption destroys rules of competition, since only the most corrupt get the best deals, rather than those with the best products and services.

So, then, we have seen that corporate ethics are likely to become even more important in future – but what about corporate governance?

20

BETTER CORPORATE GOVERNANCE

Corporate governance is an issue affecting every organization, but receives more attention if you are a publicly listed corporation: millions of people are affected when things go wrong, shares turn out to be worthless and savings or pensions are damaged.

So how can we do it better?

The essence of corporate governance is accountability: that the leaders of an organization are held responsible for their actions on a day-by-day basis, to run the organization in a profitable, responsible and ethical way.

Treating others as you would be treated and setting a good example will be the new 'Gold Standard' for corporate governance, just as for business ethics.

In recent years, institutional investors have insisted on changes to board structures, appointment procedures, remuneration and transparency. Big investors, such as pension funds, have put pressure on companies to eliminate risk in ways that sometimes go further than the requirements of the code.

So what is a good example?

- Separation of board scrutiny from management power.

- Balancing different interests and obligations.
- Assessing risk and strategies for risk reduction.

Specifically:

- At least half a company's board members should be independent non-executives, except for smaller companies.
- The roles of chair and chief executive should be separate.
- A nomination committee consisting of a majority of independent non-executives should recommend board appointments and ensure appointees have appropriate skills.
- The board's performance, including that of individuals, should be evaluated at least once a year.
- A full-time executive director should not hold more than one non-executive post in large publicly listed companies.
- Audit, nomination and remuneration committees should be independent.
- Non-executive directors should not be rewarded with share options.

Why we got in such a mess

As we have seen, free-market ideology dictated that corporations were kept responsible to customers, shareholders, workers and society by customer and investor behaviour, through the mechanism of share price. Millions of individual 'voters' in the marketplace made sure that companies behaved. 'Bad' corporations were punished by investors selling their shares. 'Good' corporations were rewarded by investors buying their shares. The rationale was: 'Market forces will sort it all out.' This ideology weakened the concept of corporate governance and accountability.

Why we still can't trust the numbers

Many company audits are marked by conflicts of interest even where consulting links are abolished. There have been concerns that some auditors are looking for jobs in the companies they audit, and of course auditors are always under pressure to get next year's audit business, so they may not be motivated to dig too deep. In addition, globalization and e-technology are making reliable audits extremely difficult.

The tendency of larger professional service firms to merge means that global corporations are running out of sources of independent advice on large complex deals. Conflicts of interest are growing rapidly – made worse by the collapse of Arthur Andersen, reducing the number of global professional firms and increasing the risk that those which remain will find themselves in danger of representing the interests of more than one party.

Compromise

Here are some examples of serious compromise, where our Gold Standard needs to apply: acting as we would like others to act, and setting good examples in everything. Regulations have been tightened in some countries, but standards remain inconsistent.

1 *CEO conflicts of interest*

Large stock options and other triggered incentives have made it too tempting for some CEOs to artificially massage the share price with specially timed release of information and other tricks. Stock options themselves have not been properly costed, allowing an ever-increasing proportion of reward packages to be given this way. But giving shares to staff does cost money: it dilutes the ownership of other shareholders who find, after a while, that they own a smaller proportion of the company than they had imagined.

Answer: all CEOs need to be accountable to strong, independent boards rather than, as it has been in some cases, to groups of their friends; all financial arrangements between the CEO and the corporation should be open and easy to understand.

2 *Employee conflicts of accountability*

A fundamental issue at the heart of many recent scandals is: who are people meant to be serving. Their boss? The boss of the boss? The CEO? The board? The shareholders? Customers' interests? The general public? The courts of law? Their own conscience? Employees can be under extreme pressure to toe the official line, and are vulnerable to harassment and threats by those above.

Answer: all staff need to be told what to do if they feel that their professional integrity is being compromised, and how they will be protected if they reveal what is going on.

3 *Compromising of consultants and professional advisers*

To whom is the consultant or adviser accountable if things

are discovered? To the individual whose budget is paying, who signed the contract, set up the arrangement and is asking for advice (and who may be part of the problem)? To his or her boss? To the CEO? To the board? To the share-holders? To the government? To the consumers? To the public? Who do you tell and when? What are the limits of confidentiality in consultancy?

Answer: in consultancy or advisory contracts it should be clear what the line of responsibility is in the event of the integrity of the consultant or adviser being compromised, and how they will be protected if they reveal what is going on. Laws protecting so-called whistleblowers can be helpful if properly drafted and applied, but often the issues are lower-grade concerns which are best resolved informally at an early stage if at all possible.

4 *Compromising of the media*

Media investigation should be a powerful corrective force, exposing wrongdoing, but the media depend on advertising, which has the potential to make story writers vulnerable, depending on the value of the advertising account. The potential bias can be huge if the story is actually about a prominent media owner.

The media are also vulnerable to news manipulation (specially timed release of information) and lobbying, including benefits of various kinds for journalists writing stories.

Answer: journalists and the editorial team including the owner(s) need to be transparent about potential conflicts of interest, significant levels of hospitality received and so on.

5 *Compromising of government*

The amount of money spent on lobbying in the US is greater than the GDP of 57 nations, and there are now over a hundred paid lobbyists per Member of Congress. This $5 billion a year industry is designed expressly to:

- create new laws or regulations
- change existing laws or regulations
- limit corporate liability
- create barriers to entry for competitors
- change who gets elected.

There is undoubtedly potential here for corrupting the democratic purpose. In addition, the US government shell-outs to business are worth more than $300 billion a year. Selective tax breaks, trade policies and spending programmes are all sensitive areas. There is always a risk of corruption and a danger of distorting free-market principles.

Lobbying rules in the UK are very strict in comparison but there is still potential for abuse. Large corporations spend heavily on events and forums to help promote their cause to government and senior civil servants, as well as in efforts to obtain the opportunity for a discreet conversation. At the same time, government needs advice from experienced captains of industry in order to shape effective policy and encourage investment. The balance needs careful monitoring.

Answer: strict rules on lobbying and declarations of interest by those in government, plus a completely transparent process for the allocation of all government contracts.

AN HOUR TO CHANGE YOUR WORLD

Passion is what makes human beings different from machines. Computers process data, but humans require more than data for a meaningful life. But how can we convert passion into rapid action, to play our part in transforming our future?

If you're not passionate about what you're doing, if you're not sure how you personally are helping to build a better world – and that matters to you – get out while you can, and get a life! As former First Lady Betty Ford said, 'Don't compromise yourself – you're all you've got'.

Making a huge difference with very little effort
The much-mentioned 80:20 rule is vital to understanding how a small effort can make big things happen.

In 1906 the Italian economist Vilfredo Pareto observed that 20 per cent of the Italian population owned 80 per cent of the wealth, and this rule was adapted by Dr Joseph M. Juran in the late 1940s in his observation that 20 per cent of something (effort, input defects and so on) is usually responsible for 80 per cent of the results.

If we want to have a greater impact, then one solution

is to concentrate on doing more of the 20 per cent that produces the 80 per cent.

And it is often the case that just 20 per cent of that 20 per cent – in other words, just 4 per cent of total effort – can yield 80 per cent of the 80 per cent – or 64 per cent. In a 50-hour week 4 per cent represents just one hour, so in an hour a week you could achieve 64 per cent of the impact of what you would manage if working full-time.

Here are five examples of the law of disproportionate returns:

Example 1

A friend of mine has a delightful habit, in an e-mail age, of writing really encouraging personal notes inside cards. They take her a couple of minutes to prepare, and mean a lot to those who receive them. Months later you will find many of them are still stuck on personal noticeboards, or above the fireplace, or on the desk at work. They are read over and again, not only by the recipient, but by those who visit her who are themselves encouraged or inspired. In an hour a week, my friend has singlehandedly raised morale across quite a wide group of people, especially as her example has become a model to others, not just of note-writing, but maybe of kind comments in meetings, appreciative e-mails, thank-you SMS messages and so on.

Example 2

There's a regular one-hour meeting that keeps cropping up in your diary, which is optional and so you rarely attend. But, this month, the agenda is directly relevant, and you realize beforehand that, in the hour following the meeting, you will be able to have informal conversations with several key people that you have been trying to find time to meet: people that could open up huge opportunities and help get things done.

Example 3

A serious personnel issue is emerging at work. Ten minutes spent with the individual concerned, plus a couple of hours more over the next two weeks, is enough to avoid a major crisis which could have wiped out many days of management time, not only for you but also for several others. What is more, the way in which you handle the situation helped win the person over so that their motivation increased. In years to come they may remember what you did and make an extra effort to be as compassionate, understanding and effective with the people they lead themselves.

Example 4

One of the things I try to do is to keep a reasonably current website which contains copies of articles, extracts of books and presentations slides plus a few videos. It was taking less than an hour a week to maintain, yet tens of thousands were visiting those pages each year. Now, with a little more time and effort on my part, the number of different visitors is up to over 2.5 million in twelve months, and is a major source of new friendships and business (www. globalchange.com).

Example 5

In my work with the AIDS agency ACET it has been impossible to respond to all invitations to speak about the epidemic in hard-hit places such as India, Russia, Nigeria and Uganda. Now, in partnership with several other organizations, we have been able to print and give away over 200,000 copies of a book I wrote back in 1989, in a new edition which has been translated into 12 languages. In most cases we can print three books for a dollar by printing in India. For the cost of a single economy air fare we can place a key training resource into the hands of a couple of thousand potential project leaders. In addition, over 800,000 book chapters have been downloaded online. New projects have started all over the place, in countries I could never have reached, by people I have never met. It was all held up for a while because I needed to find a few hours to update the book.

Taking influence to make things happen

There are two main ways of building a better world: one is acts of human kindness, the other is by taking influence.

Taking influence is about:

- inspiring other people to great things
- not only making things happen, but encouraging the best things to happen
- laying good foundations in a child's life
- imparting self-confidence to someone full of self-doubt
- encouraging others to be helpful to others
- shaping the laws which rule us
- challenging the prejudice of others

■ affecting the atmosphere at work in a positive way.

How to keep sane and cheerful

Sometimes I see people with high motives giving themselves to wide ranges of people and causes. They become crushed and overwhelmed by the nature of what they are involved in. Here are three keys to keep things in proportion:

1 *Life's too short to …*

Life's too short to … dwell on things that you cannot change when there are other things that you can. Life's too short to … become bitter and twisted because someone has hurt you. Life's too short to … allow yourself to become cynical.

2 *There's more to life than …*

There's more to life than … work. There's more to life than … the person who tries to stab you in the back. There's more to life than … failing an exam, a broken relationship, a physical disability. There's more to life than … being let down by a friend. We need to see the bigger picture – see the context of the whole of our lives and future, and be grateful for what we have.

3 *You can only do what you can do …*

You can only do what you can do. You can't be expected to do what you cannot do. We only have limited time, limited energy, limited talent and limited power. We are responsible for doing what we can do, but not for what we can't do. But so often we torture ourselves over things we can't change. I see this particularly with parents, who can be tempted to try to live their children's lives for them. But there comes a day when the older child is an adult and has to be allowed to go her own way. You can't live other people's lives. You have to let people go.

Why a single shareholder can change a corporation

I often ask the chairman and board members of public companies how many shareholders are enough to keep members of the board awake at night before an annual general meeting. The answer is usually one. And how many shares does that person own? Answer: one. And for how long has that share been owned? Answer: maybe only a few days, but …

… a single passionate individual, driven by a cause that attracts others, can be enough to create a media storm that results in public debate, censure, embarrassment and policy change.

If this is the case for a single member of the public, then most of us have far more potential influence than we realize to make things happen in a way that matters to us.

All managers of other people have huge opportunities every day to make a difference to the lives of those around them, in how they treat their staff, their attitudes to customers and a host of other ways.

> 'Spirituality is the basic desire to find ultimate meaning and purpose in one's life and to live an integrated life.'
>
> Ian Mitroff and Elizabeth Denton[1]

For many people, including myself, there's a strong spiritual dimension to life, a sense of destiny, or being here for a purpose, of being on a journey, and a question of calling. You may be a follower of Jesus, as I am, or of Mohammed or Buddha or Confucius, or of another way, or of none, but the ultimate issues of purpose are often the same – the challenge is to be true to our own sense of purpose and meaning.

We can sit back and wait for events to unfold or we can seize the day, take the opportunity and contribute in some small way to a better future – for ourselves, those we care for, our communities and our wider world. And as we do so, we join with men and women of every nation who share this common cause, expressed in a myriad different activities, and will find we are more successful in every area of life.

Take hold of your future – or the future will take hold of you.

FREQUENTLY ASKED QUESTIONS

Q: *How can I turn around a large company that has lost the plot?*

You may need a whole new structure and approach to the organization. Financial controls never inspired or created anything. Get in touch with the values of the founder. Headless chickens often need reconnecting. Sometimes the founder is marginalized – or even deceased. Take a look at the history, talk to people who are connected with how it all started out.

Q: *How can I encourage investors to take a wider view of our mission?*

It's happening already. Take courage and be your own person. That means being prepared to walk away and do something more worthwhile with your life should your most influential investors take a view of the company which you think is (a) not in the longer-term interests of shareholders and (b) incompatible with what you believe is important in life.

Remember, as we have seen, a single shareholder can be enough to keep some CEOs awake at night. So get smaller investors on your side – people who share your values and can act as a conscience for the corporation at investor level – against some of the more opportunistic approaches of fund managers and others in the professional investing community.

In addition, court the attention of ethical investment funds. Make sure that your principles are widely discussed in the media. Insist on taking the moral high ground. Then enjoy the free media coverage and strengthening of your brand.

Don't weaken in pursuit of the corporation's mission to build a better kind of world. Maximize your competitive advantage amongst those consumers, clients and customers who warm to the valued stance the corporation is taking.

Make your corporation 'business partner of choice', as well as 'employer of choice'. Beat the competition by consistently attracting the best talent around without having to spend outrageous amounts of bonus and share options to do so. Make sure that you win further advantage by enrolling all your senior managers and most important wealth-generators in the core values of your mission so that, every day in every way, they are proud to be working for the organization and cannot imagine wanting to work anywhere else.

Enjoy the affection of consumers, the public and the government as well as the respect of the analysts.

And if your career is abruptly brought to an end, comfort yourself in the knowledge that most corporate careers can easily end in tears – you could easily have been unseated a short time hence for a host of other reasons – and that there will be no shortage of other organizations in line waiting to take advantage of your courage, values, integrity, leadership and experience.

Q: Fads come and go – how enduring will the principle of building a better world be?

Since it is proving difficult or impossible to find any other basis for human or organizational behaviour, because it describes a truism about human beings, the principle is strong, timeless and will be very enduring.

It was Winston Churchill who declared that to understand the future it was necessary to study the past, and the same principle appears to fit retrospectively with past examples of organizations, business interests and civilizations since the beginning of recorded time.

Q: How can I start warming up our brand?

First, make sure that you yourself are passionate about the business you are in, and can explain in less than three or four sentences why your mission is so significant and important to people's present and future happiness.

Once you have done this effectively, the rest automatically begins to follow.

Make sure that your brand is promoted with feeling. Explain what it does or how it helps, but also how people feel about that: either as consumers or makers, being served or serving.

Analyse all your previous recent campaigns and score them according to their 'zap factor' – how much they tug at the heart because of the real benefits of what you are about.

Make sure that your brand environment (general image, media profile, corporate values) is strongly positive about making a difference at every possible level.

Use 'building a better world' as a filter through which major decisions are taken – for example, how a new project is set up in a developing country, the location of a new call centre, the package of community support that is built around such a place at the earliest planning stages.

THE $20,000 BUILDING A BETTER WORLD CHALLENGE

$20,000 donation to a charity or not-for-profit organization nominated by the winner(s)

The purpose of the building a better world challenge is to explore the strengths and weaknesses of what I believe is a universal principle of human behaviour and organizational success. The value of any theory is found, however, in defining the exceptions to it that can be said to prove the rule!

The building a better world challenge works as follows:

The challenge is to find an example of a successful advertising campaign, marketing exercise, mission statement, corporate value or leadership principle that is built upon any other common principle than the general expectation of building a better world as a result, in the sense of promising a better life or improving things in some way. It can be a better world in the present or the future or both, for an individual or individuals, those they care about, for the wider community or their wider world, or for some balance of several/all of these. A successful challenge must fit into the mainstream of human activity and motivation.

How to apply

No purchase of this book or of any other kind is needed to make a challenge, although challenges will be judged in the context of the message in this book – in other words, attempts to win by inferring a particular narrow interpretation of the words 'better' or 'world' will fail unless the spirit in which those words are being used in the challenge is entirely consistent with the spirit of the book itself, which is also described online.

Challenges can be made on the Building a Better World –

$20,000 Challenge bulletin board. There you will find all the background information needed: globalchange.com/challenge.htm.

By entering the Challenge, you agree to be bound by the rules and requirements set out on the bulletin board.

Initial judging by online community

Each challenge will be timed and dated and available for comment by the rest of the online community. From time to time the author will participate in these comments and discussions.

Independent panel to provide final assessment

Twelve months from publication of the most recent international first edition in English or any other language of the book, any challenges that are clearly undefeated by the rest of the online community including the author (publicly listed comments) will be forwarded to a panel of three independent judges to assess.

In the event that there is more than one successful challenge, the judges may either split the award equally or at their discretion, given the relative merits of the challenges.

In the event that there is more than one successful challenge, essentially variants of the same challenge, the award will be made to the person who posted the first challenge of that nature.

If no successful challenge has been made, the period of the challenge may be extended up to a maximum of five years further. If it remains the case by then that no successful challenge has been made, the $20,000 will be donated to a charity of the author's choice.

The Challenge is subject to English law and the exclusive jurisdiction of English courts. The decision of the judges will be final and binding and no correspondence can be entered into. The name of any winner or winners will be posted on the bulletin board.

Note: the publisher accepts no responsibility for the operation of this challenge.

NOTES

Chapter 1: The future feels different

1   Institute for Volunteering Research, UK survey, 2004; Volunteer Development Scotland, 2004 survey; Home Office 2003 figures.
2   European Volunteer Centre, Brussels, reports from 1999 to 2004 for various EU nations; UK Home Office figures for 2004.
3   Independent sector survey, 1998.
4   Independent sector survey of 4,000 people, 2004.
5   Institute for Volunteering Research, UK survey, 2004.
6   European Volunteer Centre, Brussels, reports from 1999 to 2004 for various EU nations.
7   Review on the back cover of Bill Shore's *The Cathedral Within: Transforming Your Life by Giving Something Back*, New York: Random House, 2001.
8   Survey of 2,500 35–45 year olds conducted by Future Laboratory for Standard Life Bank, published June 2004.
9   Ibid.
10   According to a survey conducted by Alliance & Leicester in August 2002, 59 per cent of UK workers are unhappy with their jobs and 28 per cent with long hours.
11   Peter Senge, *The Fifth Discipline – The Art and Practice of the Learning Organization*, New York: Bantam Dell, 1994.
12   Survey commissioned by the leadership charity Common Purpose, published June 2004. See *The Guardian*, 26 June 2004.
13   Ibid.
14   Survey, based on a representative sample of 5,000 US households, conducted in July 2003 for The Conference Board by NFO World Group. The NFO is one of the TNS group of companies.
15   Figures compiled from: Society for Human Resource Professionals; Sibson Consulting; Gallup Poll; Monster.com.
16   Australia Institute, *Discussion Paper 50*, January 2003.
17   Survey based on a representative sample of 5,000 US households, conducted in July 2003 for The Conference Board by NFO WorldGroup.
18   Figures compiled from: Society for Human Resource Professionals; Sibson Consulting; Gallup Poll; Monster.com.
19   Australia Institute, *Discussion Paper 50*, January 2003.
20   Work-Life Balance survey by People Management Chartered Institute of Personnel and Development online, 26 September 2002.
21   Interview, *Daily Mail*, 8 April 2004.
22   Richard Y. Chang, *The Passion Plan at Work: Building a Passion-Driven Organization*, San Francisco: Jossey Bass, 2001, p. 5.
23   Millennium Poll on Corporate Social Responsibility conducted by Environics International Ltd in cooperation with The Prince of Wales Business Leaders Forum and The Conference Board.

Chapter 2: Four words for every business

1   Jerry Kaplan, *Startup: A Silicon Valley Adventure*, Boston, MA: Houghton Mifflin, 1995, p. 15.
2   Peter Senge, 'Foreword', in A. de Geus, *The Living Company*, Cambridge, MA: Harvard Business School Press, 1997.

3   Elliott Sober and David S. Wilson, *Unto Others – The Evolution and Psychology of Unselfish Behaviour*, Cambridge, MA: Harvard University Press, 1999, p. 8.
4   Nelson Mandela, *Long Walk to Freedom: The Autobiography of Nelson Mandela*, Boston and New York: Back Bay Books, Little Brown, 1995, p. 622.
5   Studs Terkel, *Working: People Talk About What They Do All Day and How They Feel About What They Do*, New York: The New Press, 1997.
6   Daniel Goleman, *Emotional Intelligence*, London: Bloomsbury, 1996, p. 3.
7   Peter Senge, Art Kleiner and Charlotte Roberts, *The Fifth Discipline Fieldbook*, New York: Currency/Doubleday, 1994, p. 231.

Chapter 3: Better leadership

1   Interview, *The Times*, 16 October 2004.
2   Warren Bennis, 'Foreword', in Marshal Goldsmith *et al.*, *Global Leadership: The Next Generation*, London and Indiana: Financial Times/Prentice Hall, 2003, p.3.
3   Interview, *Automotive News*, 2001; see Jim Hall's speech and testimony at: http://www.ntsb.gov/speeches/former/hall/jhc000313.htm.
4   Joseph Badaracco ,'We Don't Need Another Hero', *Harvard Business Review*, 2001.
5   Ibid.
6   Article, 2003, on Detroit Regional Chamber website: http://www.detroitchamber.com/detroiter/articles.asp?cid=103&edtcid=249.
7   Kevin Freiberg and Jackie Freiberg, *Nuts! Southwest Airlines' Crazy Recipe for Business and Personal Success*, New York: Bantam Books, 1998, p. 215.
8   Cited in Richard Y. Chang, *The Passion Plan at Work: Building a Passion-Driven Organization*, San Francisco: Jossey Bass, 2001, p. vii.
9   Max Landsberg, *The Tools of Leadership: Vision, Inspiration, Momentum*, London: Profile Books, 2003.
10 See Bill Shore, *The Light of Conscience*, New York: Random House, 2004, p. 187.
11 Robert Kaplan and David Norton, *The Balanced Scorecard: Translating Strategy into Action*, Boston, MA: Harvard Business School Press, p. 34.
12 Temple Address, London, 27 October 2004.
13 From the introduction to Mihaly Csikszentmihalyi, *Good Business*, London: Coronet Books, 2003.

Chapter 4: How to develop better leaders

1   The Drucker Foundation, *The Leader of the Future: New Visions, Strategies, and Practices for the Next Era*, ed. Frances Hesselbein, Marshall Goldsmith, and Richard Beckhard, San Francisco: Jossey-Bass, 1996.
2   Jim Collins and Jerry I. Porras, *Built to Last: Successful Habits of Visionary Companies*, New York: HarperBusiness, 1994.
3   Cited in John R. Childress, *A Time for Leadership: Global Perspectives from an Accelerated European Marketplace*, New York: Leadership Press, p. 71.
4   Ibid., p. 69.
5   Speech at UK National Prayer Breakfast, 21 October 2004.
6   Jeffrey Garten, *The Mind of the CEO*, New York: Basic Books, 2001, p. 117.
7   Marcus Buckingham and Donald O. Clifton, *Now, Discover Your Strengths*, New York: Free Press, 2001, p. 112.
8   Daniel Goleman, *Emotional Intelligence*, London: Bloomsbury Publishing, 1996.
9   Andy Stanley, *Visioneering: God's Blueprint for Developing and Maintaining Vision*, Sisters, OR: Multnomah Publishers Inc, 2001.
10 Tom Peters and Nancy Austin, *Just Business*, Oxford: Oxford University Press, 2000, p. 52.

11   Peter F. Drucker, *Management Challenges for the 21st Century*, New York: Harper Business, 1999.

Chapter 5: Creating better teams

1   Frederich Reichheld, *Loyalty Rules*, Cambridge, MA: Harvard Business Books, 1996.
2   Lynda Gratton, *The Democratic Enterprise: Liberating Your Business with Freedom, Flexibility and Enterprise*, London: Financial Times/Prentice Hall, 2003.
3   Cited in Mihaly Csikszentmihalyi, *Good Business*, London : Coronet Books, p. 70.
4   Helen Alexander, cited in John R. Childress, *A Time for Leadership: Global Perspectives from an Accelerated European Marketplace*, New York: Leadership Press, p. 132.
5   Georgeanne Lamont, *The Spirited Business: Success Stories of Soul-Friendly Companies*, London: Hodder & Stoughton, 2003, p. 247.
6   Ibid., p. 247.
7   Source: NASSC India, November 2003.
8   Alfie Kohn, 'Why Incentive Plans Cannot Work' *Harvard Business Review*, September–October, 1993, pp. 54–63.
9   Frederick Herzberg, 'One More Time: How Do You Motivate Employees?', *Harvard Business Review*, January–February, 1968, pp. 53–62.

Chapter 6: Building better brands

1   Quoted on the back cover of Jesper Kunde, *Corporate Religion*, London: Financial Times/Prentice Hall, 2000.
2   Figures from the US Chamber of Commerce and UK Department of Trade and Industry.
3   Statistics from: Interbrand; JP Morgan Chase, 2002.
4   Estimates from various sources range from £0.5 million to £1.6 billion for spending on alternative therapies – partly influenced by the definition used. There are half a billion US consultations by alternative therapists – depending on how you define a consultation. If you include numbers of people who receive personal advice in a retail outlet, the figure is probably very conservative.
5   Jesper Kunde, *Corporate Religion*, London: Financial Times/Prentice Hall, 2000, pp. 3, 4.
6   This quote is from *A Time for Leadership*, p. 120, but see also the following quote from the Axel Johnson website: 'My discussion with the aspiring leaders ended up being about value-driven leadership. My talk with the young leaders was also about their views of companies and work. They were searching for a raison d'être – a job with a fast pace and high demands, but also a balance in life between work and family: a holistic picture. We agreed across generations that the companies that would prosper the most over time would be those in which the driving forces are both clearly cost-effective and value-creating.'
7   Ibid., pp. 48-49, 248.
8   Jonas Ridderstrale and Kjell Nordstrom, *Karaoke Capitalism: Managing for Mankind*, London: Financial Times/Prentice Hall, 2004, p. 255.

Chapter 7: Better marketing

1   Grey Australia survey, quoted in *Business Review Weekly*, 29 May 2003.
2   Figures from Skynet marketing department.
3   Figures from Ernan Roman and Scott Hornstein, *Opt-in Marketing*, New York: McGraw-Hill, 2004.

4   Ibid.
5   Ibid.
6   Ibid.
7   David Ogilvy, *Ogilvy on Advertising*, New York: Crown Publishers, 1983, p. 16.
8   Survey by Retail Forward, April 2003.
9   Al Ries and Jack Trout, *The 22 Immutable Laws of Marketing*, New York: HarperCollins, 1994.
10 Michael Newman, *The 22 Irrefutable Laws of Advertising*, New York: John Wiley & Sons, p. xvii.
11 Allyson Stewart-Allen, director of International Marketing Partners, speech for Management Centre Europe, 2004.
12 *Harvard Business Review on Corporate Ethics*, Harvard Business School Publications, 2003, p.29.
13 Brand Benefits survey, 2003.
14 Figures from MORI/CSR poll Europe, 2000.
15 Brand Benefits survey 2003.
16 Ibid.
17 Ibid.
18 Ibid.
19 Business in the Community survey, 1999.
20 Boys and Girls Club of America , author's own figures.
21 Cone Corporate Citizenship Study, Cone, Inc., 2002.
22 Business in the Community survey, 2003.
23 Business in the Community, research survey 'Profitable Partnerships', 2000.
24 Ibid.
25 Cone/Roper benchmark survey of 2,000 people.
26 UK Food Commission, April 2003.

Chapter 8: Better customer relations

1   Terry Leahy, speech to the British Chambers of Commerce Conference, 2000.
2   *Allianz Journal*, special issue, December 2003.
3   Benson Smith writing about futurism as a personal trait in Benson Smith and Tony Rutligiano, *Discover Your Sales Strengths: How the World's Greatest Salespeople Develop Winning Careers*, New York: Warner Business Books, 2003, p. 219.
4   Ed Keller and Jon Berry, *The Influentials: How One American in Ten Tells the Other Nine How to Vote, Where to Eat and What to Buy*, New York: Free Press, 2003.
5   Malcolm Gladwell, *The Tipping Point: How Little Things Can Make a Difference*, New York: Little Brown & Co., 2002.

Chapter 9: Better public relations

1   Temple Address, London, 27 October 2004.
2   Gallup Poll, 2002.
3   Mori Poll, April 2003.
4   Temple Address, London, 27 October 2004.

Chapter 10: Better innovation

1   Taken from *People Management*, 3 June 2004.

Chapter 11: Better people

1 Figures from McKinsey.

2 1997 McKinsey study by Ed Michaels, Helen Handfield-Jones and Beth Axelrod, surveys of 13,000 executives at more than 120 companies plus 27 case studies.

3 Ibid.

4 Survey carried out by *HR Executive* magazine, November 1999.

5 CIPD, *Recruitment, Retention and Turnover Survey*, 2004.

6 Ibid.

7 Chartered Institute of Personal Development, 17 June 2004 at: htttp://www.cipd.co.uk.

8 Figures from the Corporate Leadership Council of the Corporate Executive Board.

9 Survey carried out by *HR Executive* magazine, November 1999.

10 James Lucas, *The Passionate Organization: Igniting the Fire of Employee Commitment*, New York: Amacom Books, 1999, p.88.

11 Harris Poll, August 2001.

12 Harris Poll, July 1998.

13 Charles Woodruffe, 'Becoming an Employer of Choice: The New HR Imperative', *Training Journal*, July 2001, pp. 9–13.

14 C. William Pollard, *The Soul of the Firm*, Grand Rapids, MI: Zondervan, 1996, p. 104.

15 The Gallup Organization, *Follow this Path: How the World's Greatest Organizations Drive Growth by Unlocking Human Potential*, London: Gallup Press, 2004.

16 Marcus Buckingham and Donald O. Clifton, *Now Discover Your Strengths*, New York: Free Press, 2002.

17 As 14 and insights from a personal visit to ServiceMaster.

18 As 16.

Chapter 12: Better motivation

1 Viktor E. Frankl, *Man's Search for Meaning*, New York: Washington Square Press, Simon and Schuster, 1963, p. 127.

2 *Business Week*, 12 July 2004.

Chapter 13: Better balance

1 Gregg Easterbrook, *The Progress Paradox: How Life Gets Better While People Feel Worse*, New York: Random House, 2003.

2 GDP and HDI-UNDP, Human Development Index at: www.undp.org/hdro/98hdi.htm, quoted in Clive Hamilton, *Growth Fetish*, Sydney: Allen & Unwin, 2003.

3 See also Clive Hamilton, *Growth Fetish*.

4 Bruno S. Frey and Alois Stutzer, *Happiness and Economics*, Princeton, NJ and Oxford: Princeton University Press, 2002.

5 Ed Diener, Jeff Horwitz and Robert Emmons, 'Happiness of the Very Wealthy', *Social Indicators Research*, 16, 1985, pp. 263–74.

6 Mihaly Csikszentmihalyi, *Good Business*, London: Coronet Books, 2003, p. 24.

7 Quoted on the back cover of Clive Hamilton's *Growth Fetish*.

8 See Barry Schwartz, *The Paradox of Choice: Why More is Less*, New York: ECCO/HarperCollins, 2004.

9 Csikszentmihalyi, *Good Business*, p. 24.

10 John Kay, lecture at the Department of Trade and Industry, 13 May 2003.
11 *Journal of Clinical Psychiatry* quoted by the National Institute of Mental Health at http://www.nimh.nih.gov/publicat/numbers.cfm.
12 According to Arnold Ludwig, *The Price of Greatness: Resolving the Creativity and Madness Controversy*, New York: Guilford Press, 1995. Of course, figures depend on exact definition of mental illness. Very high achievers can be more vulnerable to becoming unwell at times of great pressure, by the nature of the personalities they have.
13 *The Financial Times*, 15 November 2001.
14 *The Age*, 11 April 2000.
15 Jeffrey Garten, *The Mind of the CEO*, New York: Basic Books, 2001, p. 183.
16 Princetown Survey, 24 June 1999.
17 CIPD survey, 2003, of 1,966 people in the UK.
18 Ibid.
19 Ananova Orange Survey, July 2002.
20 UK Wealth Watch Survey by Lloyds TSB, August 2002.
21 CIPD survey, 2003, of 1,966 people in the UK.
22 *The Times*, August 2001.
23 Ibid.
24 Internal BT survey, 1998.
25 London Metropole, 2001.
26 Judge Institute of Management survey at: http://www.jims.cam.ac.uk.
27 *Management Today* survey of 6,000 people at: http:www.clickmt.com/public/home.
28 Gallup Poll, 4 May 2001.
29 Gemini Consulting survey of UK managers, 1998.
30 Career Innovation Research Group survey, 1999.
31 Organized by Market Facts – TeleNation survey, 1999.
32 Charles Woodruffe, 'Becoming an Employer of Choice: The New HR Imperative', *Training Journal*, July 2001, pp. 9–13.
33 *People Management*, 17 June 2004.
34 Joseph Rowntree Foundation Report, May 2002 at: http://www.jrf.org.uk.
35 Quoted in Beverly Daniel Tatum, *Why Are All the Black Kids Sitting Together in the Cafeteria? And Other Conversations about Race: A Psychologist Explains the Development of Racial Identity*, rev. edn, New York: Basic Books, 2003.
36 Survey carried out by *Top Santé* magazine of 2,000 mothers with paid jobs, average age 38.
37 Figures from *Pregnancy and Birth* magazine, May 2002.
38 *Top Santé* magazine, European survey, June 2002.
39 See Sean Covey, *The 7 Habits of Highly Effective Teens*, New York: Fireside, 1998.

Chapter 14: Motivation matching
1 Curt Coffman and Gabriel Gonzalez-Molina, *Follow this Path: How the World's Greatest Organizations Drive Growth by Unleashing Human Potential*, New York: Gallup Organization/Warner Business Books, 2002.

Chapter 15: Managing change for the better
1 In a speech on Advancing Enterprise, February 2005.
2 *Irish Examiner* article, 31 May 1999.

3   Tom Peters, *Thriving on Chaos; Handbook for a Management Revolution*, New
     York: Alfred A. Knopf, 1987.
4   Nigel Nicholson, *Managing the Human Animal: Why People Behave the Way They
     Do in Corporate Settings*, New York: Texere Publishing, 2000.
5   Rolf Breuer, cited in Jeffrey Garten, *The Mind of the CEO*, New York: Basic Books,
     2001, p. 123.
6   Stephen R. Covey, *Seven Habits of Highly Effective People*, New York: Free Press,
     1990.
7   John Goossens, quoted in John R. Childress, *A Time for Leadership: Global
     Perspectives from an Accelerated European Marketplace*, New York: Leadership
     Press, p. 61.
8   Jeffrey Garten, *The Mind of the CEO*, New York: Basic Books, 2001, introduction.
9   Dolf van den Brink, quoted in Childress, *A Time for Leadership*, p. 69.

Chapter 16: Better strategy
1   *The Economist*, 20 March 1993, p. 106.
2   Michael Cusumano and Costas Markides (eds), *Strategic Thinking for the Next
     Economy*, San Francisco: Jossey Bass, 2001, p.2.
3   Ibid., p. 187.
4   Cited in Jeffrey Garten, *The Mind of the CEO*, New York: Basic Books, 2001, p.184.
5   Cited in Jim Collins, *Built to Last: Successful Habits of Visionary Companies*, New
     York: HarperBusiness, 1994, p. 46.
6   Cited in Garten, *The Mind of the CEO*, p. 167.
7   Samantra Ghoshal and Christopher A. Bartlett, 'Changing the Role of Top
     Management – Beyond Strategy to Purpose', *Harvard Business Review*,
     November–December, 1994, pp. 79–88.
8   Quoted in *Allianz Journal Special*, December 2003.
9   Prudential *Annual Report*, 2004.
10   Speech to Avodah Institute, 8 June 200.
11   Don Young and Pat Scott, *Having Their Cake: How the City and Big Bosses are
     Consuming UK Business*, London: Kogan Page, 2004.
12   Jim Collins, *Good to Great: Why Some Companies Make the Leap and Others
     Don't*, New York: HarperCollins, 2001; *Built to Last: Successful Habits of Visionary
     Companies*, New York: HarperBusiness, 1994.
13   Wayne W. Dyer, *10 Secrets for Success and Inner Peace: Your Sacred Self Making the
     Decision to be Free*, London: Hay House Publishers, 2002, p. 154.
14   Lynn Sharp Paine, *Value Shift: Why Companies Must Merge Social and Financial
     Imperatives to Achieve Success*, New York: McGraw-Hill, 2003.
15   Michael Cusumano and Costas Markides (eds), *Strategic Thinking for the Next
     Economy*.

Chapter 17: Lessons from not-for-profit organizations
1   Giving and Volunteering in the United States, 1999; Independent Sector. The
     Gallup Organization.
2   European Volunteer Centre, Brussels – reports from 1999 to 2004 for various EU
     nations.
3   Ibid.
4   Ibid.
5   Ibid.
6   Ibid.
7   ABC News and *The Washington Post*.

8   Roper Center for *Reader's Digest.*

9   CBS News and *The New York Times.*

10 Ibid.

11 Independent Sector / Gallup.

12 Princeton Survey Research Associates, April 1997.

13 CBS News and *The New York Times.*

14 Points of Light Foundation, 1999 study.

15 Volunteer Canada survey, 2003.

16 UK Home Office figures, 2004.

17 Points of Light Foundation 1999 study.

Chapter 18: Better ways to invest

1   Judge Institute of Management case study, University of Cambridge, 2003.

Chapter 19: Business values – the ultimate test

1   Mihaly Csikszentmihalyi, *Good Business,* London: Coronet Books, 2003, p. 25.

2   Work by Amitai Etzioni, Professor of Sociology at George Washington University, quoted in *Harvard Business Review on Corporate Ethics,* 2003.

3   Jeffrey Hollender and Stephen Fenichall, *What Matters Most: How a Small Group of Pioneers is Teaching Social Responsibility to Big Business and Why Big Business is Listening,* New York: Basic Books, 2004, p. 35.

4   Jeffrey Garten, *The Mind of the CEO,* New York: Basic Books, 2001, p.184.

5   *People Management,* 17 June 2004.

6   Cited in *Harvard Business Review on Corporate Ethics,* Harvard Business School Publications, 2003, p. 92.

7   Hollender and Fenichall, *What Matters Most.*

8   *Guardian,* 10 April 2004.

9   Garten, *The Mind of the CEO,* p. 184.

10 *Harvard Business Review on Corporate Ethics,* 2003.

11 See note 3 above.

12 Eckhart Tolle, *The Power of Now: A Guide to Spiritual Enlightenment,* Novato, CA: New World Library Publications, 1999, p. 168.

13 http://www.interfacesustainability.com/metrics.html.

14 World Bank, *Extraction Industries Review,* July 2003.

15 C.K. Prahalad, *The Fortune at the Bottom of the Pyramid,* Philadelphia, PA: The Wharton School, 2004.

16 *Harvard Business Review on Corporate Responsibility,* Harvard Business School Publications, 2003, p. 11.

17 Milton Friedman, *Capitalism and Freedom,* Chicago: Chicago University Press, 1962.

18 Elaine Sternberg, *Just Business: Business Ethics in Action* (2nd edn), Oxford: Oxford University Press, 2002, p. 6.

19 Speech, 5 December 2003, Windsor Leadership Trust, HSBC website.

20 Roper Study for Cone Communications.

21 American Chamber of Commerce, June 2002.

22 Cited in *Harvard Business Review on Corporate Responsibility,* 2003, p. 54.

Chapter 21: An hour to change your world

1   Ian Mitroff and Elizabeth Denton, *A Spiritual Audit of Corporate America: A Hard Look at Spirituality, Religion and Values in the Workplace,* San Francisco: Jossey Bass, 1999, p. xv.

BIBLIOGRAPHY

Badaracco , Joseph, 'We Don't Need Another Hero', *Harvard Business Review*, 79, 2001, pp. 121–26.

Bayler, Michael and Stoughton, David, *Promiscuous Customers: Invisible Brands: Delivering Value in Digital Markets*, London: Capstone Publishing, 2002.

Bennis, Warren, 'Foreword', in Marshal Goldsmith *et al.*, *Global Leadership: The Next Generation*, London and Indiana: Financial Times/Prentice Hall, 2003.

Blanchard, Ken and Bowles, Sheldon, *Raving Fans: A Revolutionary Approach to Customer Service*, New York: Blanchard Family Partnership and Ode to Joy Limited, 1993.

Blumenfeld, Yorick (ed.), *Scanning the Future: 20 Eminent Thinkers on the World of Tomorrow*, London: Thames and Hudson, 1999.

Boyett, Joseph and Boyett, Jimmie, *The Guru Guide: The Best Ideas of the Top Management Thinkers: Stephen Covey, Peter Drucker, Warren Bennis, and Others*, New York: John Wiley & Sons Inc, 1998.

Brake, Terence, *Managing Globally*, London: Dorling Kindersley Limited, 2002.

Buckingham, Marcus and Clifton, Donald O., *Now, Discover Your Strengths*, New York: Free Press, 2001.

Chang, Richard Y., *The Passion Plan at Work: Building a Passion-Driven Organization*, San Francisco: Jossey Bass, 2001.

Childress, John R., *A Time for Leadership: Global Perspectives from an Accelerated European Marketplace*, New York: Leadership Press.

Cialdini, Robert B., *Influence: Science and Practice*, 4th edn, London: Allyn & Bacon, 2001.

Coffman, Curt and Gonzalez-Molina, Gabriel, *Follow this Path: How the World's Greatest Organizations Drive Growth by Unleashing Human Potential*, New York: Gallup Organization/Warner Business Books, 2002.

Collins, Jim, *Built to Last: Successful Habits of Visionary Companies*, New York: HarperBusiness, 1994.

Collins, Jim, *Good to Great: Why Some Companies Make the Leap and Others Don't*, New York: HarperCollins, 2001.

Collins, Jim and Porras, Jerry I., *Built to Last: Successful Habits of Visionary Companies*, New York: HarperBusiness, 1994.

Covey, Sean, *The 7 Habits of Highly Effective Teens*, New York: Fireside, 1998.

Covey, Stephen R., *Seven Habits of Highly Effective People*, New York: Free Press, 1990.

Crainer, Stuart and Dearlove, Des (eds), *Financial Times Handbook of Management*, London: Pearson Education Limited, 2001.

Crainer, Stuart and Dearlove, Des, *Firestarters: Igniting the New Entrepreneurial Organization*, London: Pearson Education Limited, 2001.

Crone, Tom, *Law and the Media: An Everyday Guide for Professionals*, Boston, MA: Focal Press, 1995.

Csikszentmihalyi, Mihaly, *Good Business*, London: Coronet Books, 2003.

Cusumano, Michael and Markides, Costas (eds), *Strategic Thinking for the Next Economy*, San Francisco: Jossey Bass, 2001.

De Bono, Edward, *Simplicity*, Harmondsworth: Penguin Books, 1999.

Denny, Richard, *Motivate to Win: How to Motivate Yourself and Others*, London: Kogan Page Limited, 2004.

Diener, Ed, Horwitz, Jeff and Emmons, Robert, 'Happiness of the Very Wealthy', *Social Indicators Research*, 16, 1985, pp. 263–74.

The Drucker Foundation, *The Leader of the Future: New Visions, Strategies, and Practices for the Next Era*, ed. Frances Hesselbein, Marshall Goldsmith, and Richard Beckhard, San Francisco: Jossey-Bass, 1996.

Drucker, Peter F., *Management Challenges for the 21st Century*, New York: Harper Business, 1999.

Dyer, Wayne W., *10 Secrets for Success and Inner Peace: Your Sacred Self Making the Decision to be Free*, London: Hay House Publishers, 2002.

Easterbrook, Gregg, *The Progress Paradox: How Life Gets Better While People Feel Worse*, New York: Random House, 2003.

Eccles, Tony, *Succeeding with Change: Implementing Action-Driven Strategies*, New York: McGraw-Hill Publishing Company, 1997.

Frankl, Viktor E., *Man's Search for Meaning*, New York: Washington Square Press, Simon and Schuster, 1963.

Freiberg, Kevin and Freiberg, Jackie, *Nuts! Southwest Airlines' Crazy Recipe for Business and Personal Success*, New York: Bantam Books, 1998.

Frey, Bruno S. and Stutter, Aloes, *Happiness and Economics*, Princeton, NJ and Oxford: Princeton University Press, 2002.

Friedman, Milton, *Capitalism and Freedom*, Chicago: Chicago University Press, 1962.

The Gallup Organization, *Follow this Path: How the World's Greatest Organizations Drive Growth by Unlocking Human Potential*, London: Gallup Press, 2004.

Garten, Jeffrey, *The Mind of the CEO*, New York: Basic Books, 2001.

Gates, Bill, *The Road Ahead*, New York: Viking Press, 1995.

Gates, Bill, *Business at the Speed of Thought: Using a Digital Nervous System*, Harmondsworth: Penguin Books, 1999.

Ghoshal, Samantra and Bartlett, Christopher A., 'Changing the Role of Top Management – Beyond Strategy to Purpose', *Harvard Business Review*, November–December, 1994, pp. 79–88.

Gladwell, Michael, *The Tipping Point: How Little Things Can Make a Difference*, New York: Little Brown & Co., 2002.

Goldsmith, Marshall, Greenberg, Cathy L., Robertson, Alastair, Hu-Chan, Maya, *Global Leadership: The Next Generation*, London: Pearson Education, 2003.

Goleman, Daniel, *Emotional Intelligence*, London: Bloomsbury, 1996.

Grant, John, *The New Marketing Manifesto: The 12 Rules for Building Successful Brands in the 21st Century*, London: Orion Business, 2000.

Gratton, Lynda, *Living Strategy: Putting People at the Heart of Corporate Purpose*, London: Pearson Education Limited, 2000

Gratton, Lynda, *The Democratic Enterprise: Liberating Your Business with Freedom, Flexibility and Enterprise*, London: Financial Times/Prentice Hall, 2003.

Greene, Robert, *48 Laws of Power*, London: Profile Books Ltd, 2002.

Greene, Stephen, *Serving God, Serving Mammon? Christians and the Financial Markets*, London: Marshall Pickering, 1996.

Hamilton, Clive, *Growth Fetish*, Sydney, Allen & Unwin, 2003.

Handy, Charles, *The Age of Unreason*, London: Arrow Books, 1995.

Handy, Charles, *The Empty Raincoat: Making Sense of the Future*, London: Arrow Books, 1995.

Handy, Charles, *The Hungry Spirit: Beyond Capitalism: A Quest for Purpose in the Modern World*, London: Hutchinson Arrow Books, 1998.

Handy, Charles, *The New Alchemists: How Visionary People Make Something out of Nothing*, Hutchinson, 1999.

Harvard Business Review on Corporate Ethics, Cambridge, MA: Harvard Business School Press, 2003.

Harvard Business Review on Corporate Responsibility, Cambridge, MA: Harvard Business School Press, 2003.

Harvard Business Review on Motivating People, Cambridge, MA: Harvard Business School Press, 2003.

Harvard Business Review on Work and Life Balance, Cambridge, MA: Harvard Business School Press, 2000.

Heller, Robert, *Motivating People*, London: Dorling Kindersley, 1998.

Heller, Robert, 'Foreword' in *Movers and Shakers: The Brains and Bravado Behind Business*, London: Bloomsbury Publishing, 2003.

Herzberg, Frederick, 'One More Time: How Do You Motivate Employees?', *Harvard Business Review*, January–February, 1968, pp. 53–62.

Hofstede, Geert, *Culture's Consequences: Comparing Values, Behaviors, Institutions and Organizations Across Nations*, New York: Sage Publications, 2001.

Hollender, Jeffrey and Fenichall, Stephen, *What Matters Most: How a Small Group of Pioneers is Teaching Social Responsibility to Big Business and Why Big Business is Listening*, New York: Basic Books, 2004.

Jackson, Ben, *Poverty and the Planet: A Question of Survival*, Harmondsworth: Penguin Books, 1994.

Jacobi, Jolande, *The Psychology of C.G. Jung*, London: Chaucer Press, 1968.

Kaplan, Jerry, *Startup: A Silicon Valley Adventure*, Boston, MA: Houghton Mifflin, 1995.

Kaplan, Robert and Norton, David, *The Balanced Scorecard: Translating Strategy into Action*, Boston, MA: Harvard Business School Press.

Keller, Ed and Berry, Jon, *The Influentials: How One American in Ten Tells the Other Nine How to Vote, Where to Eat and What to Buy*, New York: Free Press, 2003.

Kennedy, Carol, *Guide to Management Gurus: Shortcuts to the Ideas of Leading Management Thinkers*, London: Century, 1991.

Klein, Maury, *The Change Makers: From Carnegie to Gates, How the Great Entrepreneurs Transformed Ideas into Industries*, New York: Times Books, 2003.

Knight, Peter, *The Highly Effective Marketing Plan: A Proven, Practical, Planning Process for Companies of All Sizes*, London: Pearson Education Limited, 2004.

Kohn, Alfie, 'Why Incentive Plans Cannot Work', *Harvard Business Review*, September–October, 1993, pp. 54–63.

Kotler, Philip, *Ten Deadly Marketing Sins: Signs and Solutions*, New York: John Wiley and Sons Inc, 2004.

Kulananda and Houlder, Dominic, *Mindfulness and Money: The Buddhist Path of Abundance*, New York: Broadway Books, 2004.

Kunde, Jesper, *Corporate Religion*, London: Financial Times/Prentice Hall, 2000.

Lamont, Georgeanne, *The Spirited Business: Success Stories of Soul-Friendly Companies*, London: Hodder & Stoughton, 2003.

Landsberg, Max, *The Tools of Leadership: Vision, Inspiration, Momentum*, London: Profile Books.

Leigh, David and Vulliamy, Ed, *Sleaze: The Corruption of Parliament*, London: Fourth Estate Limited, 1997.

Lucas, James, *The Passionate Organization: Igniting the Fire of Employee Commitment*, New York: Amacom Books, 1999.

Ludwig, Ludwig, *The Price of Greatness: Resolving the Creativity and Madness Controversy*, New York: Guilford Press, 1995.

McGraw, Dr Philip C., *Self Matters: Creating Your Life from the Inside Out*, New York: Simon & Schuster Inc, 2001.

Maister, David H., *Managing the Professional Service Firm*, New York: Free Press Paperbacks, 1997.

Maister, David H., *True Professionalism: The Courage to Care about Your People, Your Clients, and Your Career*, New York: The Free Press, 1997.

Mandela, Nelson, *Long Walk to Freedom: The Autobiography of Nelson Mandela*, Boston and New York: Back Bay Books, Little Brown, 1995.

Markides, Constantinos C., *All the Right Moves: A Guide to Crafting Breakthrough Strategy*, Cambridge, MA: Harvard Business School Press, 2000.

Meyer, Peter, *Warp-Speed Growth: Managing the Fast-Track Business without Sacrificing Time, People, and Money*, New York: AMACOM, 2000.

Micklethwait, John and Wooldridge, Adrian, *The Company: A Short History of a Revolutionary Idea*, London: Weidenfeld & Nicolson, 2003.

Miller, George A., *Psychology: The Science of Mental Life*, Harmondsworth: Penguin Books, 1991.

Mitroff , Ian and Denton, Elizabeth, *A Spiritual Audit of Corporate America: A Hard Look at Spirituality, Religion and Values in the Workplace*, San Francisco: Jossey-Bass, 1999.

Mooney, P. Kelly, *The Ten Demandments: Rules to Live by in the Age of the Demanding Customer*, New York: McGraw-Hill, 2002.

Naisbitt, John, *High Tech High Touch: Technology and our Accelerated Search for Meaning*, New York: Nicholas Brealey Limited, 2001.

Nash, Laura L., *Believers in Business: Resolving the Tensions Between Christian Faith, Business Ethics, Competition and our Definition of Success*, Nashville, TN: Thomas Nelson, 1994.

Newman, Michael, *The 22 Irrefutable Laws of Advertising*, New York: John Wiley & Sons, 2004.

Nicholson, Nigel, *Managing the Human Animal: Why People Behave the Way They Do in Corporate Settings*, New York: Texere Publishing, 2000.

Noer, David M., *Breaking Free – A Prescription for Personal Organizational Change*, San Francisco: Jossey-Bass, 1997.

O'Connell, Fergus, *Simply Brilliant: The Competitive Advantage of Common Sense*, London: Pearson Education Limited, 2001.

Ogilvy, David, *Ogilvy on Advertising*, New York: Crown Publishers, 1983.

Ogilvy, David, *Confessions of an Advertising Man*, London: Southbank Publishing, 2004.

Ohmae, Kenichi (ed.), *The Evolving Global Economy: Making Sense of the New World Order*, Cambridge, MA: Harvard Business Books, 1995.

Oxelheim, Lars, *Financial Markets in Transition: Globalization, Investment and Economic Growth*, London: ITP, 1996.

Paine, Lynn Sharp, *Value Shift: Why Companies Must Merge Social and Financial Imperatives to Achieve Success*, New York: McGraw-Hill, 2003.

Pande, Pete and Holpp, Larry, *What is Six Sigma?*, New York: Quebecor/World Martinsburg, 2002.

Pattison, Stephen, *The Faith of the Managers: When Management Becomes Religion*, London: Cassell, 1997.

Pendergrast, Mark, *Uncommon Grounds: The History of Coffee and How It Transformed Our World*, New York: Basic Books, 1999.

Peters, Tom, *Thriving on Chaos; Handbook for a Management Revolution*, New York: Alfred A. Knopf, 1987.

Peters, Tom, *The Pursuit of Wow: Every Person's Guide to Topsy-Turvy Times*, Basingstoke: Macmillan, 1994.

Peters, Tom and Austin, Nancy, *Just Business*, Oxford: Oxford University Press, 2000.

Peters, Tom and Waterman Jr, Robert H., *In Search of Excellence: Lessons from America's Best-Run Companies*, London: HarperCollins, 1995.

Plimpton, George, *The Writer's Chapbook: A Compendium of Fact, Opinion, Wit, and Advice from the 20th Century's Pre-eminent Writers*, Harmondsworth: Penguin Books, 1992.

Pollard, C. William, *The Soul of the Firm*, Grand Rapids, MI: Zondervan, 1996.

Prahalad, C.K., *The Fortune at the Bottom of the Pyramid*, Philadelphia, PA: The Wharton School, 2004.

Priest, Simon and Welch, Jim, *Creating a Stress-free Office*, Aldershot: Gower Publishing Limited, 1998.

Reicheld, Frederick, *Loyalty Rules*, Cambridge, MA: Harvard Business Books, 1996.

Ries, Al and Trout, Jack, *The 22 Immutable Laws of Marketing*, New York: HarperCollins, 1994.

Ridderstrale, Jonas and Nordstrom, Kjell, *Karaoke Capitalism: Managing for Mankind*, London: Financial Times/Prentice Hall, 2004.

Rohwer, Jim, *Asia Rising*, New York: Nicholas Brealey Publishing Limited, 1996.

Roman, Eman and Hornstein, Scott, *Opt-in Marketing*, New York: McGraw-Hill, 2004.

Schluter, Michael and Lee, David, *The R Factor*, London: Hodder and Stoughton, 1993.

Schwartz, Barry, *The Paradox of Choice: Why More is Less*, New York: ECCO/ HarperCollins, 2004.

Semler, Ricardo, *The Seven-Day Weekend: The Wisdom Revolution: Finding the Work/ Life Balance*, London: Century, 2003.

Senge, Peter, *The Fifth Discipline – The Art and Practice of the Learning Organization*, New York: Bantam Dell, 1994.

Senge, Peter, 'Foreword', in A. de Geus, *The Living Company*, Cambridge, MA: Harvard Business School Press, 1997.

Senge, Peter, Kleiner, Art and Roberts, Charlotte, *The Fifth Discipline Fieldbook*, New York: Currency/Doubleday, 1994.

Shore, Bill, *The Cathedral Within: Transforming Your Life by Giving Something Back*, New York: Random House, 2001.

Shore, Bill, *The Light of Conscience*, New York: Random House, 2004.

Smith, Benson and Rutligiano, Tony, *Discover Your Sales Strengths: How the World's Greatest Salespeople Develop Winning Careers*, New York: Warner Business Books, 2003.

Sober, Elliott and Wilson, David S., *Unto Others – The Evolution and Psychology of Unselfish Behaviour*, Cambridge, MA: Harvard University Press, 1999.

Stafford-Clark, David, *What Freud Really Said*, Harmondsworth: Penguin Books, 1965.

Stanley, Andy, *Visioneering: God's Blueprint for Developing and Maintaining Vision*, Sisters, OR: Multnomah Publishers Inc, 2001.

Sternberg, Elaine, *Just Business: Business Ethics in Action*, 2nd edn, Oxford: Oxford University Press, 2002.

Tatum, Beverly Daniel, *Why Are All the Black Kids Sitting Together in the Cafeteria? and Other Conversations About Race: A Psychologist Explains the Development of Racial Identity*, rev. edn, New York: Basic Books, 2003.

Templar, Richard, *The Rules of Work*, London: Pearson Education Limited, 2003.

Terkel, Studs, *Working: People Talk About What They Do All Day and How They Feel About What They Do*, New York: The New Press, 1997.

Tolle, Eckhart, *The Power of Now: A Guide to Spiritual Enlightenment*, Novato, CA: New World Library Publications, 1999.

Trompenaars, Fons, *Riding the Waves of Culture: Understanding Cultural Diversity in Business*, London: Nicholas Brealey Publishing Limited, 1993.

Tyson, Kirk W.M., *Competition in the 21st Century*, Florida: St Lucie Press, 1997.

Wallis, Jim, *The Soul of Politics: A Practical and Prophetic Vision for Change*, New York: HarperCollins, 1994.

Webb, Philip and Webb, Sandra, *The Small Business Handbook: The Entrepreneur's Definitive Guide to Starting and Growing a Business*, 2nd edn, London: Pearson Education Limited, 2001.

Welborn, Ralph and Kasten, Vince, *The Jericho Principle: How Companies Use Strategic Collaboration to Find New Sources of Value*, New Jersey: John Wiley & Sons Inc, 2003.

Williams, Stephen and Cooper, Lesley, *Dangerous Waters: Strategies for Improving Wellbeing at Work*, Chichester: John Wiley and Sons Ltd, 1999.

Woodruffe, Charles, 'Becoming an Employer of Choice: The New HR Imperative', *Training Journal*, July 2001, pp. 9–13.

Young, Don and Scott, Pat, *Having Their Cake: How the City and Big Bosses are Consuming UK Business*, London: Kogan Page, 2004.

Zyman, Sergio, *End of the Advertising As We Know It*, New Jersey: John Wiley & Sons Inc, 2002.

INDEX

Boxed text is indicated in *italics*.

A&P *153*
accident rates 166, 167
accountability 46, 294, 297–8
ACET (AIDS Care Education and
    Training) 226–8, *303*
achievement, sense of 156
Adler, Alfred 24
Adorers 270
advertising
    bad news sells good news *128*
    campaigns 80, 89, 94, 110, 124
    honest 117
    media dependence on 298
    slogans 91–3
    spending on 79
Africa, the poorest and most
    marginalized in 276
aftersales service 111
agape 69
Agilent Technologies 266
AIDS 226, 227, 255, 270, 276, 291
AIDS Care Education and Training *see*
    ACET
airlines 93
Alexander, Helen 67
Allen, Woody 146
Allianz 113
alternative medicine 81–2
altruism 5, 25
Alzheimer Society, The 102
American Red Cross 90
Anderson, Ray 277
Andrews, Kenneth 263
animal welfare *93*, 135
antidepressants 186
anxiety disorders 186
Apple Macintosh 84, 92
appreciation 114, 116, 156, 157, 170
Aristotle 168
Arthur Andersen 121, 122, 124, 252, 296
Asda *196*
Ashridge Business School 190
AT&T 266
auditors 296
Austin, Nancy 61
Australia, downsizing in 13

autonomy 156
Avon Cosmetics 101, *107*, 283

bad profit 264
Badaracco, Joseph 40
balance 156, 177
balanced scorecards 22, 45
bankruptcy 216
banks, bankers 93, 154, *154*
Barclays 101, *153*
Barna Research Group 13
BBC 91
behaviour, study of 24
Belgium: volunteering 249
belief 83, 85, 275
benchmarking 269–70
Bennis, Warren 58, 60, 144
    Global Leadership 31–2
Berkshire Hathaway 238
'best practice' 269
Bezos, Jeff 79
Blair, Tony 34
Blanchard, Ken 41, 64
Bloomer, Jonathan 237
board members, non-executives as 295
Body Shop 84
Boeing 242
bonuses 76–7, 156, 160, 187
boom times 217
Boys and Girls Club Movement *105*
BP 90
brainstorming 141, 144
brands 16, 79–85
    adapting 80–81
    as brittle and easily broken 94–5
    image 106
    long-lasting 80
    warming up the brand 80–85, 309
        emotional brands 84–5
        feeling-faith-brand religion 83–4
        future feeling 81–2, *82*
        ten steps to warming up a brand *85*
        the world's top ten brands (2002)
            81
Branson, Richard 263
Breakthrough Breast Cancer *107*
bribery 126–7, 292–3, *292*
British Gas 101